Selling 'em by the Sack

Selling 'em by the Sack

White Castle and the Creation of American Food

David Gerard Hogan

NEW YORK UNIVERSITY PRESS

New York and London

NEW YORK UNIVERSITY PRESS
New York and London

© 1997 New York University

Library of Congress Cataloging-in-Publication Data
Hogan, David Gerard, 1959–
Selling 'em by the sack : White Castle and the creation of
American food / David Gerard Hogan.
p.   cm.
Includes bibliographical references and index.
ISBN 0-8147-3566-5 (acid-free paper)
1. White Castle (Restaurant)—History. 2. Restaurateurs—United States.
3. Ingram, Billy, 1880-1966. 4. Anderson, J. Walter, 1880- .
I. Title.
TX945.5.W48H64   1997
338.7'616479573—dc21   97-21076
                                     CIP

New York University Press books are printed on acid-free paper,
and their binding materials are chosen for strength and durability.

Manufactured in the United States of America
10 9 8 7 6 5 4 3 2

For my parents, Ruth and Raymond Hogan

Contents

Acknowledgments

I have many people to thank for their assistance and encouragement during my research and writing of this book. First and foremost, I am grateful to Kate Kelley for teaching me about her "family business," facilitating my unrestricted access to the company records, and offering both encouragement and friendship. I also thank the helpful management and staff at White Castle, especially Kim Kelly-Bartley, MaryAnn Kelley, Wendy Tidswell, Debbie Cline, Jack Trador, Roger Post, and Therese Nolan, for opening their confidential records to me and repeatedly searching all nooks and crannies for relevant documents. Their efforts and openness made this book possible.

Many other people gave me kind assistance in my four years of research and writing. My research began in Wichita, investigating the early years of the company and industry. I am grateful to city historian Billy Ellington for guiding me through his files on White Castle and directing me to former White Castle employees still living in Wichita. One of those surviving employees was especially helpful: former manager Jimmy King and his son Wayne gave me their personal insight into the early years of White Castle in the 1920s that I could never recover from paper documents. I thank them both for their kindness and hospitality.

I also owe a debt of gratitude to many others who helped me in different locations and phases of my research, including the many unnamed archivists and librarians at the Library of Congress, several university research libraries, and the Ohio Historical Society. Because they all did their jobs with efficiency and friendliness, they made my task much easier. I am especially grateful to state archivist and fellow historian Jeff Thomas, who led the organization of White Castle's extensive papers and patiently guided me to the many documents that I needed. Without his expertise and assistance, I would still be searching through the many boxes of company records.

I am also thankful for the help and encouragement that I received from friends and colleagues during this seemingly long ordeal. Once again, I thank W. Andrew Achenbaum and Charles Forcey for their assistance. Without their guidance several years ago, there would be no book today. I also thank Peter Stearns for believing in my topic, reading many pages about hamburgers, and giving me both encouragement and crucial assistance. He made this a better book than I thought possible. I also am grateful to Timothy Bartlett at New York University Press. Throughout the long process of faxes and revisions, he showed great patience and offered innumerable ideas for improving my manuscript. I do hope that one day he will actually give in and try a White Castle hamburger.

Many of my friends and colleagues offered encouragement. First among these friends and colleagues is Tim Kelly. Four years ago we began this project together, and he has remained my closest adviser and confidant throughout. My thanks to him for reading the many different drafts of the manuscript and discussing ideas on the phone for hours at a time; thanks for always being honest about my writing and arguments; and thanks for the many years of friendship.

Above all else, I am grateful to my family for their very kind support and understanding. I thank my parents, Ruth and Ray Hogan, for their encouragement and uncharacteristic experimentation with frozen White Castles in Florida. I am also grateful to my wife Colleen for her understanding of my highs and lows during this process, for carefully reading and rereading each word, page, and chapter, and for believing in me. Thank you. I also thank my wonderful son Tim, who did more to encourage my progress than any one else. This book may never have been written had he not asked me daily, "Dad, Is your book done yet?" Yes Tim, it's done, and thanks for all the helpful reminders.

Introduction

This story is about White Castle: the company, the man who started it, and the sequence of developments that it spawned. It is social history because it analyzes how and why fast food altered American life; it is biography because it is impossible to examine White Castle without discussing the achievements and tenacity of its founder, Billy Ingram; and it is "corporate history" because it follows the company's triumphs and failures since 1921. The White Castle story cannot be told without including any of these elements. Ingram founded the company, and the significance of the company is that it drastically changed American eating patterns and, hence, American life.

The creation of White Castle in 1921 greatly affected life in America during the twentieth century. White Castle marketed the hamburger to Americans so successfully that it became their most common meal and their primary ethnic food. White Castle's success also inspired a legion of imitators and gave birth to the multi-billion-dollar fast-food industry, which continues to thrive despite America's increasing obsession with fat content. In addition to providing America with a primary food, White Castle and subsequent fast-food companies taught Americans a new and different way to eat, leading to many changes in American culture and lifestyle.

White Castle's founder Billy Ingram successfully sold to the general public the hamburger sandwich, which in 1921 was a product considered disreputable and undesirable. Because of Ingram's marketing genius, by 1930 Americans in every corner of the country accepted the hamburger as a mainstream food and eventually made it a staple of their daily diet. Ingram did not "discover" or "invent" this food, but he did introduce it to Americans at an affordable price and deliberately marketed it to specific segments of the population. He sold his hamburgers in large quantities at five cents each, telling his customers to "buy'em by the sack" and introducing and promoting both the food and the carryout format that became synonymous with fast food. Within a decade Ingram had altered the American palate and captured millions of customers. In fact, it could be said that what

Henry Ford did for the car and transportation, Billy Ingram did for the hamburger sandwich and eating.

The immediate outcome of Ingram's marketing genius was that White Castle sold a lot of hamburgers. It quickly became apparent that Americans loved them and avidly followed White Castle's advice to "buy'em by the sack." The longer-term effect was that Billy Ingram's success became well known and countless imitators started restaurant chains that were virtually identical to White Castle in product, architecture, and even name. White porcelain buildings appeared on many street corners, bearing names such as White Tower, White Clock, Royal Castle, or White Palace. This almost immediate proliferation of White Castle imitators was the beginning of the massive fast-food industry, which today ranks among the largest segments of the American economy.

Beyond the creation and promotion of a new food product and the founding of a new industry, White Castle had even greater—if less quantifiable—effects on American society. The fact that the hamburger that Ingram marketed so aggressively became America's favorite food had several important ramifications. First, millions of Americans consuming millions of hamburgers each day caused a major increase in beef production. Not only did the beef producers love the ever-growing demand for their product, but the fact that Americans were eating more meat also affected their overall diet and health.

For better or worse, White Castle started the massive consumption of hamburgers that continues unabated to the present. Its most significant contribution to American culture is that hamburgers came to be closely identified with American culture. In 1921, Billy Ingram promoted his hamburgers to an American society whose many subgroups were still deeply entrenched in and divided by their original ethnic traditions. The early 1920s was a time of intense ethnic and racial division in the United States, with few areas of "common ground" between groups. One result of this division could be found at the collective dinner table. The diverse ethnic foods consumed by people from different backgrounds often were a persistent link to their past. Many recently arrived Europeans immigrants and northward-migrating African Americans maintained their indigenous cuisines, whereas other Americans were divided gastronomically by region and class. These differences in backgrounds, customs, and tastes were a major obstacle in the formation of a homogeneous American ethnicity. One might also argue that in 1921 there was no true American ethnicity. Much happened in the next forty years, however, to bring American citizens together under a single ethnic identity. In this book I analyze the revolutionary "creation" of this new American ethnicity and discuss how Ingram's hamburger sandwich emerged as the country's principal ethnic food. I even contend that White Castle and its imitative progeny were instrumental in helping create a uniquely American ethnicity.

As a society, we still often do not consider that a unique American ethnicity exists or understand its defining characteristics. Nonetheless, there was a quiet, unheralded change in ethnic identity between 1920 and 1960, even though many Americans failed to notice it. Although we acknowledge the existence of American patriotism and nationalism, we generally do not ponder or revel in our ethnicity. In fact, many people deny the essential commonalities in our culture; indeed, some are horrified by the notion that the fast-food hamburger has come to be identified as America's premier ethnic food. If you find this hard to believe, just ask anyone from another country, "What is American food?" Nine out of ten replies will be "Hamburgers!" This outsider's perspective allows us to see what we so rarely ponder and often take for granted: the hamburger is all around us on a daily basis, comsumed by many millions. The fact that it is so close, so mundane, and unextraordinary is exactly what makes it so important and central to who we are as a people.

In some ways, the hamburger is to America what fish and chips is to Britain or the tamale is to Mexico. Each of these foods helps define the country's ethnic identity yet is usually disdained or at least is downplayed by the elites in their societies. Fish and chips, for example, is savored by much of the British working class, but rarely, if ever, is served at middle- or upper-class tables. Greasy and traditionally wrapped "to go" in old newspaper, fish and chips also became popular in the early twentieth century, appealing to the appetites of an increasingly busy British working class. These elements of speed and convenience closely parallel those of the hamburger. Common features of most true ethnic foods are that they are easily cooked, convenient, inexpensive, and tasty. Their ready accessibility and affordability, in fact, are what often identify them with the working or lower classes and hence often make them less desirable to the more affluent or more "cultured." Although usually plain and inelegant, such ethnic foods remain the sustenance of the majority of the world's population and—in conjunction with language, history, and belief systems—help define particular peoples and cultures.

In addition to documenting White Castle's extraordinary significance in terms of the American economy and ethnicity, this book also follows the company along its roller-coaster ride of business highs and lows. In essence, the history of White Castle reflects the history of twentieth-century America. Tracing the company's progress chronologically through the decades mirrors the prosperity of the 1920s, the upheaval of the Great Depression, the war years, the social explosion and demographic changes in postwar America, and the prosperity of modern times. Issues of class mobility and division, racism, changing gender roles, and demographic movement also are central to the White Castle story.

I have written about White Castle because most historians have ignored the founding of the fast-food industry and culture in America. Little scholarly work has been done on fast food, and most of what is in print focuses on the McDonald's phenomenon of the late 1950s. Although White Castle frequently receives a brief mention, or even a paragraph, in many food or cultural histories, it is often discussed interchangeably with its imitator White Tower, often confusing which chain and entrepreneur actually started the hamburger craze. For the most part, however, both White Castle and the formative years for fast-food hamburgers exist only as footnotes in scholarly works either praising or criticizing Ray Kroc and his golden arches. This misplaced emphasis has led both academics and the general public to believe, erroneously, that fast food really started in the 1950s, thereby leaving any developments before that time in an undocumented haze. While books abound about far more peripheral issues in American life, a void exists in the explanation of the basic question of how and what Americans feed themselves. Being either forgetful or elitist, historians often overlook the history of American food in general, reserving a special blind spot for the history of fast food. Telling the White Castle story is just my attempt to clarify that haze.

When I first considered White Castle as a research topic, I had never been to a Castle nor eaten a White Castle hamburger. But I knew that White Castle was an innovator in the food industry, so I decided to look into it further, with an article in mind. When investigating it, however, I discovered a rich history, as well as a company and its founder that together had left a distinctive mark on American society. In the research process, I approached my subject with balance, letting the evidence I uncovered speak for itself. If my prose sounds at times overly praising of White Castle, it's because the company has, for the most part, maintained positive business practices over its seventy-five-year history. It could afford to, as for the first half of that period, it was the undisputed leader in American fast food.

The White Castle story begins in chapter 1, though White Castle is not its focus. Instead it examines nineteenth-century American eating habits in regard to both types of restaurants and diversity of foods. To understand the significance of White Castle's economic and cultural contributions, we must first explore its culinary predecessors. Chapter 2 discusses the decade of the 1920s, when White Castle was founded, chronicling its fast rise to domination of the fast-food industry. Chapter 3 focuses on how the company endured the Great Depression, thriving and expanding while much of American business fell apart. The underlying story of this chapter is how White Castle intentionally and successfully incorporated the hamburger into the middle-class diet. World War II and its crippling effects on White Castle and the greater restaurant industry is the main topic of chapter 4. During this time, White Castle lost its lead in the fast-food industry, barely surviving wartime shortages and restrictions. Chapter 5 chronicles White Castle's slow recovery back to financial health and stability, although it was no longer a leader in the field. This was the era when White Castle assumed a different role in the industry, becoming a bastion of tradition and simplicity rather than striving for conformity and modernity. Chapter 6 tells the tale of White Castle's renewed growth and prosperity, spanning the 1960s, 1970s, and 1980s, with White Castle reemerging as a contender in the fast-food marketplace. This chapter also looks at the company and the broader fast food industry today, explaining how White Castle is faring in the midst of giant corporate competitors and why its history is still central to its daily operations. In short, this is a more complicated story than just that of a man opening a hamburger stand.

1

American Food before White Castle

White Castle changed American culture dramatically. Now, however, the company—because of its small size—and its accomplishments—today, largely forgotten—can easily be ignored, especially in comparison with fast-food giants like McDonald's. Indeed, White Castle was, and still is, a relatively small entity in the overall context of American business, dwarfed by the advertising machines and magnitude of larger competitors. Therefore, to understand how tiny White Castle changed America, we must look at Americans' eating habits and culture before 1921 to appreciate what White Castle achieved.

Some readers may be surprised that my story of White Castle begins with an extensive discussion of previous foods and ethnicities, but the primary importance of the White Castle story is how its new food and approach to eating transformed American culture. White Castle advanced food production and distribution to the volume demanded by the expanding population, and it gave an American democracy an accessible, egalitarian, and standardized style of eating. It also supplied America with a distinctive ethnic symbol: people the world over now readily identify fast-food hamburgers as the food of Americans. In short, White Castle started a new era in human eating and created a powerful ethnic identifier for the American people.

Immigrants Bring Their Foods to America

For a long time, "American food" was difficult to define precisely. One reason was that for many years there was no consensus on what factors and traits comprised American ethnicity. At the end of the nineteenth century, the ethnic ghettos in American cities allowed their residents to preserve the culture of their homelands. Second- and third-generation Americans in these enclaves often talked to one another in their language of origin and ate their favorite ethnic foods.

Those Americans of much longer tenure, living in either another section of the city or the newly created suburbs, sometimes idealized the culture of their ancestors and even adopted certain British ethnic traits. For the most part, these two groups of Americans, of dissimilar ethnic origin, did not work together, did not worship in the same church, and certainly did not dine at the same table. Those of English origin claimed that their pre-Revolutionary pedigree made them more truly American than the recently arrived immigrants, citing the English language and cultural traditions as proof.[1] Nostalgic about the good old days before the Irish, Poles, and Italians arrived, many Anglophiles joined protectionist societies dedicated to preserving "American" culture. But this culture was in reality just a warmed-over Anglo-Saxon Protestant culture that ignored a multitude of other influences. Their claims to understand better and to own the true American ethnicity were mistaken, however; by the turn of the century, American ethnicity had become an amalgam of competing interests and influences without any clear definition or face.[2] Using the popular image of the melting pot or the tossed salad provides some visual clarity, but the reality of the time was cultural confusion, with millions of people with very little in common existing under a single national flag. The apparent outcome of this cultural competition and confusion seemed to be a chronic ethnic heterogeneity, with little hope for agreement or synthesis. Indeed, it might have surprised many people that a national ethnic food would emerge in only thirty years.

Progressing from this ethnic confusion to some semblance of relative homogeneity in only three decades was not an easy task. Dramatic national events, technological breakthroughs, and the efforts of many entrepreneurs all combined to set the stage for this transformation. Social and political reform movements during the Progressive Era of the early twentieth century helped empower disadvantaged groups while at the same time ending the federal government's long-term policy of open immigration. Both the Spanish-American War and World War I caused huge disruptions in the labor force, internal migrations, changes in gender roles, and a reassessment of America's position in the world. Each of these wars caused a profound change in the American character. The Spanish-American War established the United States as a legitimate world leader when it defeated Spain, a former colonial power, and seized its empire. At least on a military and diplomatic level, this war in 1898 launched America into an era that many historians refer to as "the American Century," a period when the United States became the preeminent world power. Twenty years later, World War I affirmed this notion of world domination and caused major demographic and social upheavals in America. When the United States entered this essentially European conflict, it quickly tipped the balance of power toward the Allies and was credited with "winning" the war, which further reinforced its newly acquired status as a major power. Back on the home front, African Americans began a massive exodus out of the agrarian South to the North's industrial cities, and millions of women displaced those male workers who were inducted into the military.

At the same time, new inventions such as the telephone, the automobile, and the radio changed transportation and communication. Spanning thousands of miles from east to west, America and its people were formerly divided by immense and insurmountable distances.[3] Then, the widespread use of the telephone among Americans in the early twentieth century connected people, literally and otherwise, in a manner unprecedented in history. The invention of the automobile during this same period further enhanced this "connectedness" by providing the means to visit faraway places or even to move easily across the country. In a few years, rural island communities became linked by both road and wire to the major urban areas. Regional differences began to blur, and a sense of national identity grew. The spread of commercial radio networks in the early 1920s advanced these new national connections, bringing identical music, news, and sports to Americans across the land and building the base for a common culture.

The aggregate effect of all these monumental changes in such a short period of time was truly revolutionary in a social sense. By the end of the 1920s, America was a significantly different country and culture from what it had been at the beginning of the century.[4] Even between 1920 and 1930, America progressed from a land of cultural competition and chaos to a much more homogenized society, with its multitude of ethnicities beginning to merge into one. Coincidentally perhaps, Billy Ingram's hamburgers appeared on the scene at that very time and became part of this new ethnic culture. Fast-food hamburgers may have become America's preferred fare at this time simply because they readily fit into the rapidly changing lifestyles of the era and because Americans yearned for a common food to complement their newly found common culture.

The Rise of the American Restaurant Industry

In the late nineteenth and early twentieth century, as wars heightened nationalism and new technologies strengthened cultural bonds, Americans began eating in new and different ways. Both the many new ethnic influences and the fact that more people were dining outside the home changed American food habits. Eating had become a public activity.[5] The move toward dining away from home had actually started decades earlier but accelerated in the early twentieth century. Restaurants had always existed in some form in America, beginning with the roadside inns and urban taverns of the early colonies. Ramshackle huts serving coarse meats, salt pork, beans, and coffee appeared alongside newly dug canals and westward toll roads. Migrants to Texas bought enchiladas, tamales, and frijoles from Mexican vendors in open-air stands. Saloons sold cheap food and liquor to prospectors and cowboys on the frontier.[6]

As American affluence grew in the mid-nineteenth century, elite restaurants appeared in the larger cities, the most notable of which was Delmonico's. Opened in New York in 1845 by a Swiss immigrant, Lorenzo Delmonico, it soon developed a following of wealthy patrons and became the standard by which all restaurants in the nineteenth century were compared. Delmonico's served exquisite fare and fine European wines to notables and celebrities including Charles Dickens, Samuel Clemens, Napoleon III, the Prince of Wales, and every president holding office since the 1830s. Although catering to a select group, the food that Delmonico's served and the dining policies that it established became the pacesetters for restaurants everywhere. Delmonico's was soon joined by other fine restaurants, including newly opened dining rooms in hotels such as the Palmer House in Chicago, the St. Francis in San Francisco, and the Parker House in Boston.[7]

Most Americans never ate at Delmonico's or the hotel dining rooms, but the notion of visiting restaurants as a means of establishing status spread rapidly. In fact, dining outside the home at all in any form of restaurant became associated with leisure and recreation, in addition to sustenance.

In the mid- to late nineteenth century, common workingmen began to frequent basic urban "eating houses." In the coastal cities, these establishments featured buckets of oysters; elsewhere, they offered a variety of fried foods. On a slightly more lavish scale, hungry diners could choose "sixpenny eating houses" which offered filling meals of beefsteak and side dishes. Eating houses catering to all economic classes and ethnic groups gradually crept into most urban neighborhoods. In addition, the hundreds of boarding houses in most major cities offered meals to both their residents and other working people who came just for a meal. Catering mostly to single men and women, the boarding houses served basic fare and usually required that customers eat quickly to make room for more diners. Since boarding-house food was universally reputed to be quite poor, it is unlikely that diners would have chosen to savor their meals anyway. Nevertheless, lacking housing with adequate cooking facilities, these thousands of single workers were often wholly dependent on the food sold by these eating and boarding houses. By the end of the nineteenth century, therefore, most of the true restaurants were still reserved for those with disposable income and leisure time. In a country where most workingmen could barely feed their families, dining outside the home and the saloon was still often considered to be an extravagance.[8]

Since dining in restaurants as recreation was a rare luxury, few Americans ever had the experience. In the late nineteenth century, similar to the reasons for the saloon or boarding house crowds, people took meals outside the home only when necessary. For example, long-distance travelers needed food at regular intervals, so the first cross-country train passengers were advised to pack their own dried or preserved foods to sustain their eight-day trek. Then, in the early 1870s, George Pullman introduced both the sleeping car and the dining car to make rail journeys more comfortable. He named his first dining-car line "the Delmonico" after the restaurant and hired chefs to serve passengers fine delicacies and wines on white linen tablecloths with Turkish carpets underfoot.[9] The transcontinental routes, however, did not enjoy the same opulence; cross-country travelers often still endured a crude menu, sometimes including prairie dog stew.

The salvation for these passengers was an English immigrant, Frederick Henry Harvey, who is credited with being "the first restaurateur to understand and capitalize on the restless mobility of Americans."[10] Harvey briefly owned a restaurant in St. Louis, which failed during the Civil War. He then worked for local railroads in various capacities, ranging from mail clerk to western freight agent. As a former restaurant owner, he quickly noticed that rail travelers had limited food options, and he responded to this need by opening cafés along the routes. Eventually he struck deals directly with the rail companies, in which Harvey would fulfill the passengers' food needs and the rail lines would deliver his supplies for free. The rail systems also heavily subsidized Harvey's operation, enabling him to provide quality meals to their passengers for very low prices. By creating a restaurant service that could cover thousands of rail miles, Harvey also created the nation's first large-scale food chain, which became a corporate model for White Castle and innumerable others.[11]

From the beginning, Harvey's approach was to offer the traveling public good food and clean service, featuring fresh fruit, oysters, sea turtle, pastries, ice cream, and a wide range of other items, including charlotte of peaches with cognac sauce. Even though Harvey's establishments, called Harvey Houses, were usually at remote rail junctions, this gourmet fare was served in pristine cleanliness with fine china and polished silverware. This level of cleanliness was guaranteed by a team of quality inspectors who constantly traveled from restaurant to restaurant, thoroughly checking every aspect of the operation and firing local managers for the slightest infraction of company standards. Harvey wanted his customers to respect his efforts at quality and cleanliness and insisted that all men wear jackets in the dining rooms.

His attempt to bring refinement to the frontier was helped by the introduction of female servers to the Harvey House. These new waitresses, always referred to as "Harvey girls," were hired back east through advertisements in magazines and newspapers and were given renewable year-long contracts. Harvey felt that a female serving staff would be more stable and that their presence on the frontier would offer a civilizing influence. He preferred employing young white women in their twenties who possessed what he defined as a combination of beauty, strength, and femininity. These women were charged with a much greater task than merely serving food at railroad stations: Harvey sent them west, charged with taming the rugged, masculine wilderness. In contrast to the stereotype of the promiscuous dance-hall girls of the Old West, the Harvey girls were dressed in long black skirts and blouses with starched white aprons, always expected to display a Victorian appearance and virtue. They lived in company-owned dormitories, were governed by strict curfews and codes of behavior, and worked twelve-hour days, usually seven days a week. These women became almost legendary in their own era, popularly held up as models of female initiative and independence.[12]

The importance of Harvey's operation was more than just his numerous innovations and gimmicks; rather, it was the first chain of eating houses that could assure customers of quality and service at every unit. Such uniformity did not guarantee identical food everywhere, since by design Harvey varied the meal offerings at each stop, but customers knew that their food would always be excellent. The Harvey House chain continued to thrive along rail lines until passenger trains gave way to airplanes in the mid-twentieth century, and the chain eventually disappeared in the late 1960s. Its legacy in the restaurant industry, however, continued in every chain that catered to the needs of travelers, especially those insisting on quality food and absolute cleanliness.[13]

Despite the success of Delmonico's and the Harvey Houses, most restaurant customers in America were neither wealthy nor train passengers. Accordingly, around the beginning of the twentieth century, the number of restaurants grew rapidly, feeding people from all classes, ethnic groups, and regional tastes and resulting in a seemingly limitless number of menus and styles. No single ethnic food predominated. Instead, restaurants served an almost infinite number of foods under the broad banner of American cooking.

Class was one factor that divided diners and menus, regardless of region. Similar to the strict class division in other areas and activities of daily life, restaurants catered almost exclusively to specific class clienteles. The wealthy continued to frequent their fine eateries, consuming expensive foods and rare wines. Saloons still dominated poorer working-class neighborhoods, serving both food and drink for the pennies that factory workers could spare. The mostly male patrons of these establishments spent much of their nonworking time drinking beer and whiskey and eating stew.[14] These saloons made no pretense of serving fine foods, but they fulfilled the workers' basic needs and had a loyal following.

Between the extremes of the saloon or boarding house and Delmonico's, other restaurants opened to serve the more affluent working people of northern European descent and the growing middle class. Such restaurants usually offered a menu consisting of basic meats and other simply prepared dishes.[15] Interestingly, however, at first the middle class was less likely than even the workers to frequent restaurants. Domestic labor was still quite inexpensive during this period, and it was not unusual for middle-class homes to employ one or more servants to clean and cook. Although restaurants were numerous, this middle-class group generally preferred either to dine at home or, occasionally, to visit the more expensive urban restaurants.[16]

Many New Foods at the American Table

The restaurant industry as a whole expanded around the turn of the century, with the greatest proliferation of restaurants in the urban ethnic enclaves. Because immigrants to the United States faced terrible discrimination, poverty, and squalor, many sought the solace and security of living near other people from their home countries. Soon large sections of the biggest cities—and sometimes almost the entire cities—acquired an ethnic identity, as seen in their churches and markets. Restaurants selling Old World foods to Old World immigrants living in America opened in these neighborhoods, often starting out as food stalls in ethnic markets or as street vendors' carts.[17]

Many of these establishments eventually outgrew their original neighborhoods and spread into the mainstream culture. Food styles that were less exciting or attractive, such as that of the Irish, remained exclusively in the hearts and the kitchens of ethnic families. German restaurants were among the earliest of the successful ethnic eateries. Many German immigrants came to America between the early nineteenth century and the 1880s, often settling on farms in the Midwest or congregating in such cities as Baltimore, Cincinnati, New York, and Chicago. Although restaurants were sparse in the rural lands, the urbanized German Americans built massive, ornate restaurants featuring Old World foods such as weisswurst, sauerbraten, dark breads, and Wiener schnitzel, washed down with beer.[18] Beginning as a haven for immigrant diners, these restaurants soon built up a large non-German following who liked both the tasty beers served in decorative steins and the hearty food. With names such as Scholg's, Luchow's, and The Platzl, these ethnically German restaurants became popular in the late eighteenth century, often rivaling much older and established eating houses. Their popularity later declined because of the anti-German sentiment accompanying the two world wars.[19]

With the millions of immigrants arriving later in the century, a variety of new ethnic food sellers entered the market, often competing with the established American and German restaurants. There was a brief but significant migration of Chinese workers to the West Coast in the 1870s, resulting in the creation of small storefront "chow chow" eateries, catering to other Chinese.[20] Soon Chinese cooks adapted their fare to attract an adventurous American clientele, quickly identifying themselves as "American Chinese" and serving such non-Chinese dishes as chow mein, egg foo yung, and chop suey. As the popularity of this supposedly exotic food grew throughout America, savvy American entrepreneurs invented the fortune cookie as a further enticement to diners. Later in the twentieth century, Chinese American cuisine became further entrenched in American tastes and eventually became mainstream American fare.

Jewish immigrants also brought with them a distinctive style of cooking. Arriving mainly from eastern Europe in the early twentieth century, these immigrants favored rich, fatty foods, such as lox, bagels, and gefilte fish. Often, such foods were not actually Jewish but, rather, had been borrowed and modified from the traditions of the European nations from which the immigrants came. Instead of opening restaurants, these eastern Europeans preferred to buy both staples and prepared foods at the informal neighborhood delicatessens.[21] Originally offering modified kosher foods to mainly Jewish customers, many of these delicatessens, popularly referred to even then as "delis," eventually began to adapt their menus to appeal to a non-Jewish clientele. This trend made deli foods popular with mainstream urban dwellers and added them to the growing list of "Americanized" ethnic foods.

Italians arriving in America offered an extraordinarily popular ethnic cuisine. Restaurants featuring all types of Italian food proliferated at the turn of the century, virtually everywhere in the United States. Ranging from small, family-owned cafés to large urban restaurants, these new restaurants catered primarily to a non-Italian dining crowd, since Italian immigrants were far more likely to eat at home or with relatives. Similar to the approach of other ethnic restaurants, Italian proprietors reinvented their offerings to appeal to the buying public, once again creating a hybrid ethnic cuisine.[22] For example, pizza was promoted to diners as typical Italian fare, although in Italy it actually was eaten only in Naples and even there, only by the poor. Pizza and numerous other "Italian American" dishes—such as clams casino, turkey tetrazzini, and Caesar salad, which were not even invented by Italians—were defined in America as Italian food.[23]

Other ethnic groups introduced their foods to America on a smaller scale. Russian immigrants opened their fabled "tea rooms," serving a traditional Russian cuisine that never quite caught on in the mainstream culture. Similarly unsuccessful in incorporating their ethnic fare into the mainstream during that period were the Spanish, the Japanese, and even the French. Greek immigrants, on the other hand, built up a successful American restaurant following, serving their foods next to traditional American meat and potatoes.[24]

The combined force of these ethnic influences on America's collective palate was immense. Before the introduction of these new foods, the notion of culinary options to most Americans meant a choice between "boiled or fried." But now many urban Americans had numerous alternatives to their usual fare and were able to enjoy the cuisines of the entire world without ever leaving the country.

In addition to the endless array of ethnic restaurants in the cities, an even greater number of regional foods were available to diners across the nation. In some ways, the distinctions between ethnicity and region overlapped. For instance, the mestizo cooking of Mexico was deeply entrenched in the American Southwest, using spices and cooking styles unknown in other regions. In the Deep South, the African American fried chicken, pork barbecue, catfish, and collard greens became staples of southern white cuisine, in both restaurants and homes.[25] The foods of Minnesota and the other northern states bore the distinctive flavor of their predominantly Scandinavian immigrant populations. Indeed, Americans throughout the country ate very differently from one another, depending on their region and their ancestry.

"Quick Foods" Enter the Marketplace

Most of the restaurant fare in the early twentieth century was far less exotic than mestizo or Chinese cooking. New types of food sellers appeared in the late nineteenth and early twentieth century to accommodate the needs of the changing society, providing basic food at affordable prices. In almost every industrial city, vendors pushed lunch carts to factory gates, selling sausages and other "quick foods" to hungry workers. Clearly a forerunner to White Castle's approach to fast eating, these vendors built up a substantial following, and the more prosperous ones eventually expanded by incorporating horse-drawn wagons into their business. Temperance crusaders even set up lunch carts close to factories with the idea of offering good food to workers outside saloons, thus distracting them from potential vices.[26]

As the lunch cart-vending business grew, so did the carts themselves. In a few years, the lunch carts grew to be wagons, and then the wagons metamorphosed into large, though still mobile, horse-drawn buildings on wheels featuring refined fixtures and a variety of foods. Such food wagons were constructed in large factories on the frames for horse-drawn trolley cars and were made to seat several customers inside the wagon, at a counter on a row of fixed stools. These mobile restaurants were enormously popular, with profits to match. In turn, large lunch-wagon companies were formed, covering hundreds of cities and serving thousands of workers daily.[27]

Over time, the nature of this food-vending business changed from being primarily mobile to mainly stationary, as the wagons were parked during the night and those hours that they were not in use. To maximize their profits, the wagons began to open for business during these off-hours, often selling food throughout the night. By serving food on a more stationary basis, the wagon owners soon noticed that they could make greater profits with less effort. Thus the wheels were taken off these wagons—in "short order"—usually still close to the factories, where they established a permanent location. The new buildings looked exactly like what they were: horse-drawn trolley cars without wheels. Used and discarded street trolleys also were salvaged and converted to diners. Later expanded to include buildings intentionally made to look like stranded railroad cars, this "accidental architecture" forever became the style synonymous with this new type of eatery. Although the process was gradual and unheralded, the era of the diner had begun.[28]

The diner industry exploded in the first few years of the century, with diners appearing in nearly every urban neighborhood. Usually open twenty-four hours a day, these small restaurants attracted customers for breakfast, lunch, dinner, and snacks in between. Never before had any restaurant provided for the public's food needs in such a comprehensive way, serving tasty fare at bargain prices. Above all, the hallmark of diner food was that it was quick, cooked and served on a "short order" basis. Such speed, nocturnal availability, and low prices, however, contributed to the popular notion that diners were unsavory establishments, selling hastily prepared food of questionable quality.

Branded early on as "restaurants of ill repute," the diners often catered to the same factory workers who had formerly patronized the lunch carts, thus reinforcing their rough image. Many of the diners were operated by Greek immigrants, who often mixed together American and Old World tastes.[29] Known for their coffee and greasy foods, these diners almost cherished this questionable reputation, attracting a loyal working-class clientele and keeping the more squeamish at bay. Despite their rather sleazy aura and epithets such as "greasy spoons" or "holes-in-the-wall," diners thrived everywhere in America throughout the twentieth century, their popularity diminishing only recently with the onslaught of the big fast-food chains or their conversion to larger restaurants. But a revival of the diner nostalgia in the last decade resulted in the creation across the country of trendy, updated, faux diners, serving upscale versions of traditional fare at premium prices.

The Rise of the Hot Dog

Hot-dog stands were another culinary innovation in the early twentieth century. Hot dogs, or at least their sausage forebears, have existed since ancient times. The practice of grinding less desirable parts of an animal carcass and stuffing the mixture into washed intestinal casings certainly was not new: for years, much of German cuisine consisted of various spicy sausages. Many of these sausages came to America with the huge influx of German immigrants, their names often referring to their place of origin, such as frankfurter (Frankfurt) or wiener (Wien, or Vienna).

One such immigrant, Charles Feltman, started as a pie vendor on Coney Island, New York, but switched to the lunch cart business in 1867. For economy and ease of operation, Feltman turned to the foods with which he was most familiar, bland sausages on white rolls.[30] Hungry customers were soon attracted to the novelty, taste, and convenience of these sausages, usually buying two at a time. The "hot dog" business took off across the nation, the silly name coming from Chicago cartoonist Tad Dorgan. Dorgan drew an amusing sketch of a dachshund inside a frankfurter bun, and from that time on, the German sausage had a new American name. By 1901, Feltman's vending business had grown well beyond his original lunch cart, eventually becoming "Feltman's German Gardens," a huge Coney Island hot-dog restaurant employing twelve hundred waiters. Although Feltman's restaurant closed long ago, his successful marketing efforts will forever link Coney Island with the hot dog, with many Americans using the two words interchangeably.[31]

Riding on Charles Feltman's business coattails were other successful purveyors of the hot dog. An early imitator was Harry Magely Stevens, who introduced hot dogs to baseball fans at New York's Polo Grounds at the beginning of the century. Although Stevens has faded into the pages of food history, his idea of linking hot dogs and baseball lives on.[32]

Another such entrepreneur was the famed Nathan Handwerker, who originally worked for Feltman, recognized the popularity of hot dogs, and opened his own stand in 1916 down the street, on the corner of Stillwell and Surf Avenues. Handwerker, a Polish American, undercut Feltman's price by half, selling his hot dogs for a nickel. In addition to offering a better price, many customers believed that his Nathan's Famous Hot Dogs were the best in the city, and his business thrived.

Problems soon developed, however, with the recurrent rumors that hot dogs were unhealthy fare, filled with rotten ground meats and an array of chemicals. As business began to dwindle because of this scare, Handwerker hired a group of college students, dressed them as physicians complete with stethoscopes, and positioned them outside his stands during the lunch hours eating hot dogs. Soon the slanderous claims of poor quality were countered with new rumors that all the doctors from the local hospital ate at Nathan's, so therefore the food must be healthy. Handwerker's business weathered that storm of controversy and continues to prosper to this day. Following Feltman's and Handwerker's successes, hot dogs subsequently migrated from the boardwalks of New York City to other cities and even to small villages across the nation. New eateries opened everywhere to sell them, and they became the "fad food" of the early century.[33]

America Discovers Its "National Drinks"

Eating hot dogs on Coney Island—or anywhere else, for that matter—made consumers thirsty, and so it soon became customary to eat hot dogs along with a new generation of soft drinks. From the beginning, the leader among these drinks was an unlikely headache remedy invented in 1886 by an Atlanta pharmacist, John Styth Pemberton. Always experimenting with new products, Pemberton concocted an elixir, which he named Coca-Cola, from an extract of African kola nuts and the same leaves of the South American coca shrub from which cocaine is derived. Originally marketed as a "Wonderful Nerve and Brain Tonic and Remarkable Therapeutic Agent," Pemberton's mixture became just another patent medicine.

Five years later, however, Pemberton sold his obscure Coca-Cola recipe to fellow pharmacist Asa G. Candler, who founded the Coca-Cola Company and started selling the elixir at soda fountains as a five-cent soft drink. Candler's new company also sold the syrupy base for its beverage to restaurants, which then added carbonated water. (This carbonated water, or "soda" as it was better known, was a key ingredient in Candler's new cola and in all the other soft drinks of this generation.) The new drink became enormously popular in just a few years, almost immediately giving rise to a host of imitators.[34]

One direct imitator of Coca-Cola was Pepsi-Cola, created in North Carolina by pharmacist Caleb Bradham. The cola formula that Bradham devised and patented was different from that of Coca-Cola, was immediately successful, and by 1907 had opened forty bottling plants across America. Variations of these colas and other soft drinks were then introduced every year.[35] In Waco, Texas, chemist Robert Lazenby devised a black cherry-flavored soft drink that he called Dr. Pepper's Phos-Ferrates, supposedly after the Confederate Army surgeon Charles T. Pepper, who had invented a good-tasting mixture of mountain herbs, roots, and seltzer. Lazenby's soft drink quickly became a cultural staple in the southwestern states, only later "discovered" by the rest of America at the 1904 St. Louis world's fair.[36]

Hires Root Beer was the next soft drink to attract a following, coming soon after both Coca-Cola and Dr. Pepper. Originally sold in 1876 as a powdered herbal tea called Hires Household Extract, it was quickly reinvented as a bottled soft drink and soon won a respectable share of the market. Another twist on this new trend in drinks was Orange Crush, which first appeared on the market in 1916 (in the same year that Coca-Cola adopted its distinctive bottle shape). Made mainly of sugar and carbonated water, Orange Crush promoted its small amount of California orange concentrate as healthful, hoping to capitalize on the food purity crusades of that era. The next generation of imitators further pursued this marketing line by introducing other citrus flavors, such as lemon-lime.

The drinking public embraced all these new, soda-based drinks, regardless of whether they were colas, root beers, or citrus.[37] The combined force of these drinks changed Americans' drinking habits, often replacing coffee, tea, and even alcoholic beverages. First served as beverages accompanying foods, these soft drinks often became the end in themselves. New businesses called "root-beer stands" sprang up in small towns across the nation to serve frosty mugs of that new drink, often also doubling as the local purveyors of New York-style hot dogs. The stands appeared everywhere, from city street corners to desolate roadways. All had a very limited menu of quickly prepared, broiled or fried foods, and most always offered a choice of colas and root beer. The novelty of these stands was that customers did not have to go there to eat a meal but, rather, just for the soda drinks. Indeed, the idea of "going out for a Coca-Cola" eventually became a mainstream leisure activity and the focus of many dates.[38]

A food business that centered even more directly on the various soda drinks was aptly named the "soda fountain," which served a variety of carbonated soft drinks, ice cream, and combinations of both. Collectively, these fountains invented and standardized numerous treats, including milk shakes and banana splits. Since most of the early soda fountains began as one corner of the neighborhood drugstore, it was not a great coincidence that pharmacists such as Pemberton and Bradham invented soft drinks.

A hundred years ago, the basis of a pharmacy was a mixture of chemicals and drugs. In most of the smaller stores, pharmacists would sell medicinal preparations from one counter and then walk across the store to serve soda or ice cream. It was natural that their chemistry skills and their access to ingredients would lead to experimentation. In fact, the link between soda drinks and pharmacists was tighter than one would first imagine. In the early years, the lure of many soda drinks was their powerful narcotic and nonnarcotic additives. (When the cocaine ingredient was removed in the early twentieth century, these drinks were usually reinforced with a greatly enhanced dose of caffeine, so as not to lose their enthusiastic following.) For many reasons, the public wanted to buy what these pharmacists were selling at the fountains. By 1891 there were more soda fountains than saloons in New York City, and the fountains themselves became increasingly ornate, with marble countertops and chromium fixtures. The soda fountain industry continued to grow, publishing its own trade journal by 1900 and funding university research on fountain operations and products.[39]

Although most soda fountains remained appendages of pharmacies, some eventually expanded their food service to lunch as well. First expanding on a limited basis, these full-service fountains soon became known as lunch counters or "luncheonettes" serving sandwiches and hot foods in addition to sodas and ice cream.

In many ways, these lunch counters differed from their diner cousins only in that they usually were housed in a pharmacy or other type of store. The F. W. Woolworth dime stores were early innovators in this business, opening counters in most of their stores by 1910 and redefining them as an unique type of eatery. The concept behind this new approach was that customers could combine their shopping and eating in one stop. Because Woolworth's lunch counters usually prospered, many soon needed more space and so constructed dining rooms for their customers.

The addition of these dining rooms further redefined the lunch counters as lunchrooms. This was far more than a mere semantic change, as these new, larger lunchroom facilities were specifically designed to be utilitarian, often serving hundreds of customers at the same time, with each person sitting at a single, one-armed table called a *settle*.[40] This design intentionally discouraged group dining, trying to keep customers from lingering beyond the time it took them to finish their meal. In 1904, Harvey Kelsey began a chain of these lunchrooms, called the Waldorf Lunch, in Springfield, Massachusetts, expanding to seventy-four units in the Northeast by 1920. The other lunchroom mogul was candy maker William F. Schrafft, who built his chain by offering lunch customers more genteel surroundings than his competitors did. Regardless of decor, both Kelsey and Schrafft made fortunes selling ordinary sandwiches and pie to a hungry public and established the lunchroom as an urban institution.[41]

Adding to the many different types of restaurants opening in the early twentieth century were cafeterias, through which customers filed in military-style serving lines, and the famous Automats, where customers deposited coins into slots and removed their food choices from small cubicles with glass doors. Both businesses more resembled stores selling hot food than traditional restaurants serving meals. This no-frills, no-waitress approach appealed to an increasingly busy public that consistently preferred to buy its food in an efficient and economical manner.[42]

This broad array of restaurants altered American culture in a variety of ways. First, they together created a cultural norm for eating meals outside the home, on either an individual or a family basis. This norm set the stage for the explosion of restaurants in later years. In a sense, restaurants taught Americans how to enjoy the experience of dining out both for the food and as a leisure activity. Less positively, these restaurants usually catered to different classes or ethnic groups, helping sustain a widely fragmented and heterogeneous society.

In sum, in the first two decades of the twentieth century, food providers ranged from push carts to Automats to Delmonico's, with the range of food offerings even wider. Some Americans regularly dined on the foods of their homelands while others ate ham sandwiches at a Woolworth counter. Some people ate turkey as their Sunday meal; others ate spaghetti. All these foods thrived independently of one another, each typical of a particular ethnic or class subgroup. America was a land of many foods, yet with none able to claim to be a standard bearer of the so-called American ethnicity. If an ethnic group "is what it eats," then it was readily apparent that America still had no single unifying ethnicity. Very soon, however, one company and one food appeared that would provide the common strand linking Americans together: White Castle, which gave Americans the modern fast-food hamburger.

The Hamburger Takes Shape

We should emphasize that White Castle did not "invent" the hamburger sandwich. Rather, its accomplishment was persuading the public that hamburgers were an acceptable mainstream food and then marketing them to the entire nation. Legitimizing hamburgers, however, was not an easy task, and they did not gain a great following during the late nineteenth and early twentieth century. Appearing about the same time as hot dogs, hamburgers were slow to achieve popularity. The main reason was that the public were deeply suspicious of the quality of ground beef, believing that it was ground up because it was spoiled or because it was an inedible grade of meat. Although offered on the Delmonico's menu as early as the 1830s, the hamburger of the late nineteenth century was considered to be a food for the poor, seldom served in better restaurants. In fact, the hamburger was hardly ever served in any restaurants.

Most hamburgers consisted of a small round "meatball" placed between two slices of bread, principally sold by vendors at county and state fairs. In addition to fairs, hamburgers were sold from the lunch carts outside factories, although sausages were preferred. As a "fair food," the hamburger was quite popular, but it was not able to make the successful transition to becoming a daily-meal food.

Exactly where the hamburger came from is anybody's guess. Several claims compete for the honor of being the true "father of the hamburger," and although most probably have some merit, all are impossible to verify. Most of the would-be inventors claiming credit were avid self-promoters. Obviously, no single person or culture can claim to have discovered ground meat, since its existence definitely predates our recorded past. The label *hamburger* almost certainly harks back to the famed German city, and the earliest references to ground-beef patties in America were to "Hamburg-style steak."[43]

Nonetheless, the early purveyors of the hamburger sandwich claimed that their "invention" of the product was the true original. One such claimant was Charlie Nagreen of Seymour, Wisconsin. Known regionally as "Hamburger Charlie," Nagreen is said to have served the world's first true hamburger sandwich in 1885 at the Outgamie County Fair. Only fifteen years old at the time, he supposedly was cooking and selling meatballs to the fair goers from his ox cart. Although his meatballs sold well, many of his customers wanted a more convenient way to carry them as they walked around the fair. So Nagreen began serving the meatball between two slices of bread. Although this scenario is plausible, Nagreen also claimed to have coined the term *hamburger* at the same time, despite Delmonico's printed usage of the word fifty years earlier.[44]

Others vied for the title of being the hamburger's inventor. The town of Hamburg, New York, still insists that the sandwich originated there, citing only its rather unoriginal name as evidence.[45] Fair concessionaire Frank Menches is also said to be the founder of hamburgers, first serving them at the Akron, Ohio, County Fair in 1892. At the time of his death in 1951, the *Los Angeles Daily News* stated that Menches was "widely credited with inventing the hamburger." Exactly who did this crediting is open to debate. According to the family-promoted story, Menches regularly sold pork sandwiches until one day when his meat supplier was out of pork and could offer him only ground beef. After seasoning the ground meat, Menches began selling these new sandwiches to a hungry public, and the rest, as they say, is history. Once again, however, some of the claims seem exaggerated: Menches also boasted during his life that he invented the ice-cream cone.[46]

More verifiable and probable than either Nagreen's or Menches's claims is the story of Louis Lassen, the proprietor of Louis' Lunch in New Haven, Connecticut. Lassen supposedly fashioned the first burger in 1900, by forming discarded steak trimmings into a patty. Louis' Lunch is still a New Haven institution and insists that it is the birthplace of the hamburger.

Fletcher "Old Dave" Davis is reputed in some circles to be the true originator. A native Texan, Davis took his onion-covered hamburger sandwich to the midway at the 1904 world's fair in St. Louis, where it "caused a sensation." Indeed, Davis's burger stand was quite popular at the fair, even attracting the attention of the *New York Tribune*. Certainly Nagreen's and Menches's creations predate that of Fletcher Davis, but his stand on the midway of the world's fair was heralded in the national press as the formal introduction of the hamburger sandwich to America. (But this only is evidence that newspaper reporters had not eaten at many factory lunch carts during the previous decade.) Today, many people still credit Davis as the inventor of the hamburger.

Conflicting dates, contradictory details, and exaggerated achievements all cloud the issue of who truly created the hamburger. Although this debate still rages among people arguing a family or regional claim, for most people it is largely meaningless, in the realm of food trivia. Regardless of who was first, all these men—and many others—did help refine and popularize the hamburger. The more important discussion is how the hamburger became so popular and how its acceptance changed American life. To understand these issues, it is useful to ask who was responsible for making the hamburger our national food and fast food our preferred style of eating. On that question there is no confusion or debate: in the 1920s, Billy Ingram and his White Castle System did.

2

White Castle and
the Beginning of Fast Food

The 1920s is often called the "roaring" twenties, a time when America underwent dramatic changes in its lifestyle, values, and technology. As the decade began, the consumption and sale of alcohol were prohibited under the newly enacted Volstead Act, which temporarily slowed the use of liquor in America and had consequences that lasted for years. After a decades-long battle, the suffrage movement finally achieved victory, securing voting rights for women in national elections. With the onset of commercial radio, news and entertainment filled the airwaves over Detroit and Pittsburgh. Automobiles had become a more common sight on city streets, and highways were being constructed to accommodate the growing legions of travelers. New technology and legislation brought immediate changes in many areas of American life, such as more efficient transportation and lower alcohol consumption, and caused even a larger ripple effect that continued to alter attitudes and behavior.

Because of these significant and widespread changes, many historians point to the 1920s as the time when American culture as we know it today began. This was when many Americans bought their first automobile, their first radio, or voted in their first election. And yes, it was when most Americans tasted their first hamburger.

White Castle was created in May 1921, after which time the idea of fast food caught on very quickly. Indeed, the hamburger sandwich rose from obscurity and disrepute to prominence in less than ten years. Whereas in 1920, fast food as we know it today did not exist, by 1930, fast-food restaurants already dotted urban neighborhoods and highways across America, selling millions of hamburgers annually. Americans soon began craving White Castle-style fast-food hamburgers, and by the end of the decade they were a staple of the American diet.

The Founders of White Castle

White Castle can be traced back to a lone grill cook in Wichita, Kansas, by the name of J. Walter "Walt" Anderson. A self-described "ne'er do well" itinerant, Walt Anderson was born on a farm outside the town of St. Mary's, Kansas, in 1880, the son of Swedish immigrants. He attended a small business college in Sedalia, Missouri, and then moved to Baldwin, Kansas, enrolling for a time at Baker University. While at Baker he supported himself by working as a school janitor and living in an abandoned house. Anderson left college after two years, citing the freezing conditions in his unheated house as the reason for his withdrawal. After that, he spent years wandering throughout the Midwest, going from job to job washing dishes and cooking in restaurants.

Worried about Walt's lifestyle and future, in 1905 his father bought him his own restaurant in Marquette, Kansas. But within a year, Walt was once again struck by wanderlust. He sold the restaurant and organized a traveling stage show with a cast and orchestra of thirteen persons. " 'I soon learned that I knew nothing of the show game,' he admitted, " 'and three weeks after I started the venture the show went on the rocks and I caught a freight to Topeka where I got a job cooking in a hotel.'"[1] Although failure seemed to haunt Anderson, his two brothers back in Illinois enjoyed great success: one became a prosperous stock trader and the other, a respected newspaper editor. Walt next got a job cooking for the Southern Pacific Railroad, moving out west to Nevada and then later to Utah, where he got married. Returning in Kansas in 1912, Anderson continued to work at a series of low-paying jobs.[2]

While employed as a short-order cook in a local diner in Wichita, Anderson experimented with grilling ground meat in a variety of ways, molding the meat into different shapes and serving it with an assortment of condiments. Most popular among his customers was a flattened patty smothered with onions, seared on both sides and served on a bun instead of bread slices. Legend has it that Anderson actually stumbled onto this "patty" idea one day when he grew increasingly frustrated with a slow-cooking meatball that was sticking to the skillet. In a moment of exasperation, he supposedly smashed the meatball flat with his spatula. Anderson found that this way it did cook faster and even that many of his customers preferred it to the traditional style.[3] Whatever the circumstances, the modern hamburger sandwich was born.

As Anderson's hamburger sandwich grew in popularity, he decided to start his own restaurant business, in 1916. Since banks often considered itinerant fry cooks to be poor credit risks, Anderson and his venture were repeatedly turned down for financing. In his own words, Anderson later admitted that his "credit rating would horrify either Dunn or Bradstreet and his financial statement would chase a film of glass across the eyes of the softest-hearted banker in the city."[4] After several unsuccessful attempts, he was able to borrow $80 from a rather hazy source to buy and partially refurbish an old shoe repair stand at 800 East Douglas Avenue. He equipped his stand with a counter and three stools, a flat piece of iron to be used as a griddle, and various cooking utensils. Over the door he hung a simple sign reading "Hamburgers 5¢."

By the time Anderson had built his "shack," however, he had no money left to buy the supplies necessary to open for business. But a local grocer, William A. Dye, on nearby South Rock Island Avenue, agreed to give Anderson five pounds of ground beef, at ten cents a pound, and enough buns for his first day of operation, on the promise that Anderson would pay him by noon.[5] Anderson opened his hamburger stand on the morning of November 16, and business was so brisk that he quickly sold out all his hamburgers at five cents each. His wife later told how Anderson hawked his wares on the sidewalk, yelling "Hamburgers, a nickel apiece!"[6] True to his word, Anderson returned to Dye's store at noontime with a big bag of nickels, repaid his debt, and bought an additional five pounds of meat for the afternoon trade. By closing time in the late afternoon, Anderson had earned a profit of $3.75.[7]

In addition to making a tidy profit on his first day of business, Anderson also saw that he would have to modify the edges of his iron griddle, since grease had spilled onto the floor during his day of frying meat, making quite a mess. He soon solved this small problem and the other minor start-up difficulties that plague many new businesses and quickly discovered exactly what his customers wanted. Responding to the continued apprehension about the quality of ground meat and the cleanliness of many makeshift stands, Anderson ground his meat and grilled his hamburgers directly behind the counter in full view of his customers. Impressed by the cleanliness (once his griddle was modified) of his shop and the high quality and good taste of his hamburgers, first-time customers soon became "regulars," buying sandwiches from Anderson every day. Word of Anderson's new stand spread quickly throughout Wichita, and his hamburger business boomed virtually overnight. Anderson recalled that his initial clientele of factory workers, "transients, newsboys, and hangers-on of the district" quickly expanded to others outside the immediate area.

> Soon I noticed that little boys would come into my place asking for half dozen lots to take out. These lads were not the street urchin type, so I became curious and investigated, to learn that they would take the hamburgers around the corner and climb into big limousines. Their mothers were ashamed to drive up in front of my dinky place and would park their cars around the corner and send their lads after the sandwiches.[8]

Despite Anderson's claims of wealthy patrons "slumming" to enjoy his hamburgers, most of his customers were from the working class and lived within close walking distance of his stand. In any case, his hamburger stand did prosper in the first two years, adding two more locations in other Wichita neighborhoods and, by 1920, a fourth stand. Once established in different areas of the city, Anderson did whatever he could to maximize his business. At each location, he encouraged the practice of buying his burgers in "half-dozen lots," by adopting the slogan "Buy'em by the Sack," and his customers complied. He also contracted with the Campbell Bread Company to supply rolls for his sandwiches.[9] Realizing that some potential buyers might be discouraged by the shabby appearance of his stands, he tried to make them more presentable, recalling that "I cleaned up my place, making it neat and attractive."

Anderson's efforts bore fruit. No records survive of the details of his financial success, but by 1920 his profits enabled the former fry cook to build what was described in the *Wichita Eagle* as "an imposing $12,000 home on the Hill ... which commands a view of the east end." (This is $12,000 in 1920 dollars.) This same article goes on to proclaim Anderson as the "King of the Hamburger" and to praise his commercial contributions to Wichita. Starting to enjoy his newly acquired status as a prospering businessman, Anderson became involved in civic associations and social organizations, even serving as an officer in the local Masonic lodge.

Despite Walt Anderson's financial success with his four hamburger stands, they were still just hamburger stands: poorly constructed buildings on busy street corners. The persistent stigma attached to ground meat and the middle-class prejudice against hamburger stands were still strong, and hamburgers remained almost exclusively a working-class food, regarded with scorn by the more affluent. Seen by many as purveyors of a dubious product, hamburger stands were often identified as generally unseemly. That is, since many people viewed the sale of ground meat as unhealthy, they also assumed that other vices must be lurking nearby. Indeed, it was common for hamburger stands like Anderson's to be referred to by the disparaging slang term *joints*, implying something shabby or disreputable. In the early years of Prohibition, in fact, street-corner and storefront food stands were often suspected of being "front" operations for speakeasies or brothels. It was in this climate of questionable legitimacy that Walt Anderson sought to expand and establish his small chain of hamburger stands.

Just as the banks in Wichita usually denied loans for the purpose of opening new food stands, many property owners in Wichita hesitated before leasing space in their buildings to stand operators, and others just refused. So even though by 1921 Anderson enjoyed a good personal reputation in the Wichita community, the nature of his business was still suspect. When he tried to lease an additional property owned by a local dentist, the dentist stated his reservations about the viability of a hamburger stand and asked for additional guarantees. But the insurance and real estate broker who was negotiating the deal, Edgar Waldo "Billy" Ingram, became intrigued with what he learned about Anderson's hamburger operation. As a former employee of the financial firm of Dun and Bradstreet, Ingram was both interested in and impressed by the customer base and growth potential for the business. He thus immediately agreed to cosign the lease on the dentist's property and, with $700, became an enthusiastic principal investor in the business. Ingram next sold his interest in his insurance and real estate firm to his partner, Austin Stone, and devoted all his time and energy to the hamburger business. With Walt Anderson as president and Ingram as vice president, the new Anderson-Ingram partnership was thus forged, a partnership that would henceforth change American eating habits.

Born in Leadville, Colorado, on December 28, 1880, in a two-room slab house roofed with tin cans, Billy Ingram took a long and indirect route to the hamburger business. At the time of Billy's birth, his father, Charles W. Ingram, was a clerk in the government assayer's office. When Billy was two, Charles tried his hand at ranching, moving his family to the Travis ranch in the San Luis Valley of Colorado. Quickly becoming dissatisfied with the ranching life, two years later Charles moved his family to Omaha, securing employment in the land development department of the Union Pacific Railroad. In 1897 the family moved again, this time to St. Joseph, Missouri, where Charles became an officer of the smaller St. Joseph and Grand Island Railroad. But the small railroad soon went into receivership, and Charles, now without a job, bought a hand laundry to make ends meet.

Young Billy worked in this laundry and stayed in St. Joseph until he graduated from high school the following year and moved to Omaha. He worked there for five years in journalism, as both a livestock reporter and an editor for the *Omaha Bee*. Billy then left the *Bee* to accept a job offer from the A. I. Walker Manufacturing Company of Council Bluffs, Iowa, which manufactured patented attachments for farm implements. When the A. I. Walker factory closed the following year, Billy returned to both Omaha and journalism at the *Omaha Excelsior*, a small weekly society paper. At the *Excelsior* his job encompassed reporting and editing, the sale of advertising, bookkeeping, and occasionally even the printing of the paper. Billy stayed at the *Excelsior* for two years until he found a job in 1905 with R. G. Dun and Company (later Dun and Bradstreet), as its traveling agent for the state of Nebraska. Two years later he requested and received a transfer to R. G. Dun's Wichita office.

Soon after arriving in Wichita, Ingram realized that the city held great entrepreneurial possibilities, and he left his employment with Dun in less than a year to open an insurance agency. He cofounded the firm of Ingram, Yankey and Company and devoted the next thirteen years to building a series of profitable insurance, oil, and real estate partnerships. By 1921 Ingram was the managing partner in the insurance and real estate firm of Stone and Ingram, and he enjoyed a sound reputation in the community.

Anderson and Ingram Form the White Castle Partnership

Exactly where Walt Anderson met Billy Ingram is no longer known. Both men were avid Masons long before they formed their business partnership, and Ingram was also quite active in the local Rotary Club. They probably knew each other through Masonic activities, which may be why Anderson sought Ingram's help in buying a home and later in securing the property lease. In any event, Billy Ingram certainly was an unlikely entrant into the restaurant business. Indeed, many Wichita businessmen wondered why Ingram would leave a profitable insurance and real estate agency, and considerable status in the financial community, to go into the business of hamburger stands. Others questioned how he could significantly advance Walt Anderson's hamburger success, with no experience working in restaurants and only a minimal knowledge of advertising and promotion. But Anderson and Ingram apparently knew enough to make it work. Anderson knew how to make the hamburgers in the way that his customers liked, but his approach to business was not much different from that of other food stands and diners in the city. By the closing months of 1921, in fact, other entre-preneurs had capitalized on Anderson's success by opening numerous hamburger stands on the streets of Wichita, and the competition was grow-ing increasingly fierce.

Distinguishing Walt Anderson's business from these other upstart com-petitors is where Billy Ingram made a profound difference. He brought to the partnership a sound understanding of the financial world and a vision for growth and expansion. As soon as Ingram entered the business in 1921, he implemented many changes in both the company's philosophy and its operation. First, Ingram believed that achieving irrefutable legitimacy was a necessary step toward greater commercial success. He was convinced that hamburger stands and their ground-meat products could overcome their negative images. Ingram immediately sought "to break down the deep-seated prejudice against chopped beef."[10] To do this, he set out to create a new, more positive public image for their hamburger business.

Essentially, Ingram intended to repackage Anderson's existing operation completely. He first selected both a new company name and a symbolic ar-chitecture. Accordingly, the Anderson-Ingram partnership was legally or-ganized in March under the name of the White Castle System of Eating Houses. Ingram later explained that the rationale for this new name was to convey a more positive image of their business, with "White" signifying pu-rity and "Castle" signifying strength, stability, and permanence. He also wanted to demonstrate this positive change in the buildings themselves. Rather than opening just another shabby hamburger "stand," Ingram de-cided to create a unique structure that would represent the new company's ideals and help change the public perception of the hamburger business.

Ingram's choice of architecture for the partnership's first new restau-rant—and later for all subsequent buildings—was a white-washed struc-ture with crenellated walls and turrets, loosely modeled on Chicago's famed Water Tower. The Chicago Water Tower, which was itself styled after the turrets of medieval castles, was the only structure still standing after the disastrous Great Chicago Fire of 1871. This medieval motif was further reinforced by use of leaded stained-glass windows in some White Castles. Ingram believed that this architecture would reinforce the sym-bolism of the new company name, with the castle towers indicating strength and permanence and the white paint signifying purity and clean-liness. This cleanliness was further reinforced by employing a separate "clean-up man" to scour the woodwork and utensils each day in every White Castle restaurant.[11]

Each new restaurant, or "Castle" as the company called them, had the same layout, with a grill, a counter, and five stools and was staffed by two males employees. In fact, Ingram's insistence on standardizing every aspect of the business became the hallmark of White Castle's operations. Ingram also had the phrase "White Castle Hamburgers 5 cents" painted on the exterior on the new "Castles," along with Walt Anderson's successful slogan "Buy'em by the Sack." Featuring a streamlined menu of hamburgers, coffee, Coca-Cola, and pie, White Castle was open for business.

In addition to these architectural features, catchy phrases, and positive symbols, Billy Ingram also tried to create a solid public image by constantly publicizing good news about White Castle and its hamburgers. Ingram believed that the White Castle approach to eating was revolutionary and frequently proclaimed this fact to anyone who would listen. He was always quick to point out that White Castle had legitimized the hamburger and transformed the inexpensive-food industry, offering the rare combination of both cleanliness and speed.

On the issue of cleanliness, Ingram wrote triumphantly that

> when the word "hamburger" is mentioned, one immediately thinks of the circus . . . or [a] dirty, dingy, ill-lighted hole-in-the-wall, down in the lower districts of the city. The day of the dirty, greasy hamburger is past. No more shall we have to taste the hamburger at circuses or carnivals only, for a new system has arisen, the "White Castle System."

His response to the "dirty, dingy" stereotype was that all utensils "were to be kept scrupulously clean."[12] In regard to prompt service, he proclaimed that "a revelation in the eating business has come. Instead of having to go to a restaurant and wait half an hour for the noon lunch, one may step into a nearby hamburger establishment and partake in a hot, juicy hamburger, prepared instantaneously." Ingram sensed that this combination was attractive to Americans in the 1920s, and he promoted it at every opportunity. Although the term had yet to be coined, through Ingram's promotion efforts the fast-food revolution had begun.

Achieving legitimacy for ground beef and for his company was central to Ingram's strategy. Once again, the two main challenges in this quest were convincing the buying public that ground beef was both palatable and safe and that White Castle maintained the highest standards in the food industry. To underscore this guarantee of product quality and freshness, Ingram ordered that only special cuts of shoulder meat be used for White Castle hamburgers. (Such shoulder meat is commonly referred to today as "ground chuck.") In a 1925 article in the *Wichita Eagle*, he explained just how carefully the company selected its beef:

> Our meat must be delivered from the butcher shop from two to four times daily. All the left-over meat is sent back. Meat is never more than four or five hours from the butcher shop when fried into hamburgers. Our hamburger meat is not like the average kind purchased in a butcher shop. To start with, we buy a certain cut from the carcass and no trimmings from any other part of the beef are allowed to enter. It is not crushed to the required pulp in the ordinary manner, but cut and recut so that the food cells in the meat are not crushed and considerable food value is lost. The butcher who agreed to supply our meat was compelled to spend $1500 on additional machinery.[13]

This seemingly excessive emphasis on food quality was necessary during that era to dispel the common suspicion that meat was ground only to hide spoilage or as a means to market inferior cuts or otherwise discarded parts of the animal. A famous exposé from that era by Arthur Kallet, entitled *100,000,000 Guinea Pigs*, passionately reinforced the belief that hamburgers were a horrible health hazard:

> The hamburger habit is just about as safe as walking in a garden while the arsenic spray is being applied, and about as safe as getting your meat out of a garbage can standing in the hot sun. For beyond all doubt, the garbage can is where the chopped meat sold by most butchers belongs, as well as a large percentage of all the hamburger that goes into sandwiches.

Kallet went on to indict the purveyors of ground meat for their rampant use of preservative chemicals, such as sodium sulfite, citing a study that found sulfite in seventy-one of the seventy-six hamburgers sampled. He contended that this commonly used preservative "not only restores the color and appearance of fresh meat, but also destroys the odor of putrefaction." Kallet concluded that "eating putrid meat is not the only risk that you run when you eat a hamburger; the sulfite itself is one of the most severe of all digestive and kidney hazards."[14]

Kallet's views were supported by Frederick J. Schlink's *Eat, Drink, and Be Wary*, which further condemns the hamburger. Schlink agreed with Kallet's observations about the additives in ground meat and also questioned the use of potassium bromate in the production of white-flour buns.[15] Even the famed food writer Duncan Hines cautioned his readers about the questionable food purity of hamburgers and issues of cleanliness.[16]

In response to this very negative publicity, Ingram and White Castle constantly had to work to change the public perception of hamburgers. Interestingly, Ingram himself later used "scientific" studies to counter the critics of ground beef. In May 1928, he opened the much heralded "Food Experiment Department" on East Douglas Avenue in Wichita. Intended as both a test kitchen and a quality-control laboratory, this new "department" actually served real customers but sold the food products at greatly reduced prices.[17]

Still striving toward the appearance of even greater objectivity, in 1930 White Castle commissioned a study by the physiological chemistry department at the University of Minnesota to prove the nutritional value of White Castle hamburgers. Ingram explained that

> we arranged for a medical student to live for thirteen weeks on nothing but White Castle hamburgers and water. The student maintained good health throughout the three month period, and was eating twenty to twenty-four hamburgers a day during the last few weeks. A food scientist signed a report that a normal healthy child could eat nothing but our hamburger and water, and fully develop all its physical and mental faculties.[18]

Because we do not have the details or actual data from either Kallet's studies or Ingram's commissioned project, it is difficult to determine their validity or merits. Ingram's advantage was that he could point to "scientific evidence" that his hamburgers were not only safe but also healthy. Nonetheless, for all those potential patrons convinced by these results, some skeptics still remained. Ingram's main approach to achieving legitimacy in the marketplace was much simpler; he told the public at every opportunity that both beef and buns were delivered to each White Castle at least twice each day.

Having outgrown the capacity of Dye's grocery store as a supplier, Ingram bought his meat in Wichita during the early 1920s from the highly respected Arnold Brother's Meat Company.[19] By setting this high standard of food quality at every company location, Ingram won the public's confidence and built a loyal customer base. Every day, more and more people tasted White Castle's hamburgers, and they apparently liked them. Stressing this point of consistent superiority, Ingram stated that "our food must never vary from standard in excellence and quality . . . even if the profits are smaller."[20] With this quality-oriented approach, White Castle successfully blazed a trail that eventually allowed ground beef to gain mainstream acceptance and the once-despised hamburger to become the United States' national food.

To emphasize White Castle's positive sanitary image and its theme of ultracleanliness, Ingram also mandated that all serving employees be held to strict standards of conduct, personal hygiene, and attire. Starting with the first Castle, he sought "to hire young men between the ages of eighteen and twenty-four-years-old, of neat appearance, good character, and preferably with a high school education." Applications for employment were thorough, with questions about family background and all other aspects of personal history. Each applicant for a position with the company also had to pass a physical examination, to reassure the public that their food was being prepared by healthy workers.[21] Once they were hired, employees had to observe dress guidelines, stipulating that they wear clean white shirts with sleeves neatly folded, a clean black necktie, clean patchless white pants, and a clean white apron free of stains. The company facilitated this cleanliness by washing and pressing free of charge all its employees' uniforms and aprons.[22] The employees' (or "operators," as they were known) neatly trimmed hair was to be covered by a white linen cap, and their fingernails were to be kept short and clean. Elaborate jewelry and wristwatches were prohibited.

Ingram believed that the success of a White Castle depended on how well the operator personified the company's philosophy of quality, cleanliness, and efficiency. These virtues were stressed to new employees during an intensive, unpaid two-week training period, administered by an experienced operator.[23] A few years later, as the company continued to grow and expand into new areas, these strict rules of hygiene and cleanliness were illustrated on a poster, entitled "Look Yourself Over," diagramming the model appearance for a White Castle operator, with arrows pointing to clean and properly worn articles of clothing and boldly discussing such hygiene issues as body odor, fingernails, and bad breath. Ingram's insistence on proper personal hygiene, courtly manners, and impeccable dress for all his employees and his emphasis on cleanliness in the Castles were purposely designed to counter the stereotype of slovenly fry cooks preparing food in greasy and unsanitary conditions.

In addition to neat dress and impeccable hygiene, Ingram also insisted that his operators offer prompt and polite service to their customers. In the company newsletter, *Hot Hamburger*, Ingram exhorted his workers to be more customer oriented: "So boys let's win our business by cheerfulness, and in the end we will have more friends, more business and be happier. Laugh and the world laughs with you, but he who looks for a fight can always find one." For the next forty years, Ingram kept reinforcing this notion of building friendships between the company and its customers, and he constantly stressed that friendly and polite service was equally as important as the number of hamburgers sold.

The reason for all these initiatives and innovations was, of course, to sell more hamburgers. This goal of continually improving sales was not lost on White Castle employees, but just in case, Ingram offered frequent and pointed reminders. His basic creed was that "all service workers in the restaurant are primarily sales people . . . who must be thoroughly schooled in the methods of modern salesmanship."[24] Hence a persistent theme of the *Hot Hamburger* was how to increase the sales of each White Castle, and each month it made recommendations toward that end. Ingram especially promoted active salesmanship over passive order taking. "The most important part of our business is the selling end. Anybody can take an order and serve it decently, which some believe to be the method by which our stands are managed, but this is not true." Ingram had pointers for his employees on how nearly every aspect of their interaction with customers could be the basis for an additional sale. For example, he suggested that operators begin their salesmanship immediately when the customer entered the building and then should be constantly alert to opportunities to sell additional products.

Similar to the pivotal sales techniques that are standard practice in most fast-food and other retail establishments today, Ingram advised his operators always to try to sell another type of food that could complement or complete the customer's order. Operators routinely complied with this directive by suggesting to their customers that pie and coffee would be the ideal end to a hamburger meal. Coffee sales were particularly stressed, since coffee had the biggest profit margin. Ingram cautioned, however, that this sales approach should be subtle and not too overbearing. On the issue of suggesting multiple hamburger sales, he advised, "When a customer enters and orders one hamburger, to reply by asking 'one or two' is not only disagreeable to the patron, but impolite." Instead, Ingram suggested to operators to "put on two and you will find he will invariably ask for the extra one." He declared in the December 1925 *Hot Hamburger* that the White Castle approach to salesmanship was "to think and use our heads . . . and to get new patrons and to hold them." Ingram took pride in the fact that this very basic sales strategy was enormously successful.

Ingram Creates a White Castle Corporate Culture

Ingram's early creation of a company newsletter itself was a conscious move to foster closer relationships among the company's home office, its employees, and its customers. Originally appearing in mimeographed form and distributed as the *Hot Hamburger*, this publication had the express purpose of linking together White Castles across town and eventually across the country. Ingram felt that it was important to create a sense of camaraderie among all employees and to reinforce for the customers the concept of company uniformity. His stated purpose was to promote the notion of family among everyone involved in the company, including both employees and customers.

The newsletter was compiled in the Wichita main office from correspondence from each White Castle. Issues were printed and mailed out on the first of every month. In the editorial credits, the editor was listed merely as "Office Force," and the contributing editors were the "White Castle Boys," a common term used for the all-male Castle operators. Entries included announcements of new Castle openings, brief stories of odd or unique White Castle events, inspirational messages, limericks and jokes, and tips on how to improve customer service. Most issues also contained motivational advice from Billy Ingram regarding productivity or service or both.

For example, in the January 1, 1926, issue of *Hot Hamburger*, Ingram complimented all employees on the outstanding coffee and hamburger sales in the previous quarter, thanked everyone for their Christmas cards, and extolled the nutritional merits of the hamburger. Although the newsletter was orginally intended as a link between company employees, White Castle's regular customers also became actively involved in it, sharing their views on innumerable topics ranging from the quality of the food to national politics. Employees and customers alike anxiously awaited each monthly issue to see whether their contributions had been included and to keep track of the activities of other employees and customers at other White Castles.

As the newsletter's popularity continued to grow, Ingram decided that the readers should become even more involved. So in the December 1925 issue, he announced a contest to rename the publication: "Up to the present time no definite name has been decided on, and we are just using the name *Hot Hamburger* temporarily."[25] He offered a prize of $2.50 for the winning title, and contest entries came from all corners. Imaginative contestants, both employees and customers alike, offered such suggestions as the *Castle Builder, Castle-grams, Sales and Service Stimulator, The White Castle Digester, The Hamburger Regulator*, and even *The Smasher*. The winning entry—*The White Castle Official House Organ*—was far less inspired or creative.

With the new name came a glossy, professionally printed format. Numerous copies of every issue were mailed to each Castle to be enjoyed by employees and distributed to interested customers. This customer participation in the company newsletter was not accidental; Ingram wanted to involve customers in the confident belief that such involvement would ensure fanatical customer loyalty. Once again, his strategy was effective. Since its founding, White Castle has enjoyed a consistent following of devoted customers, who could be more accurately characterized as loyal fans.

Billy Ingram's attempts to promote company loyalty and superior employee performance extended beyond the encouragement and inspirational mottoes found in the *House Organ*. In addition to paying salaries of between $18 and $30 a week, which were extremely generous for the food industry, he believed that his employees would sell more hamburgers and strive to maximize the company's profits if he devised a tangible incentive system. Accordingly, in only the third year of operation in Wichita, Ingram established a generous bonus system that distributed a fund composed of year-end profits to all White Castle employees. He explained in the *Hot Hamburger* "that this fund recognizes the value of faithful service . . . it is considered simply an additional compensation for good service . . . and it is based entirely on the gross business of all the stands." The share of this fund that each employee received depended only on his time employed at the company, minus sick time, and not on his position or salary.[26] Ingram's purpose for the bonus, however, went beyond that of rewarding employees for a year of superior productivity. He also wanted to promote the habits of saving and thrift among his workers.

As an additional benefit to his employees, Ingram instituted a generous plan to help pay extraordinary medical bills and expenses. Started in 1924, this fund was designed to pay all or part of the health care costs for both employees and their dependents. Although this was not comprehensive health insurance coverage in the modern sense, the fund assisted with exceptional bills that would have driven the employees into debt. Such health care protection was extremely rare in business in the 1920s and especially in the restaurant industry. In addition to covering hospital and surgical costs, the company also gave paid sick days to employees for recuperation. The only penalty against the worker was that such sick days were deducted from the service time determining the year-end bonus.

Ingram extended the sick-day and medical benefit to cover "incapacity from mental turmoil or strife, uncertainty or doubt," explaining that "it is as much our duty to help administer to the ailments of the mind as it is to the ailments of the body."[27] Once again, he justified this program merely as a means to improve productivity and profit, by keeping his workers healthy and happy. Ingram later declared that

> each problem to each employee should be the problem of the company. Natural contingencies over which a man has no control can create a condition, through no fault of the man himself, whereby he is robbed of every chance of the peace of mind necessary for happiness . . . if we do not take an interest and help him with his problems, is it fair to ask him to take an interest and help us with our problem?

Ingram recognized that "if a man is laboring under a problem, it is not possible for him to give a full measure of his time, his heart and his mind to the duties to which he is engaged in a business."

This progressive approach to employee health not only created a healthy and stable workforce but also engendered a strong sense of loyalty among the employees. Operators from around the country publicly thanked both Billy Ingram and White Castle for kindnesses extended. Naturally, as a businessman, Ingram's primary motivation was probably to use benevolence as a means of ensuring a capable and loyal workforce. Nevertheless, White Castle's wages, benefits, and family atmosphere made it a popular employer in the 1920s and 1930s. Unlike fast-food work years later in the "McDonald's age," working for White Castle and its competitors before World War II was a relatively lucrative and prized occupation, especially in comparison with factory work or other heavy physical labor.

The Hamburger Booms across America

These innovations in both product and service enabled Walt Anderson's and Billy Ingram's already popular business to grow at an even more phenomenal rate. Being able to eat quickly or take their burgers "to go," combined with a good-quality product, appealed to Wichita's increasingly busy factory workers, who came to White Castle either during their brief lunch breaks or while hurrying home after work. With outlets throughout the city and eight locations in the downtown section alone, the White Castle System of Eating Houses saturated the casual food market, and hamburgers soon became the daily fare for much of the working class.

Within a year, Anderson and Ingram began to look beyond the Wichita market with an eye toward expansion. Both initially agreed that the logical expansion should be to the smaller cities in the state. Their first move beyond the Wichita city limits was eighty miles northeast to El Dorado, Kansas. There they opened two White Castles and operated them somewhat profitably for two years before selling them, minus the company name and the trademark architecture, to local investors. Undecided about where to go next, Ingram returned to his former home city of Omaha to explore its business potential. At that time, Omaha was a bustling city, known as the regional hub for the livestock trade. As a result of this visit, Anderson and Ingram opened a White Castle on the corner of Thirteenth and Dodge Streets in September 1923. Just as in Wichita, the buying public of Omaha clamored for White Castle's hamburgers, and the business flourished, with two more Castles opening before the end of that year. By the end of 1924, White Castle had a total of nine locations in Omaha and was doing a thriving business. With a Castle soon operating in every section of the city, Ingram and Anderson judged that additional growth potential there was limited, so they immediately began to consider other markets.

The company then expanded at a rapid pace, adding new a city to the White Castle empire every few months during the mid-1920s. Still targeting their five-cent hamburgers to a working-class clientele in each new market, the partners built most of their Castles in the shadow of a factory, or at least in a heavily industrialized section of the city. After their great success in Omaha, Anderson and Ingram turned their attention to the Kansas City area. Kansas City in 1924 was a prosperous agricultural center, with a population of well over half a million. Consisting of two cities spanning the boundary of Kansas and Missouri, Kansas City was an area familiar to both Anderson and Ingram. In the summer of 1924, they opened their first location at 13 West Nineteenth Street in the downtown. Once again, the hamburger craze caught on, and Kansas City had six additional Castles by the end of the year. Looking to expand still farther east, Ingram opened the first White Castle in St. Louis in early 1925, at 30 South Eighteenth Street. Using the same approach of high quality and quick service that had proved so effective elsewhere, St. Louis soon became their biggest market, with eighteen restaurants.

As more locations opened, sales naturally increased. In just one week in October 1925, White Castle's combined sales consisted of more than 84,000 hamburgers and nearly half a ton of coffee.[28] At the end of that year, Ingram described all the food that White Castle had sold:

> Picture a line of buns, laid side by side, one hundred and sixty-three miles long, forty-one truckloads of hamburger, weighing two tons each, two carloads of onions, three carloads of pickles, ninety-six-hundred five gallon urns of coffee and you have an idea of the output of the White Castle System for the year 1925.[29]

With their spectacular success in St. Louis and their phenomenal growth in less than five years, from four to forty-four restaurants, Anderson and Ingram were enthusiastic about further expanding their territory. Critics, however, predicted that the hamburger was marketable only to the beef-oriented midwestern palate. A Wichita newspaper writer commented in 1925 that "the hamburger is distinctly popular only in states west of the Mississippi River and east of the Rocky Mountains." This regional limitation did not last long, however. Ingram next expanded north to the Minneapolis-St. Paul area, with unprecedented success, opening twenty Castles by the end of 1926.

He then crossed the Mississippi in 1927 to open six restaurants in Louisville, Kentucky, ten in Cincinnati, and eleven in Indianapolis. Everywhere White Castles were built, countless hamburger sales and financial success followed. In 1929, five Castles were opened in Columbus, Ohio, and nine in Chicago. The next year, White Castles were built at twelve locations in New York City and the New Jersey metropolitan area and at nine locations in the Detroit area, despite the stock market crash. These additional markets in the summer of 1930 represented the completion of the company's territorial expansion.[30] Billy Ingram proudly declared White Castle to be "a national institution," a phrase that remained at the center of the company's advertising.

The Challenge of Managing a "National Institution"

Constructing an empire and then ruling it successfully are two very different issues, and success in one does not necessarily mean success in the other. White Castle's growth rate in the 1920s was extraordinary, and by the end of the decade the company was a dominant force in the American restaurant industry. Nonetheless, the problems multiplied as the territory of operations expanded. Growing from a relatively small business in 1921, operating in the prairie city of Wichita, to a vast company spanning twelve major cities, 116 restaurants, and a geographic area stretching 1,424 miles from east to west by 1930 meant a profound change for both the principals and the operation of the company. Supervising and maintaining control over the these distant cities was difficult at a time when phone communications and transportation were still quite primitive by modern standards.

Ingram responded to this challenge by creating a model of corporate standardization. By maintaining direct ownership of all his restaurants and forbidding franchising in any form or degree, he never relinquished control of the entire operation. Indeed, Ingram believed that control was a necessary prerequisite to successful standardization and stability, as eventually proven by the disarray and fragmentation of the many White Castle competitors who relied on franchising for their corporate growth. Rather than franchising his company—which is essentially expansion through the use of other people's capital and ownership—Ingram ran his business on a strict "pay as you go" basis. After repaying the initial $700 loan that the partnership borrowed in 1921, Ingram vowed to open new restaurants only when the company could afford to pay for them in cash. He stood by this rule throughout his long ownership of the firm, and White Castle directors honor it to this day.

Critics often claim that expanding only with the capital on hand is limiting for a national company and that this practice was why White Castle was eventually dwarfed by its franchising competitors. Ingram's conservative and careful approach to the expansion of White Castle, however, may account for why it is still thriving seventy-five years later, whereas hundreds of other hamburger chains have come and gone.

Maintaining absolute ownership was fundamental to Ingram's approach, but it was only one aspect of operating a national restaurant empire. The greatest challenges were to continue to be able to offer a consistently superior product and to keep the customers buying it. Ingram met these challenges by implementing a centralized management structure, using airplanes to facilitate corporate transportation, creating dedicated food preparation plants, and even building the company's own restaurants and making its own employees' uniforms. With the exception of actually raising its own cattle and growing its own grain for the buns, White Castle achieved almost complete vertical integration—or independence from other suppliers and industries—by becoming its own primary supplier.

Every time White Castle expanded into a new market, the company built a new meat production facility to accommodate the Castles' meat needs. Carcasses were delivered to these plants by local rendering companies, butchered by White Castle meat cutters, ground to precise specifications, formed into standardized patties, and then frozen until put on the griddle. Consistent with his almost obsessive emphasis on cleanliness and quality, Ingram required that all the meat processed through these company facilities be approved by U.S. Department of Agriculture inspectors. The buns were baked at separate, company-owned facilities in a similarly uniform fashion. This strict company control over the essential elements of the hamburger sandwich ensured that the White Castle products served in Wichita would be indistinguishable from those served in Louisville, Minneapolis, or New York. By achieving such a high level of standardization, Billy Ingram set a new standard for the restaurant industry. Furthermore, producing its own primary ingredients gave White Castle advantages beyond just standardized products; it provided greater autonomy in the marketplace and the ability to procure needed supplies at a lower cost.

Ingram also hired a group of competent managers to oversee all aspects of White Castle's expansion into new cities and to ensure standardization. Most of these managers began with the company in the early days in Wichita and had learned all facets of the operation directly from Anderson and Ingram. Most notable among this group of "supermanagers" was Larkin M. Shackelford, or "Shack" as he was affectionately known throughout the company for the next forty years. Shackelford began as the company clerk in 1923, working with a home office staff of three employees. He did the accounting, wrote correspondence for the partners, handled the miscellaneous administrative functions in the office, and worked the grills when the regular Castle operators were unavailable.

Performing all tasks in the business competently, Shackelford quickly rose to be Ingram's right-hand man. When the partners decided to expand to Omaha in 1924, Shackelford was immediately tapped to direct the new operation. After White Castle became firmly entrenched and profitable in that city, Ingram sent Shackelford to Kansas City to expand the business there. Shackelford's predecessor in Kansas City, Oscar R. Ross, was transferred to Cincinnati to open a new territory. Once again, Shackelford's competent direction achieved success.

Shackelford's greatest challenge came three years later, when Ingram transferred him to New York City to open up that huge market. Ingram's strategy in sending Shackelford and other original Wichita employees into the new territories was simple: they intimately knew all the essential White Castle company policies, the correct procedures, and the proper techniques for food preparation. Their task was to recruit a group of responsible local workers in each new city and to teach them exactly how the company operation was conducted in Wichita. Walt Anderson commented in late 1927 "that it is indeed gratifying to see the new men conducting the business in the same manner as the older well-established plants."[31]

After the initial instruction, these managers or other staff sent from Wichita would remain in residence and closely supervise the business, to ensure that the company's standards were upheld. Ingram's management team would meet each year at the Wichita home office for updated instructions and a reinforcement of company policies and philosophy. These annual "managers' meetings" consisted of fine dining, the camaraderie of old company friends, and intensive planning sessions for the next fiscal year. Moreover, these meetings were a guarantee to Ingram that each manager knew his thoughts and wishes first hand and was ready to go back to his city to implement them.

To reinforce this home office supervision, Ingram and Anderson regularly visited all the White Castle cities, believing that direct contact between the owners and their employees created greater loyalty. Personally visiting and supervising such a geographically immense company, however, was no simple task in this era when Route 66 was the only highway between east and west. Fortunately, new technologies making travel more efficient materialized in the 1920s, with the airplane being the most spectacular. Wichita was coincidentally a pioneering city in the aviation industry in that decade, so the White Castle partners were conveniently able to turn to air travel to solve their transportation needs. After initially renting airplanes and hiring pilots to fly Ingram, Anderson, and other company managers from city to city, the company eventually purchased a new maroon Curtis OX-5 Travel Air Biplane in the fall of 1927. Trimmed in silver and gold paint, the plane had the words "White Castle System" painted on each side of the fuselage and under one wing.[32] Walt Anderson immediately began flight training, and for the next decade White Castle became known for its constantly flying management staff. As more planes were added to the company fleet in the next few years, the *House Organ* ran regular stories on the flying adventures of Anderson and Ingram. Each month, company employees throughout the White Castle territory read tales of harrowing and humorous airplane vacations into the wilderness, of landing in alfalfa fields, and of navigating by railroad tracks. They also learned that the partners would occasionally just swoop down into White Castle cities for unannounced visits to their restaurants. While the vacation stories were animated and enjoyable, the mention of unexpected corporate visits sent a clear message to all managers and employees in the heretofore distant places: the owners are airborne and could be stopping in at any time. Now seventy years later, we can only speculate to what degree this pointed message reinforced company control and strict adherence to established standards.

White Castle Sets the Model for Fast-Food Standardization

A tangible example of standardization was to build every Castle so that it was identical to every other. All the original restaurants in Wichita conformed to the architectural criteria that Ingram established in 1921: a whitewashed exterior, a crenellated tower, and the slogans painted on the wall. Inside each building were five stools, a grill, and a serving counter. Beyond these similarities, however, the buildings varied somewhat in size, construction materials, and proximity to other buildings, variations that were unavoidable because some of the buildings predated the partnership.

All the Castles built between 1921 and 1925 in Wichita, Omaha, and Kansas City were constructed from cement blocks on an identical ten-by-fifteen-foot floor plan, with the same crenellated facade and whitewashed exterior. As new construction was started in St. Louis in 1925, the cement blocks were changed to white enamel brick, and basements were added to house the electrical refrigeration and heating systems. Ingram preferred constructing the Castles with white enamel brick because he believed that it better symbolized his themes of cleanliness and efficiency. In 1927, White Castle's engineering and construction superintendent, Lloyd W. Ray, commented that "the white glazed brick is the best money can buy, is artistically built . . . and is very sanitary."[33]

By the end of the decade, White Castle permanently standardized its building construction, using portable all-metal buildings with a white steel enamel exterior. Designed by Lloyd Ray and heralded as "the first in the world of this kind," these new structures were said to resemble white marble, with baked-on enamel covering both the exterior and interior of the buildings.[34] Matching white enamel and stainless steel fixtures made the entire structure easy to clean and relatively simple for one operator to run. The only deviation from this white standard was a brief experimentation with porcelain-steel exteriors that had color swirled into the material to resemble marble more closely. At the end of the decade, fifty-five Castles were built with this exterior but were soon discontinued in favor of the pristine white. The use of steel buildings was continued. Ingram was pleased that these buildings could be kept fastidiously clean and were relatively simple to disassemble, transport, and reassemble in a more profitable location. Maintaining their corporate theme of vertical integration, once the partners agreed that the portable enameled steel buildings would be the company standard, they immediately created a separate company to manufacture them, and White Castle constructed all its restaurants in an identical fashion for the next fifty years.[35]

The employees' uniforms were similarly standardized. Ingram's insistence on absolute cleanliness meant that the company was continuously laundering the white linen clothing worn by all Castle operators. A twelve-hour shift spent grilling hundreds of hamburgers and pouring gallons of coffee invariably resulted in unsightly stains on the white cloth. Ingram wanted to resolve this laundry cost problem while retaining a clean, crisp look for his operators. After considering numerous possible yet unsatisfactory solutions, he finally designed a paper cap and apron that employees could wear during the workday and then discard at the end of their shift. Once again, rather than relying on outside suppliers, Ingram secured patents on his revolutionary new clothing and opened still another factory. This new subsidiary, Paperlynen, also manufactured paper napkins, which meant an additional reduction in the company's laundry expenses. The innovations of both the paper caps and the paper napkins quickly became profitable in their own right. Casual dining restaurants enthusiastically embraced the idea of disposable paper items and began buying Paperlynen products in huge quantities.

Whether for its quality food products, architecture, or paper hats, White Castle's customers always knew what to expect. Billy Ingram was proud of his success at standardization. In a pamphlet distributed to customers, he proclaimed,

> When you sit in a White Castle, remember that you are one of several thousands; you are sitting on the same kind of stool; you are being served on the same kind of counter; the coffee you drink is made in accordance with a certain formula; the hamburger you eat is prepared exactly the same way over a gas flame of the same intensity; the cups that you drink from are identical with thousands of cups that thousands of other people are using at the same moment; the same standards of cleanliness protects your food.

Later hamburger chains tried to emulate this exact uniformity that White Castle perfected during the 1920s. McDonald's and Burger King were phenomenally successful, making standardization both a high art form and an intricate science. In actuality, however, such latecomers to the industry were merely copying and enhancing White Castle's proven approach to doing business.

Ingram's emphasis on uniformity and its spread throughout the growing hamburger industry were not confined to business but, instead, reflected the trends in American commerce and culture in the 1920s. The buying public seemed to crave standardization and uniformity in the marketplace, preferring to buy nationally merchandised products and labels advertised in magazines with a nationwide circulation and sold in large store chains. Sears Roebuck, Montgomery Ward, and S. S. Kresge sold identical hardware, clothing, and other dry goods across the country, and the A&P grocery chain sold Kellogg's Corn Flakes and Campbell's Soup from the Atlantic to the Pacific. Locally manufactured products or those made by small enterprises were considered second rate next to the national brands. Consumers now believed that "bigger" was indeed better and redirected their purchasing preferences accordingly. Retailers quickly responded to this changing demand. "A merchant who failed to carry Quaker Oats, Heinz pickles, Gillette safety razors, and Kodak cameras might find himself losing business down the street to those who did."[36]

Many Americans also turned away from traditional favorites, ethnic dishes, and regional staples, choosing instead the hamburger that "was sweeping the nation." The attraction to the hamburger was that it was inexpensive, filling, and, in many circles, even trendy. Similar to the allure of Quaker Oats, the pervasive mind-set about hamburgers was that since the whole nation was suddenly eating them, they must be worthwhile. This herd mentality led many people to try their first burger, and they usually liked it once they tried it. Within a decade, the hamburger changed from being a national fad to being a national food.

A New Industry Born in the White Castle Image

A great testimony to White Castle's originality and popularity was the rush of imitators to enter the fast-food hamburger business. Previously when White Castle entered a new market, it would be the only restaurant in that city specializing in hamburgers. But once the public developed a taste for hamburgers, this monopoly disappeared. The 1920s saw an explosion of White Castle imitators spreading across the United States both the hamburger craze and the White Castle style of eating.

Starting in Wichita only months after the White Castle's beginning, new hamburger stands appeared that were suspiciously similar in appearance and product. At first, these "clones" were poorly financed, often ramshackle operations capitalizing on the "fad-food" hamburger.[37] The most serious competition in town came from a small chain, interestingly called "Little Kastle," started in Wichita in 1925 by a local entrepreneur and restaurant supplier, Harvey Ablah. This small chain later included other hamburger restaurants throughout the Midwest with similarly suspicious names, such as Little Palaces and Little Crowns.[38] A later contender in the Wichita hamburger market was the Tulsa (Oklahoma)-based White Knight Nickel Sandwich. The White Knight restaurants had a round turret and the door in the middle of the building, whereas White Castles had a square turret and the door on the side.[39] Even in a city as small as Wichita, the similarities must have been very confusing to customers.

As the White Castle System expanded and flourished in new urban markets, other entrepreneurs took notice of their success. Small whitewashed buildings began to spring up on street corners, advertising and selling hamburgers for five cents. Turrets, towers, clocks, or some other type of ornament were typical of these enterprises. These upstart operations were usually poorly funded, and many did not even have names. Once again, the quality of these enterprises' hamburgers was often considered "questionable" and could vary greatly from day to day. The majority of these whitewashed shacks appeared quickly after the arrival of the White Castles in new cities, used similar buildings to draw a crowd of somewhat confused patrons, and then disappeared just as quickly when the White Castle chain became established.

Battling these disreputable imitators became an ongoing burden for White Castle during the 1920s and 1930s. The White Castle name, the company architecture, and the little hamburgers themselves all became fair game for imitation. Other businesses envied White Castle's success, and many even adopted the White Castle company name as their own, using it for various enterprises such as barber shops, taverns, beers, dairies, and even shoes. Although potentially confusing to customers, these misnamed bars and shoes did not represent a significant economic threat to White Castle's business or reputation. Rather, a more serious problem was the restaurants illegally calling themselves White Castle and often competing against the original in some markets. When the real White Castle discovered an illegal name usage, Earle W. Evans, its Wichita-based attorney, would send the offender a letter ordering him to stop immediately. Most quickly complied with Evans's demand and often feigned ignorance of their offense.

Ingram spared no expense at fighting to keep the White Castle name unique to his company, and he was especially passionate about attacking restaurants who unlawfully used the name. He believed that the greatest threat to his success in that battle and to his company's good name would be a flood of imitators selling inferior and unhealthy products, thereby reviving the many negative stereotypes about ground beef.

An even greater threat to White Castle's profits was the more legitimate and profitable businesses that imitated its architecture, food, or both. Often using similar names, such as Royal Castle, White Tower, or White Clock, these imitators hoped to capitalize on White Castle's success. The actual number of variations of the White Castle name and the variations of these variations seemed endless. New hamburger chains enthusiastically embraced the word *white*, adding it to an infinite array of nouns, such as White Palace, White Log, White House, White Tavern, White Hut, White Cap, White Shop, White Grille, White Cabin, White Plaza, White Wonder, White Turret, White Diamond, White Fortress, White Kitchen, White Crescent, White Spot, White Manna, and White Mill. The concept of using colors as the first word in the company name became even more common, with Blue Bells, Red Lanterns, Blue Beacons, Blue Towers, and Red Barns opening across the nation. Borrowing from the castle or royal theme, imitators opened Magic Castles, Silver Castles, Prince's Castles, White Palaces, Red Castles, Blue Castles, Klover Kastles, Little Kastles, Modern Castles, Royal Castles, and even Castle Blancas. Still other hamburger chains copied White Castle's basic architectural style almost exactly. Small white buildings with some sort of tower, such as a turret, clock tower, light house, ziggurat, or even a crystal ball, became almost synonymous with the hamburger trade.

Confusion was rife among the buying public with the proliferation of so many similar names and the rampant imitation of the White Castle architecture. To many Americans by the late 1920s, the name White Castle had become an almost generic term for a fast-food hamburger restaurant. Chicago restaurateur Henry Cassada openly used the name White Castle for his business in the early 1930s, claiming that it was, in fact, a generic name. White Castle's lawyers aggressively dissuaded Cassada of this mistaken belief and worked tirelessly to thwart many other imitators. The national onslaught of similar hamburger chains, however, was overwhelming for even a battalion of lawyers to contain, so expensive legal action was reserved for only the most blatant offenders or most harmful competitors. The first to be targeted were hamburger restaurants using the White Castle name. These imitators were always challenged, instructed to stop using the name, and warned of impending action if they did not comply. Most were small restaurant operations that quickly obeyed when faced with a lawsuit by a national company. After the initial round of threats, White Castle often helped the imitators by paying for new signs or architecture modifications, in order to expedite the change.[40]

One imitative practice that White Castle lawyers could not contain at all was the rapid spread of hamburger sales. From Wichita, the hamburger's popularity quickly exceeded White Castle's area of control or of patent protection. Since White Castle never had more than approximately three hundred restaurants, most of them east of the Mississippi, it was impossible for White Castle to serve hamburgers to all Americans. In fact, it introduced the hamburger sandwich to a only very small segment of the American people. What White Castle did do, however, was create a new fast-food industry that brought the hamburger sandwich to virtually every urban neighborhood and many rural communities. Regardless of names or architecture, thousands of restaurants across the United States began serving an almost exact copy of White Castle's hamburger sandwich during the 1920s.

Huge hamburger restaurant chains soon proliferated, both competing with White Castle in some markets and becoming the sole provider in cities that White Castle never entered. Although the White Castle lawyers and marketing staff did occasionally take notice of some of the more prosperous chains, most of them operated in other regions of the country and hence were not considered a threat. Even when confronted with competitors in one of its market cities, White Castle never chose to challenge ownership of the product patent, essentially conceding that the concept of the hamburger sandwich and the approach of selling in volume on a carryout basis were in the public domain.

Notable among these chains of imitators were the enormous White Tower Company, based in Milwaukee; the Kewpee Hotel Hamburgs, started in Flint, Michigan; Little Tavern of Louisville; Maid-Rite of Muscatine, Iowa; and later the Krystal Shops of Chattanooga, Tennessee, and the Royal Castles of Miami. Each of these chains multiplied at a rapid rate, spreading both restaurants and the hamburger craze throughout their respective regions. The common denominators of all these companies were their primary product, the hamburger sandwich; their White Castle "Buy 'em by the Sack" fast-food carryout style; and of course, their unmistakable White Castle-like architecture. Most of the big chains also shared Billy Ingram's compulsive insistence on cleanliness and advanced his quest to legitimize the hamburger in the American marketplace. Although some of these chains became fierce competitors with White Castle, most of them carved out their own territories of dominance, with only minimal overlap. With an entire country to conquer, there was enough area and customers for all these hamburger chains to make a healthy profit.

One of the earliest and most colorful of these restaurant chains was Kewpee Hotel Hamburgs. Founded by Sam Blair in Flint, Michigan, soon after World War I, it was initially just "a greasy hamburger stand" similar to Walt Anderson's original. Using the popular Kewpee doll as his company symbol and the name Kewpee Hotel (although not a hotel in any sense of the word), Blair's operation spread quickly throughout Michigan, Ohio, Illinois, Indiana, Kentucky, Wisconsin, and Pennsylvania, in addition to a confusing outlier in Utica, New York.[41] Similar to White Castle, the Kewpee stands primarily sold hamburgers and were usually small, whitewashed structures with black signage and ornamentation. Dissimilar were the large picture of the Kewpee doll on the roof and the rather innocuous and non-imitative slogan "Mity Nice Hamburg."

An even greater difference was that Blair and his successor, Ed Adams, avoided major cities and located their stands in smaller cities outside the mainstream. Under Adams's direction and through the use of franchising, the Kewpee chain grew quickly across the Midwest, opening more than two hundred restaurants by the end of the 1920s and at least four hundred by the beginning of World War II. Kewpee was among the earliest to implement a drive-up feature, or "curb service," borrowing the concept from the successful root beer stands of that era.[42] The influence of root beer stands also extended into other areas of the Kewpee operation. Root beer was a prominent item on Kewpee's menu, joining coffee as the preferred beverage to accompany hamburgers. Interestingly, surviving photos indicate that many Kewpee stands later featured ten-cent mugs of real beer as the ideal complement to a bag of burgers. Since precise details are sketchy, we have to assume that this emphasis on beer sales came after the end of Prohibition in 1933. Nevertheless, this shift toward selling beer clearly distinguished the Kewpee chain from the others, which stuck to soft drinks.

An equally colorful and far more enduring hamburger chain was The Krystal Company. Krystal's, as the company came to be known, started in October 1932 on the corner of Seventh and Cherry Streets in downtown Chattanooga, Tennessee. Known for its distinctive crystal ball trademark, Krystal's became the dominant early hamburger chain throughout the Southeast. Founders Rody B. Davenport Jr. and J. Glenn Sherrill created a company very close to the White Castle image, complete with small white porcelain enamel and stainless steel buildings; small, square, onion-coated hamburgers; and the goal that "people would patronized [*sic*] 'an establishment kept spotlessly clean, where they could get a good meal . . . with courteous service . . . at the lowest possible price.'"

Davenport, who was already well established in the textile industry, formalized his emphasis on value and quality by establishing the "Krystal Kreed' as a guide for his employees and managers. In addition to the food, the buildings, and the dedication to quality, Davenport structured his new hamburger company in a manner very similar to White Castle. Like Ingram, he retained strict control over the company's expansion and forbade franchising in any form, believing, as did Ingram, that tight control was the only way to guarantee adherence to his high standards. This broad spectrum of similarities was not mere coincidence; Davenport visited White Castle's restaurants before opening his chain and took note of their successful features.[43]

If Krystal's approach to the hamburger business was familiar by 1932, its corporate name was certainly original. Company legend recounts that one afternoon Davenport and his wife were riding

> down a mountain road when Mrs. Mary McGee Davenport saw a lawn ornament in the shape of a crystal ball. While gazing at the lawn ornament, Mrs. Davenport commented that since Davenport and Sherrill felt cleanliness was a cornerstone of the concept, they should name the restaurant Crystal for "clean as a crystal," yet with a "K" to add a little twist.[44]

Hence the chain was named "The Krystal," with a modified silvery crystal ball lawn ornament on the side of each building. In addition to this innovative name, Krystal adopted an architectural style that was sleeker and more streamlined than the industry norm, using black horizontal bands, curved corners, and rounded windows.[45] Once established, Davenport's hamburger chain spread throughout the South, eventually opening more than three hundred Krystals and helping make the White Castle-style hamburger a staple food in that region.[46]

Other chains enjoyed similar success in other areas of the country. Little Tavern was started by Harry Duncan in Louisville, Kentucky, in 1927 and quickly spread throughout the South by 1930, selling steamed White Castle-style hamburgers. Little Tavern's fare was similar to White Castle's, but its buildings' architectural style was different. Even though they were whitewashed and later made of porcelain steel, Little Taverns were topped by sloping roofs with distinctive green shingles. Rather than a small urban castle, their buildings more closely resembled a quaint country cottage.

Toddle House of Memphis also used the cottage image on the exterior and fake fireplaces on the inside to project a comfortable, "home-cooked" theme. Founded in 1930, Toddle House opened restaurants in the South and Southwest, with a heavy concentration in Texas cities. Also serving an onion-smothered, White Castle-style hamburger, Toddle House thrived in both working-class and more affluent neighborhoods because of its more sedate architecture, which had no large signs or tacky gimmickry. Although different from White Castle in its outward style, the Toddle House buildings also were constructed of porcelain steel for movability. In fact, these structures were said to "toddle" from side to side during transport, hence inspiring the rather unusual company name. Both Little Tavern and Toddle House prospered in their own regions, but neither company ever posed a significant challenge to White Castle.

The First Major Battle in the "Burger Wars"

Billy Ingram remained calm during the proliferation of these large chains, despite Kewpee's meteoric growth and Krystal's close imitation of White Castle's product and approach. His relative indifference probably stemmed from the fact that both Kewpee and Krystal occupied distinctly different regions and, for the most part, did not infringe on White Castle's established territory. Occasionally throughout the 1920s, Ingram would unleash White Castle's lawyers to enforce certain patents or copyrights or otherwise to guard White Castle's good name. But as we said earlier, White Castle seldom took legal action against smaller restaurants, saving its legal wrath for successful chains of imitators that directly challenged one of its markets.

One such transgressor was the White Tower Company of Milwaukee. White Tower, which eventually became White Castle's largest competitor in its market cities, was founded in 1926 by the father-and-son partnership of John E. Saxe and Thomas E. Saxe. Owners of a public dance hall in Minneapolis, the Saxes took notice when a new White Castle was built nearby and soon realized its profit-making potential. Upon seeing White Castle's success, the elder Saxe decided to enter the hamburger business, using White Castle as a model. From the beginning, White Tower's close resemblance to White Castle was neither accidental nor indirect. Before starting their own hamburger business, the Saxes first visited several newly opened White Castles in Minneapolis, carefully observing their restaurant operation and finally securing exact building measurements and product specifications. Returning to their home in Milwaukee, they opened virtually an exact copy of a White Castle near Marquette University, complete with a whitewashed exterior, prominent tower, and serving area with five stools and counter. In addition to selling hamburgers that were indistinguishable from the original White Castle's, the Saxes boldly positioned their slogan, "Take Home a Bagful," across the front of their stands.

The only noticeable difference was that some of the new White Towers did not have a crenellated facade. Other than that, its buildings and the business conducted inside them were identical to White Castle's. Using this proven formula for success, the Saxes soon built White Tower restaurants across the Midwest and beyond, becoming one of the largest hamburger chains in the United States by the 1930s. At the start of the decade, they owned or franchised more than 120 outlets, in cities ranging geographically from Minneapolis to Washington, D.C.

White Tower's spectacular growth was due in great part to White Castle's previous marketing campaigns and solid reputation for serving quality products. With nearly identical hamburgers, White Tower also intentionally targeted White Castle's working-class clientele by locating near factories and in working-class neighborhoods. The Saxes also capitalized on the burgeoning urban transportation systems by locating their restaurants near busy trolley and train stations. For example, "more than half of the stations on Philadelphia's Broad Street subway line had White Towers at their exit."[47] Both companies were soon competing against each other in crucial cities, often in the same neighborhoods, and customers were confused by their many similarities.[48]

White Castle took the offensive in 1929 by suing White Tower in a Minnesota state court for unfair competition. White Tower retaliated by bringing an almost ridiculous suit against White Castle in a Michigan court. The Saxes contended that White Castle had infringed on White Tower's territory and business when it expanded into the Detroit area. They based their suit on the fact that the two competitors were virtually identical and that White Tower was already entrenched in Detroit with numerous restaurants when White Castle arrived. At issue in these suits were the small, onion-covered, square hamburgers; towers, crenellated or not; and "Buy'em by the Sack" versus "Take Home a Bagful." The Saxes' contention unwisely disregarded the fact that White Castle had created the fast-food hamburger, the distinctive architecture, and the marketing approach almost five years before White Tower came on the scene.

The court proceedings in Michigan verified that White Tower had indeed copied almost every aspect of White Castle's buildings and operation, disclosing some rather questionable tactics in the process. Details were aired during the trial of how the Saxes had copied White Castle's Minneapolis restaurants and even of how they lured away a White Castle operator at princely wages to assemble their new restaurants, to steal valuable data and information, and to teach them White Castle's techniques. The court also learned that White Tower had photographed the newest White Castles in order to duplicate exactly both the interiors and exteriors of the buildings. The protracted legal battle lasted for five years, with enormous expenditures on both sides and a major title at stake.[49]

White Castle's Minnesota suit against White Tower was decided first, with a 1930 court ruling in favor of White Castle. The Minnesota court proclaimed that White Tower had misled the public by too closely copying the other company and so ordered White Tower to change its name, architecture, and slogan in that state. In 1934 the Michigan court agreed that White Tower had duplicated White Castle's products and buildings and ordered White Tower to change all resemblances to White Castle in architecture and slogan. Later upheld by the U.S. Court of Appeals of the Sixth District, this decision stated that White Tower, "with full knowledge of such priority and adoption of use . . . imitated such design and appearance in the construction of competing eating houses." Citing an earlier case, the court went on to observe that "the intentional use of another's trademark is a fraud" and that "persistence then in the use is not innocent, and the wrong is a continuing one, demanding restraint by judicial interposition."[50]

The final judgment of the court against White Tower enjoined the use of the company name; its "Take Home a Bagful" slogan; its small, white, castlelike buildings; and any other names, slogans, or architecture that "are confusingly similar" to White Castle's. This order applied to both the White Towers owned directly by the Saxe family and those owned by their franchisees.

Although this was a stunning defeat for the White Tower Company, it was not the end. With victory in hand and a public declaration of sovereignty, Billy Ingram directed White Castle's lawyers to strike a fair deal with the Saxes and their franchisees. Ingram allowed White Tower to keep its name but was adamant about the changes in architecture and slogan. In return, White Tower and its franchisees agreed to pay White Castle a lump sum of $65,000 immediately, with an additional payment of $17,000 two years later. Ingram also asked for ongoing guarantees and compensation. For each new White Tower opened, the Saxes or their franchisees had to furnish a photograph of the new unit and pay a relatively small royalty fee, ranging from $100 to $350. Ingram's final stipulation was that because the name confusion would inevitably continue, White Tower had to maintain consistently high standards and a quality product.

This decision forced White Tower to create its own corporate style and approach, abandoning the "White Castlesque" medieval facade for an updated art deco and, later, a modernistic architecture. White Tower's new art deco or modern look was often augmented with sleek clock towers and reflective materials, thereby creating a distinctive difference in appearance. After this legal showdown, the two companies branched off into different urban markets, with only minimal overlap, and never confronted each other again.

White Castle's success in establishing a truly "national institution" was spectacular. Within a decade, White Castle had become a household word across the nation, synonymous with the hamburger sandwich. Even more important, the hamburger sandwich itself had become a frequent item on the American plate.

The suddenness of White Castle's success, however, begs many questions. For example, why was Billy Ingram so good at selling hamburgers to the American public, and what was so appealing to consumers about his White Castle System, its products, or its method of delivery? Or rather, was his success merely fortunate timing? Was it the revolutionary changes during the 1920s—in areas such as transportation, communications, and national marketing—that provided an opportunity for White Castle and the greater hamburger industry to grow and prosper? Even more directly, did the hamburger help change America, or was it merely a symbol of greater change? All these questions can be answered or, rather, argued, in a variety of ways. Certainly, profound changes in family structure and lifestyle opened the door for different eating habits and foods. The ready availability of fast food appealed to the changing needs and habits of society. And there also is no doubt that enhanced transportation technologies made people more mobile, which in turn fostered a more standardized menu. Americans took to the highways in huge numbers searching for work, enjoying vacations, or just looking for a new start. Arriving in an unfamiliar city and finding a familiar food was, and still is, quite comforting for travelers. Better still, these people were even more comforted by arriving in a new city and finding their favorite restaurant open for business. Other travelers or migrants with a taste for hamburgers often introduced this ground meat delicacy to their new town or region, further spreading the national hamburger craze.

This boom in travel also caused the United States to become more culturally, ethnically, and politically homogeneous. The introduction of the radio and the spread of the telephone also helped break down the long-standing barriers between regions and people. Even small towns that had once been island communities were ushered into the mainstream society and culture. This transition accelerated in the 1920s, enhanced the sense of nationhood, and launched the modern era. Emerging from this new "Americanism" was the hamburger: a new, modern, and uniquely American food that helped define a new era and a newly homogenized culture.

3

Hamburgers during Hard Times

In the American collective memory, the 1930s is synonymous with the Great Depression. But life in the United States during the 1930s was much more than just misery and hunger. Although many companies closed and many individuals suffered, business was still transacted, farmers still grew crops, and most Americans' lives still continued more or less as usual. Americans also maintained their newfound passion for hamburgers, and this demand for burgers amid hardship was not accidental. Billy Ingram and his White Castle System thrived throughout the Depression, owing to his great resourcefulness, ingenious marketing strategies, and dedication to quality and low prices. In a decade when many Americans faced poverty and hunger, White Castle still sold hamburgers at an ever-increasing rate.

Unlike a decade earlier, the story of White Castle during the 1930s must be told in the context of the greater hamburger industry. Such an industry did not exist in 1921 when Billy Ingram began his chain. The hamburger that he popularized and the industry that White Castle spawned, however, took on lives of their own by the end of the 1920s. Millions of hamburgers were being fried and served each day, by both White Castle and innumerable other purveyors of the product. Hamburgers were everywhere, with restaurant chains, diners, and roadside drive-ins selling millions annually. So many hamburger restaurants sprang up in New York City's Times Square that some Broadway columnists began referring to the Broadway and Seventh Avenue area as "Hamburger Row."[1] Paradoxically, given the widespread hunger and increased rates of malnutrition of that time, the annual per capita consumption of beef among Americans rose from 48.9 pounds in 1930 to 53.2 pounds in 1935. The bulk of this increased consumption was due to the growing popularity of the hamburger sandwich. By the 1930s, in addition to being eaten on a daily basis across America, the hamburger was already entrenched in American popular culture, regularly appearing in the mainstream press, literature, and entertainment. Pictures of hamburgers and the word *hamburger* were commonplace, adorning billboards and restaurant facades.

Characters in both the movies and novels of the era ate hamburgers, although their consumption was often used to typify working-class behavior. Hamburgers even appeared in the comics, most prominently in the popular "Popeye the Sailor" comic strip. Created in 1929, the Popeye character J. Wellington Wimpy was a scraggly, overweight, yet endearing fellow who constantly craved hamburgers and often stated that his goal was to find "the acme of bovinity" and immortalized the phrase "I would gladly pay you Tuesday for a hamburger today." Whereas Popeye turned to spinach for strength, Wimpy, along with millions of other Americans, found his solace and nourishment in the hamburger sandwich. This slow-moving, bewhiskered sidekick of Popeye became a leading national spokesman for the hamburger.[2] In fact, this comic strip was so popular that for years the hamburger sandwich was often referred to as the "Wimpy Burger." As with any issue concerning the relationship between "art" and public attitudes and behaviors, it is difficult to discern whether Wimpy's notoriety contributed to the hamburger craze or, more likely the case, whether Americans could just as easily identify with his humble taste in foods. What is certain, however, is that by the 1930s the hamburger was extremely visible in American life, and its growth and longevity proved that it was far more than just a novelty or fad.

White Castle Weathers the Depression

White Castle benefited from the increased popularity of the hamburger in many ways. Billy Ingram's lone efforts a decade earlier to take the fear out of eating ground beef and to sell the hamburger to America were now assisted by the marketing departments and advertisers employed by the other national hamburger chains. With this growing popular acceptance, Ingram could redirect some of the attention on his campaign to sell the concept of the hamburger sandwich to competing with the other members of the industry that he created. Indeed, competition itself became the theme of White Castle's transition into the 1930s. Although Ingram was the first to sell hamburgers, he was soon joined by many tough and persistent competitors. White Tower had lost its legal battles with White Castle, yet it continued to loom large in the hamburger industry. Other imitator chains, such as Kewpee and Krystal, also thrived, each opening hundreds of hamburger restaurants around the country.

Already known as a pioneer and innovator in the food business, Ingram sought to maintain a distinctive leadership position in the hamburger marketplace. To stay ahead of the growing pack, he constantly strove to provide customers with a higher-quality product, faster and more courteous service, and a better restaurant environment than the other chains offered. Ingram knew well that keeping his customers satisfied meant maintaining healthy company profits.

In the 1930s, White Castle both defied the hardships of the era and adjusted its business approaches to accommodate them. Despite the adversity of the Depression, certain companies prospered. The Chrysler Motor Company, for example, expanded during this era while most of its competitors either laid off workers or folded. Smart and adaptable management strategies largely separated the survivors from the failures. During this decade, Ingram consolidated his control over the company, restructured some operations, and moved his corporate headquarters to Columbus, Ohio, at the geographic center of his hamburger empire.

Ingram also greatly extended his approach of "vertical integration," in which he developed additional industries to supply the needs of his hamburger restaurants. All the company's construction, paper, and food product needs were met by wholly owned White Castle subsidiaries. Such expansion further reduced the company's reliance on external suppliers and ensured greater company control over production costs. Ingram also introduced innovations in the use of print advertising and couponing during this era, establishing a marketing norm for the fast-food and other industries. Even more important, he actively sought to expand the customer base for fast-food hamburgers beyond its existing male working-class clientele to include women and the middle class. The long-term effects of these measures on the fast-food industry were to facilitate the growth of the giant chains in the 1950s. In the short run, however, this combination of new initiatives helped White Castle remain prosperous in an otherwise difficult era.

White Castle's growth during the Depression defied two very difficult problems. First, consumers, now often unemployed, had less money to spend on hamburgers. Compounding this reduction in consumer buying power was the proliferation of outlets selling hamburger sandwiches. Although several hamburger restaurants failed during this time, others opened to take their place. The numerous factory and business layoffs of the early 1930s left many men without work, forced to rely on government job programs or their own resourcefulness. Many tried opening some sort of small business, with food stands being among the most popular. As Walt Anderson had proved years earlier, opening a hamburger stand required little money and much time and hard work. In addition to the stereotypical Depression-era fruit stands selling apples for five cents, many of the unemployed set up small stands on street corners to sell the popular hamburger sandwiches. Such small enterprises did not threaten White Castle's business in the same manner as White Tower's corporate competition had, but the saturation of an already shrinking marketplace did reduce its revenues.[3]

In addition to this proliferation of small street-corner entrepreneurs, White Castle's traditional competitors were still in business. Kewpee Hamburgers remained viable throughout the decade, even though more than half its nearly four hundred franchises closed.[4] White Tower was not hurt as much by the Depression as by the legal setbacks encountered in its long-term dispute with White Castle. Both these chains did start to shift their emphasis away from customers in the downtown walking city toward the growing automobile clientele. Indeed, the most successful newcomers to the hamburger business during the 1930s were those chains that recognized the commercial potential of serving customers in their cars. Among these "drive-in" newcomers to the hamburger business during the late 1930s was a modest stand more than twelve hundred miles away from the nearest White Castle. Although it became very popular regionally throughout the 1940s, the McDonald brothers did not become a significant White Castle competitor for another twenty years.[5]

White Castle continued to grow despite the new competition and the economic realities of that time. At the end of the 1930, Billy Ingram proudly announced that White Castle had sold more than 21 million hamburgers by the first of December, surpassing the previous, "pre-Depression" year by 3 million.[6] The company continued to grow in 1931, opening five new restaurants and hiring fifty-one new employees, bringing the total number of Castles to 120 in sixteen cities. The following year was possibly the low point of the Depression, yet White Castle continued to grow and prosper. Five new Castles opened in the same year that the Bonus Marchers descended on Washington and much of the country was gripped by both economic and political panic.

In April 1933, Billy Ingram announced to the annual managers' meeting in Wichita that the system was still profitable, even though sales had leveled off somewhat.[7] Some individual Castles were especially hard hit, such as Detroit's number 9, which operated in the shadow of a now closed auto assembly plant.[8] Ever the optimist, however, Ingram maintained that the company would build an additional six Castles before the end of the year. In fact, his optimism proved to be on the conservative side: by the end of 1933, six new Castles had been built, more than fifty new men had been hired, and overall profits were up. These advances continued into 1934, amounting to 130 White Castles, a workforce of more than five hundred employees, and an annual payroll of more than $1 million. Although these numbers did not rise in 1935, profits continued at a steady pace, and Ingram proudly declared that "the White Castle System of today, with its 130 White Castles, is serving the public of over half the United States."[9]

Hamburger sales further accelerated two years later, with White Castle selling more than 40 million burgers in 1937, or almost twice the total in 1930. In September of that year, the company's vice president and treasurer, Arthur "A. C." Mechling, pointed out in the *House Organ* that White Castle had thrived while most other American companies faltered. He contrasted the huge unemployment rates in America in the early 1930s with the fact that White Castle's payroll had grown more than 100 percent, from 297 employees in 1929 to 607 employees in 1935. He was also quick to add that White Castle's wages had steadily increased during that period, that the buildings had been upgraded, and that bonuses had been paid annually to all company employees. Mechling stated that "records like this just don't 'happen'; neither are they the result of 'accidents' or luck. They are the tangible results of organization efficiency, plus the unquestioned loyalty and industry of the Castle operators."

A. C. Mechling was right. White Castle did stand out among American businesses as an unlikely success story at a time when success was rare. He also was correct in his assertion that the careful guidance of Billy Ingram and the White Castle management team was primarily responsible for this success. Perhaps such business success could just "happen" in times of plenty, but such prosperity could not be purely "accidental" during the Depression. Contemporaries marveled at how White Castle could continue profitably in such an adverse economic climate. In retrospect, the answer to this question is both simple and complex. The simplest reason that White Castle remained solvent was that the buying public truly liked its hamburgers and that they continued to buy them despite economic hardship. The fuller answer is more complicated: White Castle's spectacular success during the 1930s was due mainly to Billy Ingram's innovative management and marketing strategies. To achieve this success, Ingram and his associates did not break new ground in management theory but, rather, borrowed time-tested ideas from other large industries and applied them to the hamburger business.

Restructuring and Streamlining

The most decisive move that Billy Ingram made during the 1930s was to consolidate his control over White Castle and to make far-reaching changes in the company's operations. This move came in several quick steps between 1933 and 1935. The first step was Ingram's sudden and unexpected purchase of Walt Anderson's half of the company's stock, giving Ingram sole ownership of the corporation. The second, and possibly most dramatic, step was Ingram's announcement that the company's home office would immediately relocate to Columbus, Ohio, along with its subsidiary manufacturing operations. The final step was the sudden "discontinuation" of the Wichita and Omaha operations, closing all the earliest White Castles.

Walter Anderson's departure from the White Castle System was a surprise to most of the company's employees. During his years as the company president, Anderson was seen as the cheery ambassador from the home office in Wichita who would swoop down on a White Castle city in one of his many airplanes. *House Organ* readers were thrilled to read about when he bought new planes, and many employees were even treated to plane rides over their cities when he would come for a visit. Anderson's trips across America and up into the wilds of Canada became a point of pride for many White Castle operators, that their leader embodied a rugged, if somewhat reckless, individualism. In the April 1931 *House Organ*, Anderson told a frightening tale of a narrowly averted crash, and many readers wrote in to express their affection and support. Although the more serious and pensive Billy Ingram was loved and trusted by his White Castle employees, Walt Anderson was much admired and respected by the predominantly male staff for his daring exploits.[10]

What most of the White Castle workforce did not know—but could probably have guessed—was that from the very beginning, Walt Anderson had been only a titular president. Although he owned 50 percent of the company stock, he did little in the way of day-to-day management of the company and did not take much notice of major policy decisions. Although he started the original hamburger stand in Wichita—which by the 1930s was affectionately referred to as "the Acorn"—he handed over all important responsibilities to businessman Ingram when the initial White Castle partnership was formed. Bearing the titles of vice president and treasurer, Ingram developed the strategies that took White Castle well beyond Wichita's city limits, carefully guiding every move in its eastward expansion.

Wealth came quickly to both partners as the company's profits mushroomed in the late 1920s, and Anderson set about enjoying his prosperity. The more conservative Ingram, however, spent modestly, choosing instead to invest most of his earnings. On a personal level, the two men were cordial and occasionally even took hunting vacations together in Canada, but their visions of White Castle's future were quite different. By 1930 Anderson had tired of the hamburger business and was growing restless. His passion was for flying, and he spent more and more of his time and money pursuing it.[11] The production of small planes was booming in Wichita at that time, and Anderson became convinced that the aviation industry would grow even bigger. He made it clear that he would prefer to direct his capital and attention toward that business.[12] Ingram, on the other hand, wanted to expand White Castle's holdings even further. In the spring of 1933, Anderson and Ingram agreed to dissolve their twelve-year partnership, with Ingram buying Anderson's stake in the company for $340,000. Afterward, Anderson immediately left Wichita to vacation in California.[13]

Walt Anderson's departure from the company was one of the least noticed White Castle events during the 1930s. Unfortunately for historians, it is also the least documented event in White Castle history. The company did not make an official announcement of his leaving, and the only apparent change was in the listing of corporate officers inside the front cover of the monthly *House Organ*.[14] E. W. Ingram was now listed as president, and A. C. Mechling was elevated from the post of second vice president, assistant secretary, and general auditor to Billy's old job of vice president and treasurer. Ingram did not publicly mention the separation in the *House Organ* until two years later, and then it was only a brief mention that "in 1933 Walt disposed of his interests to Billy."[15] Even the minutes of the directors' meetings fail to shed any additional light on the circumstances or details of his departure. Perhaps Anderson's rapport and popularity with the Castle operators can explain why his sudden departure was quietly downplayed in company circles. Perhaps Ingram and his White Castle management staff realized Anderson's popularity among the workers and wanted to minimize any disappointment. Regardless of the reason, however, one of the founding fathers of American fast food quickly and unceremoniously faded into obscurity.

The greatest change during the 1930s was far more open and celebrated.

In 1934 the company announced that all home office operations, including the research and development program, the test kitchen, and all manufacturing functions, would immediately be moved to Columbus, Ohio. In July of that year, the *House Organ* reprinted articles, editorials, and even cartoons from the *Columbus Citizen* and the *Columbus Dispatch* outlining the purchase of the new headquarters building, a brief history of the company, an overview of its holdings and operations, and the timetable for the move. These articles and editorials heaped praise on Ingram and his White Castle operation, appropriately crediting them with originating the fast-food hamburger industry. The newspapers reflected the pleasure that the Columbus city fathers felt at attracting a major company and new jobs to their town. Columbus would have appreciated the additional tax revenue and job openings at any time, but they were a godsend during the Depression years.

Ingram decided to move his company for several reasons. First was the fact that the White Castle operation had already spread to sixteen major cities in eleven states between Kansas and New York. Since all its expansion was east of Wichita, the home office was now on the western margin of the company's territory. This location caused more and more logistical problems for the corporation: mailing correspondence between cities during that era could be quite slow and unpredictable; support and management personnel had to travel great distances to reach eastern plants; and supplies had to be procured regionally, which was much less cost efficient than Ingram's preferred practice of centralized purchasing.

Although Ingram was deeply rooted in the Wichita community through his business and organizational ties, he realized that moving to another city would both better position White Castle for future growth and further centralize his control over its current operations. Ingram also may have been bothered that White Castle called itself a "national institution," yet the company was still run out of rented office space in a relatively insignificant city. Just as a state's capital usually is located in the geographic center of the state, Ingram chose Columbus principally because it was almost in the center of White Castle's territory.

Ingram also chose this city because he liked it. Columbus was a city that had been quite profitable for White Castle, with seven thriving Castles by 1934. He also was attracted to what the city offered. With a population of more than 300,000 people in 1930, Columbus was the state capital, boasted a major university and numerous colleges, and had an established and prosperous business community. Ingram even found what he believed to be the perfect building for consolidating all the company's functions under one roof. He purchased a recently closed two-story, red-brick factory and ten acres of land at 555 Goodale Street, formerly occupied by the bankrupt Columbus Rolling Door Company. Ingram decided to make extensive renovations in the building, installing an air-conditioning system, acoustical tile, and manufacturing areas for the Porcelain Steel Buildings division on the ground floor. On the second floor, he built ten private offices and conference rooms—all paneled in dark mahogany—larger work areas for the accounting, sales, and drafting departments, and a production area for Paperlynen.[16]

September 1, 1934, was Ingram's target date to begin operations in the new building. Much work needed to be done in the few months before 555 Goodale Street could open for business. Ingram assigned the newly promoted A. C. Mechling to plan and orchestrate the entire project. Aside from almost wholly renovating an enormous building, numerous other obstacles had to be overcome. Physically transporting the heavy manufacturing machines from Wichita and Green Bay was certain to be a monumental task. There were innumerable smaller details, such as buying new company letterhead stationery, distributing new communications information to area offices, purchasing state-of-the-art Dictaphone equipment, and arranging for a battery of telephones. But Ingram knew that the most difficult problem would be to convince his key people in Wichita to move to Columbus. Although he paid generous wages to his home office staff, most were native Kansans or Oklahomans who had never ventured far from home. Those who had been exposed to cities like Chicago or New York through company travel were not enthusiastic about permanently leaving Wichita's clean prairie air, safe streets, and relaxed atmosphere. The female employees in the office were mostly unmarried and were hesitant about leaving their parents and extended families for a city almost a thousand miles away. Despite their reluctance, however, most of the home office staff finally made the move to Columbus, for the simple reason that they would only earn a fraction of their White Castle paychecks elsewhere in Wichita, if they found new employment at all.

Not all these key employees, however, made the move. Jimmy King was one who opted to stay. King first joined White Castle in 1927, was soon promoted to area manager of the Wichita plant, and was frequently Ingram's right-hand man for solving problems and developing new products.[17] When Ingram announced the move to Columbus, he personally asked King to move there to head up an expanded and formalized research and development department. Originally from rural Kansas, King recalls that he was skeptical about moving eastward, but he agreed to give it a try. Together with his young son Wayne, King traveled to Columbus to look for a house and make the necessary moving arrangements. They stayed only a short time. Young Wayne wore a new white suit for his first day in town, and it was quickly soiled by the Columbus air, which was saturated with coal smoke from homes and factories. King immediately realized that he did not want to live or raise his children in Columbus, and he promptly returned to his manager's position in Wichita.[18]

With the exception of King and a few others who chose to stay behind, however, the home office workforce migrated en masse to Columbus during the summer of 1934 and immediately resumed their direction of White Castle from the new city. Although inconveniences such as "dangling cans of paint" and "the pounding of hammers" plagued their first few weeks, business was soon being conducted as usual, and most of the Wichitans quickly acclimated to their new surroundings. Ingram announced in the October *House Organ* that "throughout it all there has been evidence of cheerfulness, of earnestness, of helpfulness and cooperation." By the fall of 1934, White Castle had officially become a Columbus-based "national institution."[19]

Soon after the move to Columbus, Ingram began developing new strategies to increase overall profits. He had become concerned that even though annual sales remained strong, the corporation's net profitability was gradually shrinking. Ingram studied the company statistics to determine which areas of the business were succeeding and which could be improved. He looked at the cost versus profit for every food item sold, examined the profitability of the manufacturing divisions, and compared the relative productivity of all White Castle plants across the country. What he found was that not all White Castle cities contributed sufficient earnings to the overall bottom line. The plants in New York City, Newark, St. Louis, and Chicago consistently led the company in profitability, whereas most of the other cities reported significantly lower profits each month. These statistics indicated a positive correlation between an area's population density and the number of Castles operating there and their net profitability. In short, the bigger the city was, the more hamburgers were sold.

The two cities that consistently showed the smallest profits also had the smallest populations. These cities were Wichita and Omaha, the two first cities in the company empire and both former hometowns of Billy Ingram. In addition to being mediocre producers, Wichita and Omaha were geographically distant from the more highly concentrated company cities east of the Mississippi River. This point became more obvious when the home office finally left Wichita, hence reducing the city's importance to and status in the company. In addition, both cities were hundreds of miles from the next closest company city, hampering Ingram's plans for tightly centralized distribution systems and streamlined operations.

Accordingly, in the fall of 1936 Ingram decided to shut down the Castles and distribution systems in Wichita and Omaha in order to cut costs.[20] Although he was sentimentally attached to both places, he realized that these closures were for the good of the entire company, and this goal had to be his primary consideration.[21] The Wichita operation was closed first, in June 1938. Ingram's original intention was to shut down all the Castles in that city at the same time and then sell all the properties to nonrestaurants, so that the buyers of those locations could not try to capitalize on White Castle's hamburger legacy. He changed his plans, however, when Jimmy King approached him during a game of bridge with a purchase offer for four of the restaurants. King recounts that Ingram responded to his offer with the question, "Buy them with what?" implying, of course, that the salaried King could not afford the price. Nevertheless, Ingram had always had great respect for Jimmy King, and he admired his initiative. He also knew that selling to King would salvage the jobs of numerous Castle operators. So Ingram finally agreed to sell the Castles to King on the condition that the name be changed, the distinctive architecture altered, and no reference be made to a linkage between the two companies. King arranged for financial backing and quickly agreed to Ingram's terms. With the signing of their contract, White Castle disappeared from its hometown of Wichita, and King's new chain, called "Kings-X," appeared, rehiring most of the old Castle operators and successfully continuing in the hamburger business.[22]

Unfortunately, the Omaha plant did not fare so well. Ingram proceeded with his shutdown plans for that city, with all the Castles closing by late 1938. Ironically, a *House Organ* article only a few years earlier had praised Omaha, recalling how White Castle had introduced the now popular hamburger to that city. Nostalgia about better days, however, could not alter the fiscal realities of that time. Dozens of workers were laid off, and soon all trace of White Castle was gone. No official mention of either Wichita's or Omaha's closures was ever made in the *House Organ*, with the only evidence of the loss being the absence of printed correspondence from the employees of those plants in the monthly publication. White Castle employees throughout the country certainly knew of this downsizing, but none of their comments was ever printed. In the economic environment of the 1930s, layoffs and closures were quite common, and most employees were just thankful to be personally spared.

The Beginning of Paperlynen and Porcelain Steel Buildings

In addition to downsizing, Ingram had to develop other strategies for increasing White Castle's profits. One successful strategy was to lower the overall costs of doing business. For decades, management theorists had stressed the logic of minimizing production costs as a means of increasing profits. And as a businessman, Billy Ingram knew this even before starting the White Castle System, but he became more conscious of this reasoning as his company continued to grow. By the late 1920s he realized that becoming his own supplier of needed commodities, such as meat and bakery goods, would simultaneously guarantee the highest-quality products and reduce the middleman costs. Ingram thus built meat plants and bakeries to supply the Castle's operations, which ensured the stability of his fixed expenses. By the end of the decade, he was ready to complete his plan of "vertical integration."

This strategy was to make the White Castle System virtually self-sufficient, eventually creating in-house sources for its food products, for the manufacture and construction of its buildings, and even for the paper products used in its restaurants. As a further hedge against the economic instability of the Depression, these subsidiary companies, the Paperlynen Company and the Porcelain Steel Building Company, themselves soon became profit-making enterprises.

Although they are an integral part of the White Castle story, both Paperlynen and Porcelain Steel Building are significant in their own right. In quiet ways, both companies had a notable effect on American business, introducing innovative, money-making products to a broad spectrum of retailing and manufacturing companies. The Paperlynen Company began as a solution to what Billy Ingram perceived to be problems of both uniformity and cleanliness. From the outset, Ingram had established and enforced a strict company dress code for all Castle operators, insisting that all his operators wear crisp and clean white uniforms while on the job. But in the food service business, white uniforms quickly became stained and discolored. The item that became soiled most quickly was the operator's cap, mainly because of the fashion preference among men of that era for oily hair tonics. Ingram found that he had to keep replacing these caps at a rapid rate and at a surprisingly high cost. But after some informal experimentation in his office, Ingram designed an inexpensive, disposable paper cap that would look good for a short time and then could be replaced when soiled. Ingram toyed with this paper cap idea for the next three years until 1928 when he finally contracted with the mechanical contracting firm of Shaffer and Wirtz to examine the feasibility of manufacturing the caps. Experts in the paper industry, Shaffer and Wirtz were able—after almost two years of trial-and error attempts—to come up with a machine to make the caps. Company partner Frank H. Wirtz personally supervised the White Castle project, overseeing the lengthy experimentation process and conducting the first successful test run in May 1930. When the design and construction process was completed, White Castle owned the only paper cap-making machine in the world.

Once perfected, this machine could produce hundreds of caps each day. Wirtz grew so excited about the potential applications for paper products that he left the engineering business and became the first director of Ingram's new Paperlynen Company, which opened in Green Bay, Wisconsin, in March 1932. The initial production was designed to satisfy only the needs of the company itself, but it soon became clear that Paperlynen's production capabilities were far greater.[23]

After operating for two years in Green Bay, the Paperlynen factory moved to Columbus in September 1934. With the move came enhanced production, in both volume and product line. Paperlynen was soon supplying the Castles with paper napkins, paperboard hamburger cartons, and other miscellaneous paper products such as the "cutout booklets." To use its full production capabilities, Paperlynen also began producing paper headwear for a long list of food manufacturers and retailers, such as Coca Cola, Swift and Company, Borden's, Rath's Packing, the Kroger Grocery and Baking Company, H. J. Heinz, Kraft-Phoenix Cheese, Safeway Stores, Wonder, Dr. Pepper, and Ovaltine. Advertised in trade magazines for many food-related industries, these Paperlynen caps could be easily customized with the company's name or logo. But the caps could not accommodate the fuller hairstyles of most of the workers in these food industries, who were women. In response, Paperlynen expanded its product line in 1935 to include headbands for women workers. These were essentially the original caps' bands without the confining crown paper. These new headbands proved to be just as popular and profitable as the original caps, and Paperlynen became an established name in food service headwear, eventually supplying caps and headbands to more than sixteen hundred companies. Even more important to the parent-company White Castle, Paperlynen greatly surpassed original expectations and became its own profit-making industry, offering still greater fiscal stability to the entire corporation during the Depression years.

The other area where Ingram sought to minimize overhead costs was in new building construction. Once again, he turned to vertical integration to save money and retain control. Ingram had employed Lloyd Ray as his superintendent of construction since the early years of the company, and it was Ray who advanced Castle construction from the original fifteen-by-ten cement block structure to a larger white enamel brick building to a still larger fourteen-by-thirty glazed brick Castle. Ray directed the construction crew that traveled from city to city building new Castles or renovating old ones. His new designs or experimentation with alternative construction materials were frequently discussed in the *House Organ*, and they were obviously a point of company pride. Ray was constantly trying to improve the physical structure of the Castles, both their exteriors and interiors, as a means of enhancing efficiency and lowering overall operating costs. Ingram was thus pleased when Ray perfected a movable, all-metal Castle, proclaimed in the *House Organ* in May 1929 as "a dream come true" and "a true monument to White Castle ideals and White Castle achievement."[24]

Ray's new design also received rave reviews in metal industry trade journals. As the White Castle chain continued to grow, Lloyd Ray's construction department became an increasingly busy and steadily growing division of the company, responsible for ongoing research and development, on-site construction of the Castles, and regular upkeep and renovations. In 1931, Ray, in conjunction with the Allegheny Metal Company, devised a process of fusing a porcelain enamel coating onto a metal surface. Ingram had long recognized that Ray's efficiency and knack for invention could used be beyond just servicing company needs. Once Ray developed porcelain steel, Ingram immediately saw its commercial potential and began plans for a separate company, which he named the Porcelain Steel Building Company, to start large-scale production.[25]

The development of the Porcelain Steel Building Company was quite similar to that of Paperlynen. Both enterprises began as ideas of Billy Ingram, and both blossomed into successful industry leaders a decade later. The only real difference is that Ingram originally conceived of Paperlynen as a service department of the company and only later realized its vast commercial potential.

Porcelain Steel Buildings, commonly referred to as simply "PSB," began as a separate, freestanding industry, designed to build structures and interiors for both White Castle and other companies. When PSB was moved to Columbus, Ohio, in 1935, Lloyd Ray chose to remain as superintendent of construction, and the management of both PSB and Paperlynen was combined under the able direction of Frank Wirtz. Porcelain Steel employee Dean A. Myers described the operation as

> craftsmen working with their hands and a minimum of necessary mechanical devices shaping and cutting steel, planning and fitting fixtures, welding and soldering piece to piece, working through the mass of detail by blueprint and chart until the entire Castle stands were crated, ready to be shipped and assembled on its foundation in some distant city.

After providing all the needed Castles for company use, PSB then actively advertised its products and designs in trade journals, targeting all sorts of retail and service businesses. These ads emphasized the buildings' gleaming porcelain exteriors, their convertibility to a variety of uses, and their relatively low cost for both purchase and maintenance. They also stressed that these buildings could be customized to meet clients' specifications.[26]

Porcelain Steel's advertising campaign was effective. The company began selling units that were used as grocery stores and even as other restaurants. The most prosperous market for porcelain steel buildings was the burgeoning petroleum industry. More and more filling stations were needed in the mid-1930s as the number of automobiles continued to soar.[27] PSB's metal buildings were perfect for this new industry: they were inexpensive and portable, yet their porcelain finish projected a bright appearance and was easily cleaned. Most of the larger oil companies bought at least a few of Porcelain Steel's structures for their retail operation. By the end of the decade, hundreds of these buildings had been constructed as gas stations from coast to coast and remained, in the words of Billy Ingram, as "monuments to White Castle's achievements" for many years to come.

Ingram Introduces Newspaper Advertising and Coupons

In addition to streamlining operations and diversifying to manufacturing, Ingram sought ways to sell more hamburgers to consumers whose buying power was shrinking. Throughout the 1920s the traditional way of selling any product on the retail level was to open for business, hang out a sign, and let word-of-mouth recommendations spread among potential buyers. That was how Walt Anderson's early stands became so popular in Wichita, and that was what happened as White Castle spread to new cities. Then in the mid-1920s Ingram supplemented this passive approach by printing millions of small booklets shaped like castles and distributing them to all White Castle customers. These booklets listed all the White Castles across the country, described the nutritional value and ingredients of White Castle's products, and carried a message from Ingram. Referred to by Castle operators as simply "the cut-out booklet," they were designed as a marketing strategy to bond customers to White Castle.[28] Although these booklets were thought to be effective in retaining existing customers, they missed potential customers, since they were distributed in Castles by Castle operators.

Until that time, no systematic print or radio advertising had ever been attempted in the fast-food hamburger business. Ingram had dabbled in radio advertising in 1927 on St. Louis's KMOX, but he found few resulting benefits and quickly discontinued it. By the early 1930s, however, the hamburger industry was quite large and the market was already competitive. New customers became increasingly difficult to attract, and Ingram became concerned when sales grew very slowly in the first few years of the Depression. He believed that if people tasted a White Castle hamburger just once, they would become loyal customers, frequently returning for more and more. His goal, therefore, was to just get the potential customers into his Castles.[29]

One day Ingram noticed the special-sale prices for certain grocery items featured in the newspaper ad for a local food market. Grocer Bernard Kroger had pioneered advertising food prices in daily newspapers in the early 1920s, and by the end of the decade, the practice had caught on nationally in the grocery industry. Ingram saw these ads and quickly realized their potential application to the hamburger business. But he knew that merely trumpeting the merits of a particular food store was not what was bringing customers in. Rather, it was the prices advertised. Ingram became convinced that if this worked for grocery stores, it would work for the hamburger business.

Therefore, in the summer of 1933, Ingram began what the Castle operators affectionately referred to as "our big sale."[30] On June 3 he ran advertisements for White Castle in the major newspapers of all the company cities. The ads offered a coupon for five hamburgers at a sale price of ten cents, on a "carryout" basis only. Ingram would lose money selling his hamburgers at two cents a piece, but he predicted that creating a larger customer base would more than compensate for the loss. The response to this offer was enormous. Millions of coupons were clipped out of the newspapers and presented at White Castle counters everywhere. This experimental "five for a dime" sale ran for approximately one week.

At first the coupon campaign may have been too successful. The newspaper ad announced that the sale would begin the following day at 2:00 P.M., and so the Castles stocked up with a slightly larger amount of raw provisions for the day's business. Assured by their advertising consultants that the response would be healthy but not overwhelming, the area managers made few extraordinary preparations. But operators from all across the country reported that customers were lined up for blocks, even hours before the sale was set to begin, patiently waiting to get their discounted sacks of hamburgers. One Castle employee in Wichita commented that he "turned out burgers so fast that the customers all got dizzy watching them" and that "many a satisfied customer received his sack."[31] The rush was so intense at some Castles that they ran out of food in just an hour, sending their local supply houses into a frenzied effort to keep pace.

Just as Ingram had hoped, many people responded to the ad who had never eaten at White Castle before, often remarking on how much they liked it. A few voiced their displeasure over the extended wait and temporary shortages, but such criticism was minimal. Because the newspaper coupon campaign was so successful, Ingram decided to repeat it the following summer. In the interim, he continued to run more passive ads to remind the public about White Castle. The following May, the "five for a dime" coupons reappeared for two weeks, from May 7 to 20, in newspapers throughout the White Castle sales area.[32] Once again, customers lined the blocks surrounding each Castle. This time, however, the company and its operators were prepared for the onslaught, and they handled it easily. A St. Louis operator reported, "Nothing unusual has happened during the hamburger sale . . . extending the sale over two weeks has helped to prevent any great strain on the boys, consequently the coupon customers have been handled in great style." He added, "The new boys were somewhat nervous preceding the sale, the old boys having told them about the huge deluges of people who came to our Castles during the other sale, but after it started they acted like a bunch of veterans." Additional "relief men" were employed to handle the overflow. Once again, Ingram's sale was a great success, proving that giving potential customers a huge, yet brief, price incentive would result in a significant increase in long-term profits. Even more important, he demonstrated to his competitors in the fast-food hamburger industry that newspaper advertising and coupons were effective. This lesson was not lost on his contemporaries or the other fast-food companies that later entered the industry. Indeed, Ingram's coupons started a fast-food "media blitz" that continued for decades and today is worth billions of dollars each year.

Ingram Markets Hamburgers to the Middle Class

Perhaps Ingram's greatest achievement during the 1930s was that he successfully marketed his hamburgers to the middle class, overcoming the working-class stigma previously attached to them. His goal, naturally, was to increase his customer base and to sell more hamburgers, and his new marketing strategy was a conscious effort to make the entire American population avid hamburger eaters, regardless of class or ethnic background. To do this, Ingram knew that certain groups had to be coaxed into accepting hamburgers as healthy and wholesome food. Accordingly, in 1931 he began a concerted effort to convince more affluent middle-class women that hamburgers were indeed good food and could be safely made part of their family's diet. By the end of the decade, he was successful; the fast-food hamburger had shed most of its negative connotations and was finally accepted by consumers from all classes.

Selling hamburgers to America as acceptable family fare was not easy, however. The hamburger's popularity grew enormously during the 1920s, but its following was still limited in regard to class and gender. By 1930, White Castle and most of its competitors were aware that the most of their customers were working-class males, and so they aimed most of their marketing efforts toward them. Similar to the food carts of fifty years earlier, most of the new Castles were built within sight of a factory or in an otherwise industrialized area, whereas White Tower built most of its restaurants along the trolley lines frequented by commuting workers.

Ingram knew, however, that this marketing approach was a double-edged sword, that by successfully marketing to working-class men, women and even men from other classes would not come to White Castle. Since most of White Castle's clientele was male, Ingram did not permit women to be hired as operators, explaining that the male customers were apt to use inappropriate language and that employing women in that role would result in "too many problems." Castles were often filled with cigarette smoke, with constant banter between the operators and the customers about sports, hunting, and other stereotypically male discussion topics.[33] Ingram viewed this working-class male clientele and resulting male culture as positive and stable as long as these men had money to spend. As the Depression progressed, however, many manufacturing plants closed, impoverishing much of the industrial workforce.

With the buying power of his principal customer base diminishing, Ingram needed to find other customers who still had money to spend. Just as he had known for years exactly who was buying his hamburgers, he also knew who was not buying them. Ingram became convinced that the middle class could become hamburger customers, and he was determined to win them over. He also realized that this would not be easy.

Ingram knew that much of the middle class, especially the women, still considered ground meat to be essentially inedible and the hamburger sandwich to be the food of the working masses. Most of this group had read about meat in Upton Sinclair's *The Jungle*, and although Ingram had already dispelled the widely held prejudice against ground beef, the middle class still distrusted the quality and nutritional value of hamburgers. Their deep-seated apprehension about this food was exacerbated by the class associations that it earned during the 1920s. At the start of the Depression, the middle class did not consider hamburgers to be an appropriate or desirable food. Then *Advertising Age*, at that time the national publication of the advertising industry, became aware of White Castle's new tactics and pessimistically commented that "the company was handicapped in the endeavor aimed at the 'white collar' class because nobody in the industry had ever done anything in the area and there was no precedent to follow." Never a man to be thwarted, Billy Ingram decided to change their minds.

In the summer of 1932, Ingram intensified his quest to legitimize the hamburger, beginning with a campaign to make White Castle more attractive to the middle class. In doing so, he was walking a fine line. Although he wanted to change the public image of his company and its products in order to attract new customers, he did not want to alienate his current following. Ingram already took great pride in the fact that his White Castles were spotlessly clean and that they served only the finest beef. He sincerely believed that in terms of cleanliness and quality, his restaurants and products were unsurpassed at any price. In that respect, therefore, he saw no reason to "upgrade" his facilities or his food offerings.

Thus, the main challenge was to get the middle class to appreciate what he was already offering. To do this, he hired Ella Louise Agniel in July 1932 for the newly created position of "White Castle hostess." Agniel was an out-going and confident person, and before coming to White Castle, she had served in a variety of secretarial capacities, with the Illinois Central Rail-road in Chicago, the Great Western Smelting Company of Seattle, the Merchant's Navigation Company in New York, and for attorneys in New Mexico. Although Agniel had no direct experience in the food industry, her company biography in the *House Organ* mentioned that "her practical experience as a housewife gave her valuable first-hand knowledge of foods and dietetics." Ingram wanted Agniel to bring more women and the middle class to White Castle, or least to bring White Castle to them.[34]

Few White Castle people beyond the home office managers who actually hired her knew the name Ella Louise Agniel, because from the first moment of her employment, Agniel was given the pseudonym Julia Joyce for all her official company duties. All references to her in private company correspondence, press releases, and articles in the *House Organ* used only the name Julia Joyce. Remarkably, even her closest friends and associates in the company called her by her pseudonym, as most never knew her real name. Only Ingram, a few members of his management inner circle, and her employee personnel file knew the truth.

The use of corporate hostesses operating under assumed names was quite common during that era. Large national companies, especially the big food producers, frequently employed attractive and dignified women to showcase their products and to represent their public interests across the country. The first company to pioneer such image making through a representative hostess was General Mills. In 1921 General Mills, then known as Washburn, Crosby, and Company, was becoming frustrated with the growing negative publicity about the white bread made from its bleached Gold Medal flour. White bread was being denounced as having no nutritional value and being full of additives. In response, that company created the popular yet fictional gray-haired "Betty Crocker," who was portrayed to the public as both an expert on nutritional issues and the ideal role model of the feminine and organized homemaker. Beginning as merely one secretary signing this pseudonym to all public relations correspondence, the Betty Crocker personality grew to include personal appearances, the publication of numerous cookbooks, and even weekly radio shows concerning meal preparation and nutritional advice. "Crocker" would host Hollywood stars on her program to share their culinary secrets, nutritional experts to discuss new research in food, and housewives to talk about using General Mills's products. Since promoting these products was the aim of the programs—and of Betty Crocker's fictional existence itself, the merits of bread items, Wheaties cereal, and pasta were frequent topics of Crocker's shows.

Other companies and industries used similar strategies to promote the virtues of their products. The National Association of Canners hired an actual food expert, University of Chicago home economics professor Ruth Atwater, to be their industry spokesperson, proclaiming the nutritional virtues of canned products. Atwater crisscrossed the nation, speaking to women's organizations and always stressing that "research has shown conclusively that canned foods have the same food value as similar foods made in home kitchens, with the possibility of added energy value due to the presence of sugar syrups in many canned fruits and a few canned vegetables." As a result of their "hostess" efforts, both the real-life Atwater and "Betty Crocker" caused sales to boom in their respective industries.[35] After observing the success of these corporate hostesses in legitimizing distrusted food products, Ingram hired the articulate and attractive Agniel, made her into the hostess Julia Joyce, and charged her with making hamburgers a mainstream middle-class food.

Julia Joyce's sole task was to spread the good word about White Castle to the uninformed or nonbelievers. After learning about the company from top to bottom, she set out to educate the women of America—specifically the middle class—about the virtues of the White Castle hamburger sandwich. To do this, Joyce followed the successful lead of the other corporate hostesses: she traveled constantly from city to city, speaking to women's clubs and charitable organizations, made up mainly of middle-class women. She would usually be the featured speaker at these clubs' meetings, often starting her talks with the admission that she too had been reluctant at first to try hamburgers. Next she usually described the nutritional benefits of White Castle's products, explaining how hamburgers could be regularly incorporated into the family diet.

For example, Joyce cited research showing that White Castle's buns were not fattening, were completely digestible, enhanced energy and strength, and "provided vitamins for good teeth."[36] Joyce taught women how to plan their weekly menus using White Castle's hamburgers as the main course, stressing the ease of not having to cook them and the sure approval of their families. Since entire families were not likely to come to dine at a seven- or eight-stool White Castle, she emphasized the "to go" style of buying hamburgers.

After discussing the food, Joyce would read parts of Billy Ingram's "White Castle Code" to convince her listeners of White Castle's strong moral commitment to quality and value. Joyce would also joke about the old axiom that "the way to a man's heart is through his stomach."[37] Not relying on persuasive rhetoric alone, however, Joyce would also show up at these meetings with sacks full of hamburgers, to demonstrate at first hand their taste and quality. Following a series of club and organization meetings, she would next invite all the women that she had addressed to go to the nearest White Castle to inspect the sanitary conditions, the food preparation techniques, and even the ambience. Joyce's favorite features to highlight were the new under-the-counter electric dishwashers that ensured sterile dishes and coffee mugs, and the stainless steel (then known as "Allegheny metal") utensils, pans, and coffee urns. When seeing the gleaming metal, one visitor incorrectly remarked to her mother, "It's just so beautiful! It's all done up in platinum!" Joyce reinforced her addresses and these visits by giving those attending the company-printed "Menu Suggestion" book, which further elaborated on the dietary possibilities of White Castle's hamburgers. The usual outcome of Joyce's three-pronged approach was that she convinced these middle-class women that White Castle hamburgers were, in fact, delicious and high-quality food that could be safely served to their families, and as a result, many became regular customers.[38]

Ingram quickly realized that he had chosen the right person to represent his company to new segments of the buying public. He surmised that the key to Joyce's success was her relentless determination and energy. She often spoke to several clubs in one day, in addition to hosting sessions at various Castle restaurants. Although she was the company's official liaison to the middle class, Joyce was also responsible for virtually all White Castle's public relations functions, and in this capacity, her contacts extended to all classes of society.

For example, in late 1932 Joyce held a holiday party for the Salvation Army in Columbus, in conjunction with local Castle operators, distributing hundreds of free hamburgers to the poor people attending. This was the first of many charitable events over which she presided. She served 150 hamburgers to the "Just Kids Safety Club" for their summer picnic. Joyce's largest Christmas meal for charity was also for the Salvation Army, held in 1935 at its Pontiac Street Settlement House in Detroit. There she served hundreds of hamburgers to poor women and children. Known for her warmth and compassion, Joyce seemed to enjoy this charitable aspect of her job even more than her marketing duties. By all accounts, Julia Joyce was even more cordial and respectful to these meal recipients than she was to the more affluent middle-class ladies.[39]

But Joyce's or White Castle's motives for charity work were not completely altruistic. Their highly visible charitable acts had the dual purpose of helping the less fortunate while also enhancing the company's image in its market cities. Decades before the highly publicized charitable initiatives by Ronald McDonald and his company, Billy Ingram was already aware of the value of corporate giving, designating Joyce to be the company's lead person in these activities.

In addition to effectively marketing White Castle, Julia Joyce also was important to the company as almost a mother or sister figure for the all-male Castle workforce. She was the only high-profile woman in an otherwise male company world. Although some other women were employed by the company as secretaries and bookkeepers, most worked in local plant or home offices and were rarely ever visible to Castle operators. Joyce, on the other hand, was a company celebrity who regularly traveled, meeting virtually every counterman on each trip. *House Organ* correspondents would often detail her activities and successes in their cities for the entire system to read about.

Joyce was also a regular contributor to the *House Organ*, outlining her travels and describing her vacation trips with her husband. She always attended the annual managers' meetings, reporting on her progress for that year and discussing plans for the next year. Although not technically a company manager, Julia Joyce held the status of a "manager at large," and her success and competence gave her much power. It was widely known in company circles that Billy Ingram valued her judgment and asked her advice on many issues. Possibly because of her gender and popularity, Joyce was also called on to mediate some internal problems or bitter feelings that accompanied events such as the home office move to Columbus and the closing of the two company cities.

Although Julia Joyce was always successful during the 1930s, in marketing White Castle to the middle class, reaching out to the poor, and solving company problems, her greatest and most lasting achievement was that she brought much of the middle class into the ranks of White Castle customers. Before her arrival, both Ingram and the rest of the hamburger industry acknowledged that they did not have a middle-class following. Once Joyce began her club work, however, White Castle hamburgers gained acceptance in a very short time. By the end of the decade it was not unusual to see businessmen and housewives standing in line next to construction workers, policemen, and taxi drivers. By exposing thousands of middle-class women to the White Castle hamburger, Julia Joyce was able to break down many of the class barriers that seemed so impermeable just a few years before.

Despite her great success, Julia Joyce's efforts were probably not the sole factor in White Castle's gaining commercial acceptance among the middle class during the 1930s. Another, less deliberate route toward the middle-class palate came through college students. Beginning in the late 1920s, Ingram built some of his Castles strategically within walking distance of large state university campuses in company cities. His obvious short-term goals for these placements was to attract students to the Castle counters, offering hearty and inexpensive food. These campus-area Castles prospered, with hordes of students from the University of Minnesota, Ohio State University, the University of Nebraska, and smaller colleges coming each day and especially after events such as football games and dances. Most college students in the 1930s were exposed to fast-food hamburgers, whether from White Castle or a competitor, and unconsciously accepted burgers as a part of their regular diet. By developing this "hamburger habit" during their college years, these college students continued to crave the familiar sandwiches after graduation. Since most college students during the 1930s were already the children of the middle class and a bachelor's degree was almost a guarantee of middle-class standing, these new graduates were immediately becoming the next generation of the American middle class.

Much to Billy Ingram's pleasure, the fast-food hamburger was fast becoming more of a universal "American food," devoid of class stigmas or prejudice. The hamburger's legitimization was corroborated in 1937 by R. D. Clark, then president of the National Restaurant Association, who proclaimed that it was truly a national food, joining only apple pie and coffee on that very short list. He held that opposition to the hamburger had "crumbled under the weight of popular demand."[40]

Above everything else, White Castle had successfully weathered the Depression because Billy Ingram insisted that quality, in regard to product and service, never be diminished. In addition, his strategies of diversifying into manufacturing, restructuring the corporation, and appealing to new markets all increased the company's cash flow, even though its fundamental business still was selling hamburgers.

By popular demand, Ingram maintained the same basic menu of hamburgers, Coca Cola, coffee, pie, pastries, and buttermilk that had been so successful in the 1920s. He kept a watchful eye on all facets of this business, adjusting his products and service to meet customer demand and maximize his profits. If customers wanted "doubles," which became a fad in the late 1930s, then operators served up sandwiches with two patties. Ingram also introduced "curb service" in 1935 to accommodate the growing automobile traffic past his Castles and to emphasize the "to go" style of buying hamburgers. Customers simply had to drive up to the Castle, toot their car horn, and a smiling Castle operator would emerge to take their orders. By adopting this newly expanded service approach, Ingram was also recognizing and responding to the growing competition from new hamburger chains that catered specifically to automobile customers. He also introduced forty-foot-long roadside billboards to attract motorists and to announce the distance to the nearest Castle.

Always stressing cleanliness, Ingram was constantly modifying the Castles' interiors to present a cleaner, more pleasant image. He also test-marketed new food products in certain cities to gauge their acceptance, although none of these test foods was adopted for the regular menu during this decade. Ingram continued to tell everyone within earshot about the virtues of the hamburger. By the end of the 1930s, however, he was declaring these facts with even greater confidence and enthusiasm than he had twenty years before, now secure in the knowledge that his fast-food hamburger was already a mainstream American food. He also knew that White Castle sold more of them than anyone else.

Despite his great success with White Castle during this era, Billy Ingram was sensitive to the plight of the impoverished. As Ingram's company travels took him across the nation, he witnessed the devastation and poverty first hand, often writing about what he saw in the *House Organ*. Local *House Organ* correspondents from across the country added their own stories about hardship and poverty in their communities, always stating their gratitude to Ingram for keeping their jobs secure. White Castle's vice president, A. C. Mechling, who seemed far less sensitive to the needy, regularly provided *House Organ* readers with statistical information on unemployment rates and the signs of recovery.

Ingram believed that White Castle was a positive force in this time of despair, taking pride in the fact that he kept hundreds of men working at a time when their neighbors were unemployed. As mentioned earlier, he also frequently directed Julia Joyce and local operators to give away hundreds of hamburgers, coffee, and pies to the poor at charity events. In addition to these food donations, Ingram contributed large amounts of money to relief efforts in Wichita, Columbus, and throughout the nation. In fact, such charitable giving became a habit for Ingram, who a decade later founded a family philanthropic foundation to distribute millions of dollars to the needy and to nonprofit organizations. Whereas such giving is relatively common in corporate America today, Ingram was among the earliest American corporate philanthropists and was certainly the first in the fast-food industry to sponsor charitable events. In a less obvious way, he also believed that White Castle contributed to the public good by selling its hamburgers to the public for an affordable price. Furthermore, he felt that he was providing nutritious food to an American people who would otherwise be eating less healthy fare. On many levels, he believed that White Castle was actively helping those suffering most in the Depression. At the same time, he took every occasion to express his gratitude to the buying public for their continued support and to his entire White Castle staff "for a job well done."

Ingram did have much to be thankful for. During the Great Depression of the 1930s, White Castle prospered while many other chains failed. The company enjoyed a record sales year in 1937, and all indicators pointed to continued prosperity. Ingram personally emerged from the decade as the sole proprietor of the largest fast-food company in the country, a millionaire many times over, and "the father of America's food." Having survived the Depression in relative comfort, both Ingram and White Castle looked forward to the next decade. The hamburger was booming as the United States' national food and the company's reputation was firmly established throughout its business areas. In addition, Ingram's only son, Edgar, had recently graduated from Cornell University and joined him in the business. By all estimates, the 1940s was destined to be the best decade yet for White Castle.

4

White Castle Goes to War

Billy Ingram was optimistic as the 1940s began. After surviving the Depression, he was confident that his company could overcome any future obstacles and continue to prosper. Despite the widespread economic decay throughout American society in the 1930s, White Castle ended the decade larger and more solvent than any time in its past. With an economic revival forecast, Ingram and the rest of the White Castle management team predicted that the coming decade would be their best yet. Selling more than 38 million hamburgers in 1939, 41,040,750 in 1940, and a record 50,192,785 in 1941, such optimism seemed to be warranted. But with the outbreak of World War II, these predictions of greater success were not realized.[1] Instead, unseen setbacks such as labor shortages, food scarcity, and changing social patterns greatly affected the marketplace. Although workers' incomes surged upward along with wartime employment rates, White Castle's sales plummeted, forcing the company to close many restaurants. By the mid-1940s, both White Castle and the entire restaurant industry were suffering. Just as the Depression largely defined the 1930s, World War II and its aftermath shaped the 1940s.

The Road to War

Despite their outward optimism in the late 1930s, Billy Ingram and White Castle were not surprised by the outbreak of war. Beginning as early as 1937, local plant correspondents to the *House Organ* reported military aggression in other countries,[2] and in his monthly column, Billy Ingram began discussing the militarism in Central Europe, which he continued doing until the war began. Later, taking an "isolationist" position, Ingram joined a large and powerful group of business and political leaders lobbying against intervention in the war. Other White Castle leaders agreed with Ingram, and referring to White Castle's popularity, one operator even joked that "we can't go to war in Europe, because there are no White Castles there for our boys to eat at."

As the prospect of war drew nearer, however, this isolationist rhetoric immediately subsided and was quickly replaced by more patriotic calls for military involvement. The National Conscription Act reinstituted the draft in the summer of 1940, convincing everyone of the seriousness of the situation and the inevitability of the war.[3] Now instead of urging restraint, Ingram and others enthusiastically expressed support for a victory in the coming struggle.

The conscription of men began to escalate during 1941, and most people had a family member or close friend inducted into the service. Similarly, White Castles everywhere lost operators to the draft, with those departing usually saying a public farewell to their company coworkers in the *House Organ*. Before long, the tone of the publication became increasingly somber in anticipation of the coming war. Nonetheless, other issues still concentrated on positive aspects of the company and the now-rebounding economy. Leo White, a St. Louis Castle operator, stressed that the only concern of White Castle and its workforce should be "to familiarize the public with the White Castle hamburger sandwich," for the purpose of having "a much bigger and brighter 1941."[4] These Castle operators believed that the continued prosperity of their company would protect them.

Since late 1940, Castle operators, bakers, delivery drivers, and supervisors from local plants either had been enlisting or were drafted. The exodus was so great, in fact, that by September 1941 the *House Organ* began running a lengthy monthly column entitled "White Castle in the Army."[5] This column consisted of letters from soldiers and sailors away at training camps or overseas. Also featured were photos of some of these servicemen in their dress uniforms, each with his garrison cap worn at a jaunty angle, reminiscent of how they once wore their paper White Castle caps. Each column would also have some commentary by the White Castle's marketing director, Maurice "Benny" Benfer, who explained that the purpose of the column was "to hear regularly from the White Castle men who at the present are in active service." Benfer quipped that he considered these former Castle operators to be "either in spirit or in fact, 'absent without leave' . . . from their White Castle employment." From the beginning of the mass conscription, Benfer had copies of the *House Organ* mailed overseas each month to former employees, a policy maintained for the duration of the war. Over time, Benfer even personally corresponded with a large number of servicemen, often printing both his letters and their replies in the column.[6]

Switching from Uncle Billy to Uncle Sam

Already by November 1941, White Castle's workforce had been decimated by the military mobilization. Since Castle operators traditionally were healthy young males, all were prime candidates for conscription into the service. As early as two months before the start of the war, only one-tenth of all Castle operators had more than one year of service with the company. All the others had either entered the military or left the company for higher-paying defense plant jobs.

Once the war actually began, the transfer from White Castle to the military was almost complete. With hundreds of former operators now in uniform, White Castle had to turn to younger workers and to other workers who might not have been hired in earlier times. In early 1942 Billy Ingram noted that more than 325 of his operators were off fighting for their country.[7] By June 1943, that number had risen to more than six hundred, out of a workforce of only seven hundred men.[8] Both Ingram and White Castle constantly expressed their support for the war and their desire to assist the effort in every way possible. This patriotic enthusiasm at White Castle and throughout the country, however, was soon tempered by telegrams conveying news of loved ones' deaths.

Trying not to focus all its praise and attention on the White Castle operators departing for the war, the company took measures to reinforce the importance of the work of those employees staying behind. This gap between those men who were in the military and those who remained behind during the war because of physical limitation, "essential" job status, or family necessity was a sensitive issue. The prevailing culture was that everyone should contribute to the war effort, with military service being the most prized way to do so.

Accordingly, Billy Ingram, Benny Benfer, and others stressed that they considered Castle work to be "essential" even if the government did not classify it as such. Even before the war began, Ingram frequently stated that White Castle was crucial to feeding the growing legions of defense industry workers. A Castle operator from Newark agreed with this premise, authoritatively asserting that "good nutrition . . . would be enough to produce 10,000 heavy bombers, 20,000 fighter planes, 30,000 light tanks, and 20 battleships."[9] Ingram continued this theme throughout the early years of the war, always contending that White Castle provided the fuel to make the industrial workforce productive.

Despite this encouragement, during the first year of the war even many of the recently hired replacement operators left White Castle for more respected and lucrative defense-related jobs. Although White Castle increased its operators' wages early in the war, it could not keep up with the much higher pay offered by industry, which more than doubled between 1941 and 1942. In only two years, the United States progressed from operating in a Depression-era economy, with an unemployment rate of almost 20 percent, to suffering from a labor shortage, with workers needed in every area of the economy. Healthy white males earned top wages at war production facilities, draining much of the available labor power.

Castle operators left the company for the vehicle plants of Detroit, which were churning out jeeps, trucks, and tanks; for Goodyear Tire and Rubber, which was making precious tires; and for countless shipyards and munitions factories across America. In the company's General Letter to its managers, Louisville's W. A. Offner complained that "we have difficulty keeping boys . . . the Reynolds Metal Company takes a good many of our boys and I understand the wages there are about $40 a week." At Minneapolis's Northern Pump, workers were being paid more than eighty dollars a week. Such wages must have seemed exorbitant to White Castle operators, whose top pay scale was twenty-four dollars per week for sixty hours of work, and to "curb boys," who made only twenty-five cents per hour. The lure of higher wages was exacerbated by the fact that in some cities, factory representatives actually came around to White Castles specifically recruiting the operators. In addition, the local draft boards in some areas even required that certain civilian workers report for "service" at defense-related industries. The turnover of employees at White Castle therefore remained high, and the company could do little to stop it. At the outset, White Castle appealed to its employees' loyalty, constantly reminding them of White Castle's stability and prosperity during the Depression and emphasizing that although more money could now be made elsewhere, there were no guarantees that the war—and hence this lucrative wartime employment—would last beyond a few months. One *House Organ* commentary asked, "How long will these other jobs last?' and "Will you have a job after the war?"[10] Nonetheless, White Castle continued to lose men to industry and was now in the precarious position of not having enough employees to staff its Castles.

New Men at the Griddle

White Castle responded to this predicament by hiring younger male workers and less desirable individuals. For the first time, many area managers re-

Illustrations

This prototype Anderson and Ingram White Castle building opened in March 1921 on Douglas Avenue in Wichita. Before this building, Walt Anderson owned three hamburger "stands," though without the whitewashed crenellated walls and turret, all of which were incorporated into the partners' new chain.

All Castles in the early 1920s had spartan interiors, featuring a serving counter, five stools, and a back bar and grill area for food preparation. Since customer seating was quite limited, most patrons soon learned to carry away their hamburger purchases "by the sack."

Stressing freshness and quality, White Castle originally contracted in the 1920s with local bakeries and butchers for daily, or even twice daily, deliveries. In the 1930s White Castle built its own production and distribution plants to supply its needs.

Since much of its business was on a carryout basis, White Castle constantly experimented with different types of paper bags. For many years, the insulated sack (shown here) was the White Castle standard.

Pioneers in the use of aircraft as tools of business management, partners Anderson and Ingram proudly display their first plane, a Curtis OX-5 Travel Air Biplane, in 1927. With Anderson in the pilot's seat, the company's airplanes enabled them to travel easily around their company's territory, for firsthand supervision of White Castle's operations.

Following the lead of the grocery industry and other retailers, in the late 1920s White Castle began advertising in the leading newspapers in its market cities, frequently including heavily discounted coupons in its ads. The ad shown here is from the Depression years of the early 1930s, encouraging more female customers to patronize the previously predominantly male Castles.

Proud Castle operators line up for the photo on opening day in front of Chicago's first White Castle. The company began its Chicago operation in 1929, and Chicago quickly became one of White Castle's most profitable areas.

The Castles changed continually in the company's first twenty years, in size, building materials, and architecture. When one Castle was deemed to be either outdated or too small, a replacement Castle was usually quickly erected nearby. In many cases, such as this one in Chicago, the new Castle was built right next to the old one and often on the same lot.

Until World War II, White Castle employed only adult males to work as operators behind the counters. Castle operators typically worked alone, although they were sometimes teamed together during peak mealtimes or at exceptionally busy locations. Pictured here is a Castle staff of mostly teenage male operators in the late 1940s.

Endlessly stressing that customers should "Buy'em by the Sack," the company's advertising often promoted the concept of carryout purchases. This advertising photo from the early 1930s depicts White Castle hamburgers as the main course of a middle-class family's dinner. Once the Depression caused widespread industrial layoffs and impoverished many in the working class, White Castle's marketing efforts specifically targeted the middle-class consumer.

Once thought in the 1920s to be an environment dominated by working-class males, shrinking profits at the onset of the Depression forced White Castle to broaden its customer base to include more women. The company hired a corporate hostess, with the pseudonym of Julia Joyce, and sent her out with scores of hamburgers to visit women's clubs and organizations in every White Castle area. Her goal was to introduce White Castle and hamburgers to middle-class women, to convince them of the hamburgers' quality, and to encourage their regular patronage of White Castle.

To ensure architectural standardization, White Castle had nearly all its Castles constructed at the Porcelain Steel Buildings factory in Columbus. Here workers are fabricating the crenellated turrets, which became the distinctive company symbol.

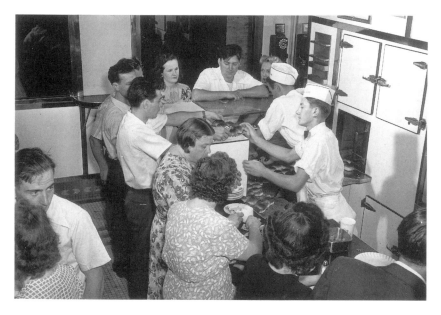

Staying open around the clock, White Castle has long attracted late-shift workers and an assortment of other late-night customers. Often the only source of food in the early hours of the morning, White Castles became popular gathering places for nocturnal city dwellers.

After World War II, the company refocused its marketing campaigns to attract more children to the Castles. By sponsoring local children's programs in the early years of television, White Castle and its competitors nurtured an entirely new generation of hamburger-hungry customers.

In the early 1930s, Billy Ingram shrewdly positioned Castles within close walking distance of large state universities and colleges. By the end of that decade, an after-hours stop for hamburgers became the weekly tradition for many students. This tradition has lived on at many campuses ever since and is often among the fond reminiscences at alumni gatherings.

White Castles began by serving a walking-city clientele in the 1920s, and by the late 1930s the company had positioned all its new restaurants on busy urban intersections or thoroughfares for the sole purpose of attracting drive-up customers. The Castle shown here reflects these changing trends, positioned between an urban commuter train station and a main artery.

One drawback of teaching Americans how to buy their hamburgers "to go" was the chronic litter problem around most White Castles. Responding to demands by local authorities, White Castle employees each morning had to clean up hundreds of discarded hamburger boxes on the streets around the Castles.

Between 1936 and 1972, competing with the carhop service offered by other quick-service restaurants such as the franchised Big Boy chain, White Castle delivered food directly to customers' automobiles.

The giant fast-food chains that proliferated in the late 1950s and early 1960s featured larger and more modern structures, usually constructed with futuristic angles, looming arches, and large expanses of glass. White Castle responded to this trend by building larger, more modern versions of its traditionally styled structures. The Castle pictured here is the original unit in the Miami area, built in the early 1960s.

Still a haven for late-night revelers and nighttime workers, many White Castles remain just as busy at midnight as at noon. This line of hungry customers is a typical postmidnight scene at virtually every White Castle.

Now featuring a modified crenellated roof but still relatively simple in comparison with its competitors' buildings, this Cincinnati Castle opened for business in 1995. Although the White Castle chain itself ranks far below the franchised fast-food giants in overall size, it is among the most profitable companies in the industry on a "per unit" basis.

White Castle founder Billy Ingram directed most of the company's operations right up to his death in 1966. He led the company on its roller-coaster ride from prosperity to near disaster and finally back to economic viability. More important, he gave America its national food.

sorted to recruiting teenagers for their workforces, first dropping the minimum age requirement to eighteen, then later in the war to sixteen, and then even lower in certain places where allowed by law.

In addition to employing teenagers, White Castle was forced to relax some of its other strict standards in hiring replacement workers. Some of the new men were of dubious quality, and not surprisingly, a new set of problems quickly developed. Since the company began, Billy Ingram had always taken great pride in the caliber, work ethic, and honesty of his operators. White Castle had always been extremely selective in its hiring process, usually accepting only attractive, physically fit, and articulate young men. Once hired, these young men were held to the strictest standards of efficiency, cleanliness, and polite service. Those who did not measure up to Ingram's standards were immediately fired.

But by 1942 the luxury of being able to be so selective was long past. Area managers ran ads in their local newspapers simply reading, "Young men; no exper. necessary. Steady work; good salary. Apply White Castle System." During such a severe labor shortage, White Castle's hiring managers had to settle for whatever workers responded to its advertisements. Many of the new employees were unmotivated and even incompetent compared with the former operators. When one supervisor chided a curb operator for serving a customer too slowly, the employee responded, "For twelve dollars a week, plus tips, I don't feel that I should have to do very much." A Cincinnati manager remarked, "It is hard, if not impossible, to get the type of men we like to hire." A veteran Castle operator, frustrated with his younger coworkers, commented that "many of these operators wouldn't have held a job for five minutes with White Castle two years ago."

Both productivity and profits fell significantly because of the less efficient operators. Moreover, these new workers frequently quit their jobs without notifying the company. W. A. Offner observed that only "50% of our boys fail to show up for work" on any given day. Even worse than this inefficiency, laziness, and absenteeism, White Castle also experienced its first rash of employee thefts and other crimes. A teenage runaway, having lied about his age to be hired in Indianapolis, stole money from both the Castle cash register and his coworkers. Two weeks later a Detroit operator emptied the till and departed before the end of his shift. Such thefts became more and more common but were difficult to stop, since operators were often alone in their Castles. Managers also discovered that the operators' practice of giving away free food to friends was becoming increasingly common.

In addition to the growing theft problem, White Castle also experienced unprecedented occurrences of employee violence. In early 1942, two unhappy and drunk Chicago operators struck their area supervisor, Jim Corr, in the head with a iron pipe and vandalized their Castle.[11] That same year, two Cincinnati Castle operators robbed a Castle in another city. An operator in New York was convicted of manslaughter and sentenced to prison. Another New Yorker was arrested for robbing grocery stores. In all, this new crop of Castle operators certainly was not upholding the sterling reputation established by their predecessors, who were now off in the military. Trying to be optimistic in the face of deteriorating circumstances, New York City manager L. M. Shackelford admitted, "I realize that we have lowered our standards somewhat . . . but our personnel are of a considerably higher type than our competitors. Many places are changing to female employees."

White Castle and other fast-food hamburger chains were not the only businesses hit hard by wartime labor shortages. Other industries, ranging from agriculture to auto plants, lost millions of their regular workers to either the military or other jobs. Even high-paying heavy-industry jobs often remained vacant, with many companies having to bring in trainloads of workers from other regions of the country to fill them. Rural African Americans working as sharecroppers in the South and whites from the hills of Tennessee and Kentucky were drawn to the factories of Detroit, Chicago, Cleveland, Pittsburgh, and elsewhere with the promise of big money.[12] Millions of Americans left their traditional homes and lifestyles to travel north in pursuit of this perceived fortune, but not for the comparatively low wages paid by the restaurant industry. For both White Castle and other restaurants, it became clear that alternative labor sources were needed.[13]

White Castle Welcomes Women Castle Operators

When the traditional worker pools had been exhausted by mid-1940, White Castle finally followed the lead of other American businesses in hiring women as workers. This practice of employing women was not new to wartime America. During World War I, millions of women briefly entered the labor force, filling jobs previously held by men.[14] Thus after the attack at Pearl Harbor, American business and industry quickly turned to women as workers, and with a far greater number of men in uniform during World War II, many more job vacancies needed to be filled. Soon women held a wide array of jobs that were traditionally bastions of male power, such as those in steelworking, heavy production, and shiploading.[15]

Nevertheless, since founding the company, Billy Ingram had adamantly refused to allow women to become operators, long setting the standard for the fast-food hamburger industry. (Throughout the United States, hamburger stands were traditionally operated by males.) Then Shackelford reported from New York that competitor White Tower "hires and works girls behind the counter and many other small eating places are doing likewise." Despite this apparent trend, Shackelford assured his fellow managers that "I do not believe that it will be necessary to hire women to work at White Castle," and area manager Bruce LaPlante harshly condemned the idea of hiring women. But with the increasing labor shortage, Shackelford, LaPlante, and others were forced to reconsider their views because area supervisors could not hire enough male employees to keep the Castles open. Their choice was between hiring women or closing entire city operations.

Given these options, Ingram relented in his opposition to female operators and changed his hiring policy. On September 24, 1942, without any prior announcement to the public, the first female White Castle operators began working at White Castles in the Minneapolis-St. Paul area. Ingram may also have reversed his policy because the gender of White Castle's customer base was changing significantly: contrasting sharply with the previous decade, by 1942 the "typical customer" was just as likely to be female.[16]

The transition from male to female Castle operators took only a few months to be completed. During the summer of 1942, only males fried and served White Castle hamburgers,[17] but by the spring of 1943, most Castle operators across the country were women. By the end of the war, the Castle counter workers were almost entirely female and remained so for many years.

Although this transition was extremely quick and almost complete by 1945, it did not occur without problems. At first, the managers disagreed whether younger or older women would be better suited for such jobs. The initial newspaper advertisements asked for "Women, thirty-five years and up," with most of the respondents being between the ages of forty and sixty. These managers then decided that the appearance of such older women was not suitable for the image that they wanted to project, so next time they advertised for "Women, twenty-five to thirty-five years of age." But few responded, since women in this age group had more employment options or more child care responsibilities. Finally, the minimum age was lowered to twenty years old, which produced enough applicants to staff the Castles.

In addition to finding the right pool of workers, another obstacle to employing women in the Castles was a legal one. In the 1940s, some cities and states still had laws limiting the areas and conditions in which women could work. First enacted as benevolent reforms after the tragic Triangle Shirtwaist Fire of 1912, such laws were designed to protect women from unscrupulous employers and dangerous working conditions.[18] But then restrictions on women in the workplace were further reinforced during the 1930s for less generous reasons, designed to give male breadwinners an advantage in the job market. By the start of the 1940s, several localities still had strict limitations on women in the workplace. In New York City, for example, labor regulations specified that women could work only during specific daytime hours, that they must have seating, and that they must be served full-course meals at precise times. Such restrictions were not conducive to a business open twenty-four hours each day, requiring employees to stand for twelve hours, often with no time for rest breaks or meals. As time went on, however, most municipalities relaxed their ordinances, or the companies made accommodations such as shorter work shifts.

One problem of sexism was largely avoided, however. As expected, not all White Castle staff and customers embraced the gender change, but the opposition was minimal and short lived. Months before the first women were hired, one longtime Castle operator from Kansas City, D. E. Stockstill, stated that "White Castle is an American institution, run by American *manhood*."[19] And when women first appeared in the Castles, some customers asked, "Where have the boys gone?" Some male customers called the new operators disrespectful names such as "Babe" and "Toots" or worse. Some of the women operators faced outright abuse from some customers and often felt unsafe working alone late at night.

Most people's reactions, however, were positive. From his post in Pearl Harbor, Private E. R. Toomey, a Castle operator turned marine, was the first to welcome publicly the newly hired women to the greatly extended "White Castle family." Writing in the "With White Castle in the Armed Forces" column, Toomey told the new women that "a great responsibility rests upon your shoulders . . . to keep up the standards and reputation that the White Castle System has held among leading organizations for many years." He also congratulated them, noting that "many of you have already taken hold and mastered the job that the public thought only men could handle."[20] Other positive comments soon appeared in the *House Organ*. Chicago operator W. F. Tretinyak echoed Toomey's sentiments, adding, "From the time war was declared women have been taking over the positions formerly held by men, and they proved that they can do these jobs efficiently. A short time ago White Castle began to employ women, and these women are doing a splendid job. . . . May they keep up the good work." Chicago's Dick Lettner agreed that "since the girls have taken over they have done a very good job . . . and it has been proven that they are capable of doing the work." Leland Butler observed that "the girls . . . are keeping up White Castle's traditions and expectations."

In addition to their fellow operators' acceptance, White Castle's customers also approved of the women operators. One operator wrote, "If there was any doubt about women's replacing men in the great White Castle System, the officials and everyone concerned can rest assured that the public has readily accepted them, in fact complimented them on more than one occasion." More important, the White Castle management was very satisfied with their new employees. In the monthly General Letter, one area manager explained, "They catch on to the work a little more readily than boys and are more enthusiastic about their jobs than any boys that we have been able to hire for quite some time . . . these girls are doing an exceptionally fine job, and we are well pleased with them."

These women's enthusiasm for their work may have been the reason for their immediate success as Castle operators. In many cases, White Castle was their first workplace outside their homes, and they relished their newly found independence. From the beginning, the *House Organ* was full of grateful letters from female operators expressing their thanks for the opportunity to work at White Castle. Elizabeth Ramos of Cincinnati triumphantly announced that "a new era has begun; girls have invaded White Castle." Evelyn Fournier commented, "We girls are all new and I'm sure everyone is wondering just how well we will turn out. So come on girls, let's show them what we can do!" Irene Wietgrefe wrote, "After 21 years, we girls are now the operators of White Castle. We'll keep 'em frying, while they keep 'em flying!"[21]

Most of these letters were also deferential to the current and previous male employees. Operator Evelyn Mueller remarked, " I only hope that we can be an asset to the system, as the men have been in the past . . . for twenty-one years men were the backbone and the soul of White Castle." Colleen Henderson of St. Paul voiced a similar tribute: "I hope we can keep up with the good work that the boys have been doing." On a lighter note, Minneapolis's Doris Arnold joked that "most of us have dreamed of being in or having a castle. Little did I know that mine would be a White Castle, but it's O.K. with me."

After a short adjustment period for ironing out new issues such hair nets, wartime marriages, and local employment laws, women operators became the norm behind Castle counters. The feminization of White Castle did not end there, however; within two years women were promoted to Castle and area supervisors in some cities, becoming even further entrenched in the occupation of fast-food service.[22]

This shift from male to female employees in the Castles and in the fast-food hamburger industry in general worked so well that women and teenage workers soon became the permanent backbone of the fast-food labor force. Aside from a few brief attempts to "remasculinize" the Castles in the years immediately after the war, women remained behind the counters. Even though many company traditionalists yearned for a return to a all-male White Castle, for the most part, suitable men in postwar America could be employed elsewhere at much higher wages. Nonetheless, the majority of company officials were satisfied with the women employees, citing their greater efficiency and dependability. Mainly, they were pleased that the Castles were staffed and the hamburgers were cooked by competent operators, regardless of gender.

Gender, however, did became a major factor in fast-food employment, both at White Castle and throughout the industry. Because women comprised the bulk of the fast-food industry's workforce from the 1940s onward, fast-food employment was quickly reclassified in the collective public mind and in corporate personnel manuals as "women's work," thus allowing, in the long run, significantly lower wages and diminished respect associated with the job. In addition, once this stigma of "women's work" was applied, employment in fast food became even less desirable for potential male workers.

American companies thought it perfectly acceptable in the 1940s, and even up through the 1960s, to pay women less than their male counterparts for the same job and also to keep wages uniformly low in industries or professions mainly employing women. Such blatant gender discrimination was commonly justified by the pervasive belief that the primary job responsibility of American women should be that of wife and mother in the home. Any employment outside the home was viewed as a temporary necessity, such as during the war or at specific intervals throughout a woman's life, like before marriage, in widowhood, or during times of family financial hardship. The notion of women having careers and aspiring toward professional fulfillment was uncommon at this time and often ridiculed. With this sexist mentality in place, women did not have much status or bargaining power in their workplaces. As a result, mostly female occupations, especially unskilled ones such as fast-food work, remained low paid and poorly regarded.

Similar to other employers of that time, White Castle's managers consistently paid their female workers proportionately less than they had their previous, all-male workforce. The plight of women and teenagers working in fast food grew even worse several years later. As the larger franchised chains blossomed in the late 1950s and early 1960s, the federal minimum wage became the standard pay rate throughout the industry, and these chains offered no employee benefits. Being able to pay these low wages, in fact, enabled many of these franchises to grow, and prosper, at such phenomenal rates. To its credit, however, White Castle never lowered its insurance coverage or other benefits, despite the gender shift and other subsequent changes in the industry. Although not recognized at the time, when women entered the Castles and other restaurants during the war, fast-food work was permanently reduced from a predominantly male and adequately paid, working-class career to being an often part-time, temporary, and low-paying job.

Even after hiring women as Castle operators, White Castle still had a severe labor shortage in many areas. In some cities, White Castle and other restaurant chains could not recruit anyone—men, women, or teenagers—for employment. Competitor White Tower made the first drastic move, closing its previously twenty-hour stands at midnight each day. At White Castle it was now common for supervisors and area managers to work full-day shifts at the griddle. The shortage was so severe in Louisville that several Castles were closed, with large signs posted on the front stating, "This Castle will reopen whenever conditions permit." Having been burdened by labor troubles throughout the war, the Louisville area manager sadly reported that these closures occurred "only after persistent effort had failed to produce enough capable operators." The managers in Kansas City were plagued by similar problems. They first informed the company's home office in early 1942 that "overall restaurants sales are running quite a bit below . . . the same period a year ago" and that "quite a few restaurants in the outlying districts have closed their doors for the duration." The next news coming from Kansas City was that most of White Castle's fast-food hamburger competitors were already out of business because of labor shortages and poor sales. In October 1942, Kansas City manager E. P. Ferguson reported that "a good many of the restaurants are hiring colored girls as waitresses." The labor situation was desperate. In some cases, the Castles opened for only a few hours, and hamburger sales in that city plummeted. This bad situation worsened when the area's food-rationing authorization forms were lost in a fire at its food supplier's warehouse, leaving the restaurants without supplies or even the means to acquire more. Although sentimental about the last of the original "western" White Castle cities, Billy Ingram decided in late 1943 to close the entire Kansas City operation. He knew that his once-solid empire was beginning to crumble.[23]

Restaurants with No Food to Sell

The labor problem was not the only reason for White Castle's declining sales and closures. Shortages of certain foods and the subsequent government-rationing programs for those commodities also were hurting White Castle. Since White Castle was in the business of selling food on a retail level, it was essential that it maintain adequate supplies of all the items on its already very limited menu. During the war, however, nearly all its products were limited, thus forcing the restaurants to choose among offering alternative items, restricting the quantities sold to each customer, or, once again, closing.

The first hint of a food shortage came even before the war started. As early as 1941, the United States' Lend-Lease aid program was sending food and needed matériel to Britain, the Soviet Union, and other Allies. By the end of that year, the United States had supplied these nations with more than 1 million tons of foodstuffs, in addition to other items, ranging from warships to petroleum. The federal government urged all Americans to conserve essential foods for the sake of the other rationed or starving nations.[24] As more and more American food was sent abroad, the grocery shelves in the United States became increasingly bare. In 1941 alone, food prices across the country jumped more than 61 percent. With shortages looming, President Franklin D. Roosevelt created the Office of Price Administration and Civilian Supply (OPA) to coordinate the prices and supply of food and other consumer goods. When America finally entered the war, the OPA was already in place to supervise hastily organized wage and price freezes, in addition to commodity-rationing programs. In January, Congress bolstered the OPA's authority by passing the Emergency Price Control Act.[25]

White Castle Coffee without Sugar?

The first food that the OPA formally rationed was sugar. In the first months of the war, Japan conquered both the Philippines and the Indonesian island of Java, depriving America of two major sugar sources. Fearing a scarcity of sugar, consumers began to hoard hundred-pound bags, and institutional users bought up entire warehouses. The OPA responded by ordering local rationing boards to issue ration stamps immediately, limiting every consumer to only eight ounces of sugar each week. Institutional users, such as restaurants, universities, and hospitals, were allocated rations based on a percentage of the previous year's consumption rate. Each institutional user was required to complete a lengthy application to its local rationing boards, documenting its past usage, a realistic forecast of future needs, and recent price increases.[26]

Billy Ingram's son Edgar and his general counsel U. Grant Sain processed this application for White Castle. White Castle was granted only 75 percent of the amount of sugar it had used during the preceding year. The home office immediately issued an order to conserve sugar—drastically—in all Castle functions. Company bakeries decreased the amount used in baking pies, and individual Castle operators were given strict instructions how they should apportion sugar for coffee.[27]

Sugar rationing became a major point of contention between White Castle and many of its customers. The first step was removing the sugar bowls from the counter and placing them behind the operator on the back bar. Customers received only one sugar cube or tablet with each cup of coffee but were given a second cube if they requested it. For granular sugar, the operators were supposed to bring the sugar bowl to the seated customer and dispense one teaspoon of sugar but, just as with cubes, would provide a second if asked. The customers' reaction to this new policy was mixed. One area manager reported enthusiastic customer cooperation, with only minor dissatisfaction. Russ Moore in Minneapolis reported to the Columbus headquarters that "the boys behind the counter are continuously listening to complaints." Detroit manager Les Sampson said that he saw "instances where customers threatened to crawl over the counter to get extra sugar" and that "we have had a certain amount of sugar stolen from the Castles."[28]

The customers' complaints, however, proved to be the least of White Castle's worries during this sugar crisis. By the summer of 1942, some White Castle cities were on the verge of running out of sugar completely. Detroit was the first to announce that its supply would soon be exhausted. Its local supplier offered to give White Castle "an advance" on its future allocations, but White Castle's attorney, Sain, discouraged this idea, calling it "a technical violation of the law."[29] Instead, Sain first sent a "special-purpose application" to the Detroit area rationing board in hopes of getting an emergency increase in White Castle's allotment. When he was turned down, Sain sent a desperate telegram to all area managers: "Detroit virtually out of sugar. Will you have any sugar surplus that you could supply Detroit plant without inconvenience to you. If so, wire quantity you could release Detroit immediately." Chicago still had a relative abundance of sugar and quickly responded to the plea, shipping hundreds of pounds eastward to Detroit. Other plants did likewise, and so Detroit was able to conduct business as usual.

Although this disaster was averted, the shortage of sugar continued to be a problem throughout the war. In addition to the reduction in sugar imports from the cane-growing countries in the Pacific, much of the domestic sugar supply was being diverted to the military. In fact, some historians contend that there was never a shortage at all; rather, too much of the existing supply was sent off to the soldiers. Indeed, at one point, White Castle had to forfeit a much needed shipment of sugar cubes because the army laid claim to all available supplies.

There was some disagreement as to exactly how much food the military truly needed. Many records show that American soldiers and sailors ate in abundance during this war, sometimes consuming three times the daily calories of the average civilian back home.[30] Depending on how widespread this knowledge was, this disparity could better explain Americans' ambivalence toward imposed rationing. On the one hand, there was much popular support for the concept of rationing, with conserving food and other scarce materials often equated "with fighting the war on the homefront." Rationing and recycling were widely touted as ways to support the troops abroad, and those violating the measures were often publicly condemned by their peers as greedy or even "traitorous." Patriotic slogans and names supporting the rationing effort were common. Posters urging "Back the Attack," "Your Boy Gives 100%. How About You?" and "Keep'em Firing" all were intended to foster cooperation with rationing. White Castle and other restaurants, in fact, promoted the practice of drinking "Victory Coffee," the straight black version without cream and sugar. But on the other hand, not everyone was convinced.[31] Despite such calls for support, many consumers did everything in their power to acquire the most food possible. Cheating was rampant, with a booming black market trade in both sugar ration stamps and sugar itself. Many Americans were determined to get sugar any way possible, legally or not. Organized crime syndicates made huge profits during the war by illegally selling food and other rationed commodities.

Anything but the Real Thing

Related to the sugar scarcity was an acute shortage of Coca-Cola and other major cola brands. Defined by ration boards as a form of liquid sugar, Coca-Cola syrup was in short supply immediately after the attack on Pearl Harbor, and it continued to be scarce until the war's end. Similar to the situation with raw sugar, much of the Coca-Cola supply was redirected to the military. The Coca-Cola Company even constructed bottling plants overseas in recently liberated areas to keep the men on the front lines amply supplied. Servicemen everywhere cherished their beloved "Coke," further institutionalizing it as the American ethnic beverage.[32]

Supplies on the homefront, however, slowed to a trickle. In February 1942 Benny Benfer announced to all area managers that "the 'pinch' on Coca-Cola seems to be even worse than expected." This news meant an inconvenience for some companies, but for White Castle it was a crisis, since Coca-Cola was a mainstay of its business. Since White Castle's founding in 1921, Coca-Cola and coffee had been the principal beverages served with their hamburgers. Benfer tried to reassure managers that this Coca-Cola shortage would not hurt business because "the condition is universal and the public during the past few weeks has built up a surprising acceptance of the inevitable shortages." He reminded managers that supplies of Orange Crush, milk, and coffee were still abundant. For the next few years, White Castle experimented with different substitute drinks, none of which ever fully satisfied its customers.

Most Castle operators took down their Coca-Cola signs and stored them in their backrooms. The newly installed Coca-Cola dispensers, however, were kept busy with new and different drink formulas. White Castle's first attempt at alternative soft drinks was "Castle Cola," an imitation drink devised by a baker in the St. Louis plant. Although popular among St. Louis customers, the company was hesitant to use it in other cities because of confusing rationing guidelines and Food and Drug Administration rules. Also, the New York Castles could not legally sell this new Castle Cola, because artificially colored drinks needed a special state license.[33]

Fearing too many complications with the company-created drink, White Castle next tried to use cola syrup from Ford's Kola, a small, Texas-based company. The relationship between White Castle and Ford's did not last, though, because the cola supplier wanted to sell only unsweetened syrup, forcing White Castle to add its own precious sugar to the mixture. Since sugar supplies were too valuable for this use, some White Castles switched briefly to "Bev-Cola," which many customers said tasted much like the real item. Kansas City Castles briefly served "Bob's Cola" from Atlanta, which claimed to be Coca-Cola's chief competitor in that city. Unable to get a sufficient amount of either of these drinks, White Castle then switched to the peculiarly named "Co-ed Cola," which now-desperate soda drinkers claimed tasted exactly like Coca-Cola. This Co-ed Cola became a mainstay for White Castle for the duration of the war, served whenever genuine Coca-Cola syrup was unavailable. By the end of the war, most customers did develop a taste for these other drinks, but the majority switched right back to Coke when supplies once again became abundant.

"Victory Coffee" without the Coffee

Coffee was another popular drink in short supply. Similar to the shortage of sugar, coffee first was in short supply only because consumers feared that rationing would soon begin. In the early summer of 1942, coffee-addicted Americans fulfilled their own prophecy of scarcity by clearing grocery shelves and hoarding coffee in their cupboards. By the time rationing was imposed a few months later, many consumers were already accustomed to having little or no coffee.

This shortage was a true hardship for White Castle because the company always took great pride in the quality of its coffee. Billy Ingram believed even the poorest working man deserved the highest grade, and his test kitchen staff constantly experimented with different blends of beans and different types of coffee makers. Although a longtime seller of Coca-Cola, Ingram bragged only about the excellence of White Castle hamburgers and coffee. Coffee was also the most profitable item on the company's menu. Consequently, Ingram worried about the effects of an acute coffee shortage.

White Castle first responded to the initial coffee shortage by using smaller coffee mugs—six versus eight ounces.[34] Benny Benfer thought that this would be a subtle and noncontroversial way to reduce coffee usage by 25 percent while also protecting the integrity of the coffee blend itself.

Benfer's next suggestion to area managers was that they slightly dilute the coffee mixture, but some White Castle veterans strongly rejected this idea. Chicago's H. R. Lewis commented that "it seems like a shame to serve a weak cup of coffee." Sometimes this strategy did produce a very weak cup. The Minneapolis plant, for example, reduced the amount of ground coffee that it used for a one-gallon urn from twelve ounces to seven. Although the company standard remained at nine ounces per gallon, the Louisville plant was using only three ounces for a half-gallon urn, making its coffee the weakest in the system.[35] Other plants avoided such extreme dilution but contemplated a price increase from five to ten cents.

As supplies diminished, Benfer directed that the new, smaller mugs be only three-quarters filled, further saving scarce coffee. In some areas, customers were limited to only one cup per visit, and all coffee had to be consumed on the premises. Then the shortage became so severe that Castle operators were warned not to sell or give away even used coffee grounds. White Castle's entire 1942 allocation was only 65 percent of the amount it had sold in 1941. Making matters worse, one operator noted that "business was especially brisk . . . due to the fact that many of our customers do not have coffee at home." (Individuals were limited to only one pound every five weeks for home consumption.) Despite White Castle's efforts to conserve coffee, however, many restaurants had run out completely by early 1943.

Facing the possibility of no coffee at all, White Castle began experimenting with substitute drinks, as it was doing with cola drinks. Realizing that radical action was necessary, a frustrated Benny Benfer conceded "that no matter which alternative we choose, we are doing something we would rather not do, something which violates the principles . . . as we have propounded them during all these years in the White Castle System." The first idea Benfer considered was to extend the existing coffee supply by adding other substances such as chicory or soy meal. Although it was an available alternative, some wholesalers refused to put chicory or any other additives in their coffee. Benfer even admitted that "it was quite painful" for him "to discuss the use of chicory."[36] Nevertheless, other purveyors started adding it because they had little else to sell. Thus it became common for wholesale roasters to add between 6 and 8 percent chicory to their mix, which did not greatly alter the taste. White Castle soon adopted this "chicoried" coffee in most Castles throughout the country. The company considered posting a sign announcing the addition of chicory, but the idea was vetoed, based on the belief that it would cause business to decline.

In addition to chicory, White Castle tried a variety of other hot drinks to fill the void created by the coffee shortage. Its first choice was NesCafe, a coffee derivative. The problem with NesCafe was that it was also quite popular with the army and hence difficult to obtain. Another option was an extract from roasted bran called Postum.[37] Created by the C. W. Post Company in 1903 and marketed during the war by General Foods, Postum was essentially a cereal flavored with molasses that could be brewed into a drink similar to coffee. Since it also was sweetened by the molasses during its production, Postum could not only replace coffee but also alleviate some of the need for sugar. It was quite inexpensive, too, with a twenty-five-cent package making more than fifty, eight-ounce cups. It was ideal in almost every way, except that it just was not coffee. It was too mild for most coffee drinkers, and it lacked the caffeine that many craved. Although Postum was offered in many Castles during times of extreme shortage, most customers chose not to drink it.

Other coffee substitutes that White Castle considered, tested, and then rejected were Soykee, a soy derivative sold by the Battle Creek Food Company; Soyfee from the Cubison Company; and Kofy Sub, another soy-based substitute. The only one that White Castle seriously considered was a soy, bran, fig, wheat, and honey combination called Breakfast Cup. Sold by Loma Linda Foods in twelve-ounce packages, this brew was deemed to have a pleasant taste but was eventually dismissed for the same reasons that Postum was. Finally White Castle concluded that dedicated coffee drinkers would not accept substitutes, and so it tried to get all the coffee it could.

The company also found that more effective methods for conserving coffee included closing the Castles at night, selling coffee only before noon, and limiting all customers to one cup. (This one-cup rule was a radical departure for a company that formerly stressed to operators that all customers should order at least two cups.) These measures stretched out the available coffee far better than did chicory additives or other substitutes, but there still were severe shortages. Fortunately for both White Castle and its coffee-loving customers, in late 1943—after two years of uncertain supplies and periodic shortages—the government suddenly lifted all restrictions on coffee, and it immediately became plentiful once again.

Other shortages also plagued White Castle during the war, ranging from mild nuisances to situations that threatened the company's very existence. Several spot shortages were common, depriving the Castles of one or more food items. Inexplicably, pickles was the first food to run short; in fact, pickle suppliers cut shipments to White Castles even before the war began. Used by the company only as a condiment on the hamburgers, pickles were not a necessity. Nevertheless, their first brief disappearance signaled White Castle that further shortages were imminent. Thereafter, pickles kept disappearing and reappearing throughout the war.

The next unlikely item to disappear was ketchup. In November 1942 Heinz cut White Castle's ketchup allocation by more than 50 percent, causing great concern among Castle managers and operators.[38] Whereas pickles were considered somewhat of a luxury, with their absence only minimally noticed, ketchup was thought to be a necessity for the hamburger business. Most White Castle customers used ample amounts of both ketchup and mustard on each burger. As with sugar, ketchup was now metered out in small doses. Operators were instructed to take the Heinz bottle off the counter and place it on the back bar. Then in January 1943, Heinz announced to some Castle areas that no more ketchup would be delivered for months. The thought of no ketchup horrified both the Columbus home office and Castles everywhere. The crisis was averted, however, when Bruce LaPlante in St. Louis proudly announced to area managers that he had five thousand pounds in storage and would be glad to share his treasure with the other areas. Even so, White Castle continued to experience periodic shortages for the remainder of the war.[39]

Cream was another food item that regularly became scarce. Although not essential to Castle operations, this shortage caused an inconvenience because many customers liked a lot of cream in their daily coffee. As with other rationed items, the company's initial approach was to limit its use, allowing only one ounce of cream per cup of coffee. The problem was eventually solved when the Cincinnati plant devised a formula mixing two quarts of cream with one quart of whole milk, thereby stretching the supply by a third. Other areas followed suit, often adding even a greater amount of milk to the mixture. Although not original to White Castle, this new mixture eventually acquired the generic name "half & half," becoming the standard "creamer" for millions of coffee-drinking Americans.

The scarcity or unavailability of other foods hurt even more. Running out of onions was much more serious for White Castle than running out of cream. Ever since Walt Anderson sold his first one on the streets of Wichita, White Castle hamburgers had been distinctive for their abundance of onions. As the war progressed, the price of onions began to skyrocket, and the OPA imposed a temporary "price ceiling" to halt the upsurge. In response, brokers held back their onions, waiting for the end of the freeze. Unable to buy any onions, White Castle continued to fry their burgers and their customers continued to eat them. For a while, these periodic onion shortages were considered to be just another obstacle to conducting business as usual. Eventually, however, White Castle decided to switch to dehydrated onions because they always were available. As with other emergency wartime measures, this switch to dehydrated onions became a permanent change in White Castle's hamburger recipe.[40]

White Castle also suffered annoying and debilitating shortages in non-food commodities. Some were relatively minor, such as the scarcity of white leather shoes to match the women operators' uniforms, and others were more serious, such as not being able to buy uniforms for the new operators at all. These minor problems, however, were easily worked out and did not threaten the life of the company. But other problems, such as the shortage of rubber and gasoline, were far more severe. Anticipating a shortage of rubber, most White Castle area managers outfitted all their cars and delivery trucks with new tires at the start of the war. This foresight was fortunate, since tires became virtually impossible to buy legally during the war. Another nonfood item that was sorely missed was White Castle's distinctive cardboard hamburger carton. Cardboard was soon in short supply, so the company opted to not wrap orders of take-out hamburgers, instead placing them in a paper bag with folded paper napkins between them. Although not as insulating or neat as the boxes, the new system worked well, with only a few customer complaints.

White Castle could not solve all wartime hardships so easily. One commodity that could be neither improvised nor bought in advance was gasoline to fuel the company's vehicles. In early 1942, the government imposed severe restrictions on all petroleum products, owing to the growing military needs and the sinking of American oil tankers by German submarines in the Atlantic. With no gas to sell, gas stations closed by the hundreds. White Castle was hit by these restrictions in two ways. First, it became increasingly difficult for company bakers and meat suppliers to deliver provisions to the Castles on a dependable basis. Area managers scrambled to secure coveted "C" stickers for their vehicles, which authorized larger rations of fuel and allowed for higher odometer readings.[41] In most cases this scrambling was not successful; the restaurant industry in most cities was still deemed to be nonessential, thus limiting White Castle's allocations and vehicle movement. As time went on, the shortage became worse, often forcing delivery trucks to remain parked in the bakery lots. Company managers and deliverymen often had to use their personal vehicles or public streetcars to reach outlying Castles. Although this system was cumbersome, it enabled the Castles to remain open longer.

White Castle's profits were hurt far more by another effect of gas rationing. During the 1930s, many new Castles were constructed along popular motor routes, to attract the growing "curb service," as opposed to earlier restaurants situated in crowded neighborhoods. This strategy proved profitable when gas was cheap and plentiful, with motorists going everywhere in their cars. But once the wartime restrictions were imposed, the driving public greatly reduced their automobile usage. As a result, much of White Castle's automobile business quickly disappeared, causing company profits to drop and forcing the closure of some Castles. Many of them never re-opened, since gasoline remained strictly rationed throughout the war. By the end of 1942, virtually everything used in the Castles was in short supply, but White Castle officials hoped that the worst of government intervention was over. Little did they know that the most severe blow was yet to come.

White Castle with No Hamburgers?

Far more threatening to a hamburger chain than shortages of sugar, cola, or coffee was the dwindling supply of meat. From the beginning of the war, ration stamps were issued for most common foods, with consumers receiving "red stamps" for the purchase of all meat, poultry, and fat products. These stamps were redeemed for both raw or processed meat at grocery stores, butcher shops, or restaurants. As with sugar, each retailer was assigned a certain wholesale allocation of meat and, in turn, had to produce enough consumer stamps to prove its compliance with the rationing laws.

Although the OPA's rationing stamp program began right after the attack on Pearl Harbor, the actual rationing of meat did not begin immediately, lagging considerably behind other commodities. At first the government urged Americans to conserve meat voluntarily, but most of the public was uncooperative, and the OPA finally imposed strict rationing restrictions on March 29, 1943. In addition, it instituted regular "meatless days" when no meat could be served in restaurants. Rationing stamps were required for any purchase of meat or animal fat. Both wholesalers and retailers frantically bought all available meat, from any source possible. White Castle was especially concerned because most of its retail profits came from the sale of hamburgers.

Facing a severe reduction in its meat supply, White Castle immediately took steps to control the potential damage. First, it reexamined its methods of distribution, food preparation, and serving in order to minimize waste. After years of perfecting a centralized supply system, Ingram directed area managers to start buying all available foods and other products from local sources.

In a further attempt to save meat, Ingram also introduced a new method for cooking the hamburgers. He personally traveled around to every Castle demonstrating this new technique, referred to as "the New York style" for its place of origin, which differed from the old one in that the patty was flipped to cook on both sides. With this new method, onions were spread all over the griddle, and the patty was placed on top of them, with the buns directly on top of the patties. The reason for this change was both to save time by cooking all the sandwich components together and to minimize the waste from the patties, which broke apart while being flipped.

In addition to analyzing all aspects of its hamburger supply and preparation, White Castle Company officials also quickly compiled a list of possible food alternatives to the hamburger. In a memo to Billy Ingram, Benny Benfer suggested cheese sandwiches, baked beans, fish patties, hot dogs, spaghetti, chop suey, and eggs. Although the options seemed to vary greatly, Benfer's intention was to select those items that could be easily prepared with the existing Castle equipment. Even though White Castle's supply of meat had not yet been interrupted, managers prepared for the worst.

In time, the realities of meat rationing began to take hold. By late 1942, there were spot shortages, and the area managers did all they could to keep meat in their Castles. In the summer of 1943, White Castle started buying large quantities of "pre-chilled" beef from Swift, even though some customers were openly skeptical about its meat content. One customer complained that Swift's meat was made from veal loaf and that it caused him "ptomaine poisoning."[42] He was later dismissed as a crank. In the New York area, White Castle began negotiations to purchase a slaughter house in hopes of guaranteeing a stable supply for its Castles in that area. In some areas, the company was already buying entire carcasses, boning them, using all the edible meat, and selling the remainder to other vendors.

One longtime company employee even tells the story (probably apocryphal) of accidentally hitting a steer with his car, tying it to the hood, and bringing it White Castle's meat plant. More believable was the way in which the New York plant procured some of the meat for its operation. For months, much of New York's hamburger was coming from a source described in company invoices only as "the Lombardi brothers." When he finally learned about this arrangement, White Castle Vice President Bill Bauerle sent a letter to Shackelford in New York, saying "when I noticed the firm name of Lombardi Brothers I had a chill. I believe my flesh was covered with goose pimples as that firm name spelled 'Black Market' to me."[43] Bauerle knew that getting caught in black market meat deals would jeopardize legal allocations and effectively ruin the company. Shackelford responded by return mail that he had "had jitters all week" and that "the situation is pretty bad and I have had some uneasy moments." He ended his letter stating that "the only thing that I can say is that we have had hamburgers in the Castles at all times."

This desire to stock the Castles at all cost became almost obsessive. During the worst times, White Castle would buy beef at exorbitantly high rates, often taking a significant loss on each hamburger sold. Later in the war, it quietly reduced the size of the meat patty. The Detroit managers, confronting extreme shortages and especially high prices in their city, raised the price of their hamburgers to a dime, breaking the company-imposed price ceiling. At times, however, there was just no meat for sale, and company managers grew even more desperate.

With the first spot shortages of hamburger, several Castles began experimenting with alternative food items. Baked beans were tried first and actually proved to be very popular with customers. However, as St. Louis manager Bruce LaPlante reported, the beans were profitable, but they created horrible dishwashing problems, "making a smeary paste of starch, sugar, and grease on the plate which is hard to wash off, gums up the dishwasher and settles on other dishes . . . especially the glasses."[44] After a short while, the company switched to serving these beans in a three-and-a-half-ounce bowl instead of on a plate, but washing the bowl was still a problem. Regardless of the mess and inconvenience, most Castles adopted baked beans as a staple food during the war, usually contracting with local bakeries to prepare and deliver them. The only other drawback to baked beans was that most customers liked to add a lot of ketchup to them, thus increasing the use of another scarce commodity. This situation was not unusual: just as White Castle found a suitable new product, at least some rumors circulated about its pending restrictions. Beans, however, proved to be a safe and lasting choice.

In addition to beans, another early substitute was the grilled cheese sandwich. Once again serving as the official demonstrator, Billy Ingram visited each Castle to show operators how to toast a cheese sandwich properly. Cheese was in short supply at the beginning of the war, but soon afterward, it was easy to find. With an ample supply of cheese, this sandwich also became a White Castle mainstay during the lean years of the war.

Spaghetti was also used when hamburgers were not available. Sold for ten cents and served in the same bowls used for baked beans, spaghetti started as an experiment in Cincinnati and soon spread to most other areas. A Minnesota manager commented that "we have been serving spaghetti at six of our Castles, and the customers' acceptance of this item has been exceptionally good." Since White Castle used whatever foods were plentiful, some of the new items added to the menu seemed a bit unusual. Cole slaw became a staple offering at most Castles. Some New York Castles resorted to selling cod cakes for a dime but quickly discontinued them. Shackelford commented that they were a good idea, but "we were not successful in getting the public to buy them."

Two items that did do well were hot dogs and egg sandwiches. Hot dogs already enjoyed a national following, in some cities even rivaling hamburgers in popularity. Customers loved them, but the competition in some markets was fierce. Many other vendors also sold hot dogs, and they too were a rationed item. The only substitute that was both plentiful and popular was the fried egg sandwich. Since there was never a scarcity of either poultry or eggs, the egg sandwich was the one item on which White Castle could depend. First perfected by Bruce LaPlante in the St. Louis area, these sandwiches resembled McDonald's Egg McMuffin, with the egg fried in a metal ring. The egg was then served on a bun exactly like a hamburger patty.

When meat was in short supply, White Castle's strategy was to serve egg sandwiches at night and in the morning, switching to hamburgers only between noon and dinnertime and then resuming with eggs when the meat ran out. Although customers certainly preferred hamburgers, many settled for an egg sandwich. An Indianapolis operator observed that "when a customer comes in for a hamburger, but finds none, he will take an egg." Unfortunately, eggs could not be White Castle's salvation during this bleak time. White Castle sold its egg sandwiches for a nickel each, but the wholesale price for eggs was usually more than fifty cents a dozen. Adding to this the cost of the bun, seasonings, and labor, each egg sandwich was sold at a considerable loss.

The company continued to search for an inexpensive product that was available in sufficient and stable quantities. In the last few months of the war, White Castle turned to chili and egg salad, and even to bologna and lettuce-and-tomato sandwiches. The chili was made at the central bakery, transported to the Castles in frozen five-pound blocks, heated, and sold in eight-ounce bowls. Both the chili and egg salad sold moderately well but were immediately abandoned when the rationing ended.

Not all items died so easily. One food that was introduced as an emergency measure but gained a lasting place on the White Castle menu was french fries. The company first turned to french fries because potatoes were abundant and cheap. White Castle managers observed that other restaurants had had differing degrees of success with fries, so they decided to use them on a trial basis. The only drawback to selling french fries was properly training operators how to make them. Bruce LaPlante warned all employees that the fryer itself was dangerous because the fat had to be kept at a constant temperature of between 340 and 370 degrees. Gradually, however, the area managers solved these safety problems, taking sufficient precautions to avoid accidents. Before long, White Castle patrons grew accustomed to eating an order of french fries with their hamburgers or egg sandwiches, and the demand for them kept increasing, even when the shortages disappeared after the war.

In addition to substituting alternative foods for their hamburgers, White Castle also seriously considered serving "meatless" hamburger sandwiches. Benny Benfer started exploring these alternatives even before rationing began and discovered a wide array of choices. He found that many major food producers were already marketing meatless sandwich patties, with John Harvey Kellogg's Battle Creek Foods offering the largest selection. Battle Creek offered two nonmeat patties, one made from yeast and vegetable juices and the other from wheat, peanuts, and salt. Columbus neighbor Special Foods also offered a meat alternative named "Numete." It consisted of peanuts, corn flour, salt, and seasonings and was said to taste like beef.

The most abundant option was the soy burger offered by numerous companies. Loma Linda Foods offered "Vegelona"—a mixture of soy beans, tomatoes, onions, and peanuts—and "Proteena"—a concoction of soy, tomato juice, and yeast extract. After a thorough investigation, the product toward which Benfer leaned was not a meat replacement but a meat extender called Soya Flour. Made by the Central Soya Company, Soya Flour was high in both fat and protein and was very inexpensive. Benfer actually bought three, twenty-five pound bags with which to experiment, but no record exists that White Castle ever mixed its meat with soy flour or anything else.[45] With egg sandwiches to fall back on, White Castle never had to resort to a vegetarian menu.

White Castle's mediocre egg sandwich sales and marginal success selling other products reaffirmed that their customers were still hamburger fans. Most Castle veterans agreed that the company could not survive long without meat on the menu. In his usual direct manner, New York's Shackelford put the matter bluntly: "Doing business without hamburgers has presented quite a problem." He went on to confess that "in fact, we have not found anything so far that we can sell" and that "we have some customers who get really nasty because we do not have hamburgers. . . . During the past few weeks, it hasn't been a matter of trying to operate the Castles in any particular manner, but has just been a case of trying to keep the doors open."

Many of the doors, in fact, did not stay open. Whether because of labor shortages or food scarcity, dozens of Castles were boarded up during the last two years of the war. In his area's monthly status report, one White Castle manager bleakly announced, "Conditions the same as last month, only more of it." As the war dragged on, that was about the best news that White Castle officials could hope for. Naturally Billy Ingram saw a bright side to this gloomy situation:

> We sell eggs. We don't like to sell eggs; we have no experience selling eggs, but when necessity demands it we can sell eggs and do a good job of it. We have done an excellent job over the years introducing, preparing, and dispensing our now generally accepted "White Castle hamburger sandwich." The lack of this item makes its broad public acceptance stand out vividly.

Despite plummeting sales, Ingram was buoyed by the customers' disappointment over the absence of hamburgers, thus demonstrating that his twenty-year-long sales job to the American consumer had been a success.

The most interesting aspect of this meat crisis was that technically there never was a shortage of meat in America at all. The production of all types of meat during the war was at a much higher level than ever before. Similar to other commodities, a combination of hoarding, military needs, price controls, and black marketeering all created a meat shortage that did not need to happen. The armed forces received a generous allocation of America's meat supply, with each soldier and sailor consuming more than 360 pounds each year, whereas the average adult male civilian was limited to only 125 pounds.[46]

The War's Toll on White Castle

As the war continued and the hardships multiplied, most Americans grew increasingly discouraged, many White Castle employees among them. Despite the closures of Castles, the drop in profits, and the trend of overall decline, Billy Ingram joked in the General Letter of April 1943, "If we had some ham we could have some ham and eggs if we had some eggs. If we had enough help we could do a good business if we had something to sell."

Ingram spoke in a different tone by the end of 1944, announcing that "it has been a hectic year, and I hope we never live another one as bad. . . . Each day I have felt more and more helpless in my ability to cure it. So let's look on the good side . . . we can't say it was dull and uninteresting." More changes were yet to come. Japan's surrender in 1945 was a joyous day for all Americans, but as the country enjoyed the excitement of victory, Billy Ingram had to face the fact that his White Castle System had shrunk by almost half during the four years of war.

Even though his company had managed to survive the economic ravages of the Depression, the combination of wartime labor and commodity shortages were devastating White Castle. In 1935 Ingram owned 130 Castles in sixteen cities in 1935, but ten years later this number had dropped to only eighty-seven Castles in twelve cities. Sales had fallen by almost 30 percent in three years. By 1945, Ingram's White Castle was a vastly different company than it had been a few years before, for the first time playing the role of the underdog. Nevertheless, Ingram always remained an optimist. At year's end he gave a positive forecast for the coming year: "If we get enough meat; if our equipment does not break down . . . (I hope, I hope, I hope) that 1946 will prove to be more enjoyable than any of the several years in the recent past."

As the troops returned, more dark days appeared ahead for White Castle. With most of the world in shambles, American factories were still producing needed items at maximum rates, absorbing all available labor. Many of the former soldiers either relocated to other regions of the country or opted to go to college on their GI Bill benefits. Even former operators who had regularly corresponded with the *House Organ* throughout the war refused reemployment with White Castle. With high factory wages still attracting workers and setting the economic pace, White Castle once again had to accept inferior employees. At the same time, many of the good women operators got married and left the workforce to begin their families. Many Castles remained understaffed or poorly operated, resulting in growing customer discontent. In addition to the continuing or even worsening labor difficulties, the government continued asking consumers and restaurants to observe meat conservation measures. Just as during the war, the United States was feeding millions of starving people abroad whose own economies and food production systems had been destroyed.

Formal rationing ended in November 1946, but White Castle and other restaurants were asked to observe more "meatless days." Billy Ingram respectfully declined. White Castle had already been ravaged by the effects of government rationing, and he felt that it could not endure any further restrictions. Ingram's feelings were similar to those of most other Americans at that time. All were tired of sacrifice and government rules, and all wanted to enjoy their newly regained bounty. As a result, Americans ate 20 percent more beef in 1946 than they had in 1940 and, as a result, renewed fears of more shortages and rationing. Instead, President Harry Truman lifted price controls on beef in an effort to reduce the growing consumption, and prices skyrocketed.

White Castle reacted to this huge price increase in the only way it could afford to: the Columbus home office ordered all areas to double the price of the hamburger sandwich to ten cents. (As mentioned earlier, certain areas had already done so, out of necessity, during in the war. This 1946 directive only set a uniform price companywide.) Despite the price hikes and the shadow of the government looming over the restaurant business, White Castle briefly rebounded in 1946. Its customers willingly paid the extra nickel for a hamburger, and they returned in droves.

5

White Castle Rises Again

The 1940s ended bleakly for White Castle. Billy Ingram's hamburger empire was reduced to virtually half its previous size, with little hope for recovery. Although White Castle's sales rebounded immediately after the war in 1946, this good fortune was short lived. Meat shortages, government-imposed price ceilings, and wage freezes continued to plague company operations. Worse still was the continuing shortage of qualified labor to run the Castles, resulting in more closures. During the eight years following World War II, sales rose and fell sharply, buffeted by still another war, fluctuating food prices, and the mixed blessing of a healthy economy. Having endured both the Depression and World War II, White Castle's managers began to tire of the prolonged years of hardship and uncertainty. Even the optimistic Billy Ingram expressed some regret and a fear of the future. "Our cash is way down, about half of last year, and our hamburger sales show a decrease of twelve percent." He felt that this decline was "our greatest danger."

White Castle in the 1950s had even more troubles, compounding its already existing difficulties. As the decade began, White Castle soon faced additional worker and food shortages due to the Korean War, intensified government regulation at all levels, a growing crime problem, and the growth of regional and giant national fast-food hamburger chains. At the start of the decade Ingram wanted White Castle to regain its competitive edge and once again to become the industry leader. The external forces of regulation, competition, and inflation, however, made his goal difficult to achieve. After trying several strategies for recovery, which largely imitated those of the newly appearing hamburger chains, Ingram decided to regain the lead by reinforcing his original business principles from 1921: offering customers cleanliness, quality, and service. Although his strategy never brought phenomenal profits during the 1950s or even a return to being the industry's leader, Ingram was able to navigate his company through still another stressful and potentially devastating era.

The 1950s: The Cold War, Suburbia, and Conformity

This dismal picture for White Castle was painted on the backdrop of a turbulent and confusing era in American history. Buoyed by the victory of World War II, the American people enjoyed an unprecedented level of prosperity and optimism, but at the same time, they confronted new problems and greater threats than ever before. Americans took great pride in the fact that their country had emerged from the war relatively unscathed as the undisputed victor and the sole possessor of the atomic bomb. This reassurance of military dominance was soon accompanied by a growing sense of American economic and cultural superiority. Life was good in postwar America. Returning soldiers married their wartime sweethearts and immediately began their families, many taking advantage of government-guaranteed mortgages to buy their own homes. In earlier times, buying a house was an elusive plateau of success for many working Americans, achieved only after years of saving money. But now the government suddenly made home ownership available to millions of people, who quickly rushed out to buy their new houses. Their rush to buy homes resulted in a boom in the building industry, which further resonated throughout the economy. Rural cornfields gave way to housing tracts as the growing suburbs expanded far out into the countryside. These burgeoning suburbs created both new communities and an entirely different American subculture. Other veterans' benefits also caused drastic changes in American society. The GI Bill provided all veterans with access to a fully paid college education, which before the war was available only to the economic elite. To the government's surprise, many former servicemen used this benefit to go to college, causing a great expansion of colleges and universities across America. These veterans' benefits transformed American society virtually overnight. Social and economic mobility became more elastic than any time in the past. Huge numbers of poor men went off to college, emerging as educated and employed candidates for the newly forming middle class. Young working-class families bought houses in record numbers, creating the suburban community for this new class. Women once again departed from the workforce, assuming roles as wives and mothers in this new community. Motherhood, in fact, became a dominant occupation in suburbanizing America. Beginning in the late-1940s, the nation experienced a gigantic surge in the birthrate that was sustained throughout the next decade and that was popularly dubbed "the Baby Boom." Children and family soon became pivotal themes in American society, and most Americans were looking forward to an even brighter future. But at the same time, they were faced with new problems and threats.

While the economy boomed and the American standard of living rose steadily during the postwar era, the nation was confronted by a whole new set of problems. Social critics contended, and historians today agree, that this widespread quest for prosperity went well beyond reasonable limits, often verging on obsessive materialism. Even the trend toward suburbanization created problems. When young householders took their growing wealth and tax base with them from the cities to the suburbs, they created a economic, generational, and cultural division between them and the cities.[1] Urban neighborhoods deteriorated; stores and businesses eventually closed or relocated outside the city; and crime and violence climbed.

In addition to these internal social changes, Americans also had to contend with threats from abroad. Historians argue as to the extent that the cold war invaded American life, but all agree that the looming threat of communism and nuclear annihilation put a damper on the celebration of American prosperity in the postwar era and the 1950s.

White Castle in Times of Upheaval

White Castle faced both old and new problems. For years, Billy Ingram had predicted brighter days ahead, relentlessly pushing forward despite all forms of adversity. During the economic hardship of the Depression, he forecast that prosperity would soon arrive. During the lean years of World War II, he reassured his employees and customers that the days of abundance would soon return. Ingram never wavered in his capitalist faith that the economy would soon right itself, the war would end, and his hamburger business would once again thrive. When the American economy became healthy again, however, his business was still fraught with seemingly endless problems. Ingram grew increasingly frustrated that new problems appeared while old problems still remained unsolved.

Renewed Shortages: Help Always Wanted

A continuing problem for White Castle during the late 1940s and into the early 1950s was the persistent shortage of food commodities and labor power. In terms of employing workers, the prosperity of the postwar era proved to be disastrous for the relatively low paying industries such as hamburger outlets and other restaurants. With the continued need for the United States to supply manufactured goods to much of the world, factories still paid exorbitantly high wages, attracting much of the male workforce.[2] When the auto industry revived, some White Castles in Detroit experienced a 75 percent monthly turnover rate. At the same time, millions of women returned to working only in their homes.[3]

In many ways, the employment situation in the postwar era was worse than the labor shortage of World War II. Although the healthy young men had returned from war, most opted for higher-paying jobs than fast food could offer. Many White Castle managers idealized the days of their all-male workforce and believed that a return to men in the Castles would resolve their current problems. L. M. Shackelford observed, "We still feel that if we can have married men with families, they will be much more dependable. However, we still have considerable difficulty in getting these men to apply. It runs our labor cost quite high . . . when we give them enough overtime to provide them with a weekly salary on which they can support their families."[4] After several short and fruitless attempts to recreate all-male Castles, the managers admitted that they simply had to get whom they could afford. Detroit was one area that mounted a major recruiting effort to hire men and also learned a hard lesson:

> The type of men that we were able to hire, by comparison, are not as high class as the female operators. We have hired approximately 200 male operators during the past three months, and to date we have only two male operators behind the counters. [We] are going to stick to the female . . . and we will spend the next few months trying to gain back the ground we lost.

Gone too were many of the capable women who had sustained White Castle throughout the war. Once again, White Castle and the greater fast-food industry had to choose from young, single women and men who could not get or hold on to more lucrative factory jobs. The frequent complaints about labor quality heard from White Castle managers during World War II only increased by the late 1940s. Reminiscent of the war years, Chicago's Howard R. Lewis wrote in 1948, "It seems we can get help, but not the kind that we want."[5] Often Lewis's best solution was hiring the most capable high school students that he could find. Other areas did likewise. The Cincinnati area manager accepted applicants as young as fourteen years old. Later in that year, Cincinnati's Oscar Ross conceded in the monthly General Letter that we "can't hire any girls at this time, let alone any men.

We are going to get some handicapped people to work . . . as this might solve our problem."

With the beginning of the Korean War, the labor situation went from bad to worse. As had happened during World War II, a hiring agent from the local Western Electric plant lured away most of Indianapolis's operators. Detroit's Pete Westberg confessed that "the response to our ad was small, and the applicants are, in most cases, from the bottom of the barrel." Despite the constant labor shortage, however, White Castle never tapped the abundant supply of available African American workers, with the exception of one cleaning woman hired during World War II. In 1953, Louisville's Willard Offner observed that "colored people who are looking for a job congregate on the sidewalk next to the filling station across from my office," but he never seemed to connect their job search with his labor shortage.[6] White Castle also continued to have an insufficient number of staff, a problem that in some areas was exacerbated by the constant threat of union organization. Minneapolis was the first White Castle area to face restaurant unionization, but this trend soon spread to other company cities. Although the unions never succeeded in organizing White Castle's workforce, they never stopped trying.

In an effort to attract a better pool of applicants and to thwart the union's inroads, White Castle offered its workers more incentives. In 1951, the starting wage for an operator was increased to ninety cents an hour. Although this rate was still sometimes only half that of factory workers, White Castle stressed the additional earnings from the year-end bonus. The company also distributed packets and booklets to all employees, outlining the array of company benefits available to them, including health insurance coverage, a retirement plan, paid vacations, and a savings program. At the top of the list was the comprehensive Blue Cross/Blue Shield health insurance plan for all full-time employees. Initially, employees had to pay $6.25 each month for their premiums, but eventually Billy Ingram decided to pay the full cost for all employees and their families.[7] Even with these generous benefits, however, White Castle was not able to attract and retain the higher-quality employee that had long been the backbone of the company's success. By the 1950s, working as a fast-food hamburger operator meant comparatively low wages and increasingly lower status. Shackelford jokingly suggested that more good people would apply if the company retitled the position from "operator" to "Salisbury Steak Technician and Purveyor." His proposal was never adopted, and White Castle remained troubled throughout the decade by a very marginal workforce.

Renewed Fears of Rationing and Restrictions

At the beginning of the 1950s, White Castle had even greater concerns than maintaining a stable workforce. When the Korean War broke out in early 1950, White Castle feared that once again it would not have enough food to sell. Supplies of meat and other staple products had remained erratic throughout most of the 1940s, but the fear of renewed war sent the food industry into a panic. Recent memories of rationing and acute shortages caused Billy Ingram and his White Castle managers to brace for another catastrophe. On the eve of war, Ingram announced, "There is much for us in the White Castle System to be thankful for today, and it seems to me that we can face whatever the future holds." Howard Lewis commented that "none of us can predict the length or extent of this war. It might well become World War III. . . . Probably the greatest problem will be coping with the price situation . . . and we may also have a serious problem regarding rationing."

Fortunately, the feared shortages never reached the extent of those during World War II, and government rationing programs for food never materialized. The first hint of shortages during the Korean War came when the chemical manufacturer Du Pont announced that it was voluntarily rationing the cellophane wrapping that White Castle used to ship hamburger buns and to cover pies and pastries. In addition, just the scare of war caused food prices to rise rapidly.

The division of White Castle hurt most by the war was Porcelain Steel Buildings (PSB) and, in turn, the interior renovations of many of the older Castles. What hurt PSB most was a government ban on the use of nickel for any use other than the production of war matériel. Since nickel was a key element in PSB's stainless steel products, many of its operations were halted.[8] The company remained busy with other types of production work, such as the manufacture of lawn spreaders, but the ban on nickel delayed the installation of many new stainless steel Castle interiors.

In the White Castle division, "prerationing" measures disrupted the smooth flow of business, in what Ingram termed "a merry-go-round on meat." In the summer of 1951, Swift informed the Columbus and Cincinnati plants that it could not supply them with sufficient meat. In anticipation of such spot shortages, Ingram had had the foresight to hold fifty thousand pounds of frozen meat in reserve, from which he supplied the two plants. Fearing continued shortages, White Castle searched for ways to further extend its existing meat supplies. Egg sandwiches were once again discussed but never actually revived. In 1952, a brief shortage of Idaho potatoes resulted in the discontinuation of french fries in many White Castle areas.

Even more frustrating for White Castle than these actual shortages were the suppliers who profited from them. The government imposed price ceilings on basic food commodities as a means to forestall skyrocketing prices, but many wholesale suppliers disregarded the ceilings and demanded higher prices anyway. White Castle, in turn, had to observe these price ceilings on the retail level while still paying inflated prices to many of its suppliers, consistently taking losses just to have food to sell. Chicago's Lewis referred to these unscrupulous wholesalers as "scavengers," but White Castle still had to buy from them to survive. As both labor and meat prices crept upward, the company scrambled to find a way to cut costs. In 1951, the home office leadership decided to take the unprecedented step of trimming the size of its hamburger patty from one to eight-tenths of an ounce, effectively getting two additional patties from each pound of ground beef. To achieve this reduction in size, White Castle made its square patty thinner and bored its distinctive five holes into the meat.

Originally proposed on an anonymous employee suggestion sheet in 1947 by Cincinnati operator Earl Howell, this five-hole concept was slow to catch the attention or interest of company officials.[9] But when White Castle finally "downsized" its patty in 1951, it publicly touted the inclusion of the holes as a way to make the meat cook faster, in less than a minute, while also allowing more steam and juices into the bun on top. Billy Ingram praised this new innovation for its speed and efficiency. The publicized rationale was accurate, as the patty did cook faster, but the main purpose for the five holes was to use 10 percent less meat—while still charging the same price as before. With retail price controls in force and wholesale prices skyrocketing, White Castle had few other options.

Few customers either noticed or cared about the smaller size. Some employees themselves had fun with the new product. Bruce LaPlante in St. Louis joked to other managers that "we are using our trial shipment of 'Holy Hamburger.'" In a more serious tone, he added, "So far it has met with unusually good acceptance, with little, if any comment from the customers as we expected. Many of the employees think that the flavor of the finished product is improved by its use." Within a few months, all the White Castle areas had adopted this new patty, officially known on company order forms as the "perforated meat."[10] Chicago reported that "compliments are coming with repeat orders." Indianapolis operators generally liked the new patties but commented that the meat now broke apart more easily. Despite some dissent, the initial overall acceptance of this "perforated meat" by both customers and operators was quite positive.

Almost immediately after the introduction of the patties with holes, the government lifted its price ceilings on retail food, and White Castle boosted the price of its hamburger to twelve cents. Since White Castle was virtually the last restaurant offering dime hamburgers, nobody thought that this increase would be controversial. Most other hamburger chains already charged twelve or fifteen cents or even more for their sandwiches, albeit usually for a larger piece of meat. In a few months though, White Castle was serving a 10 percent smaller sandwich for a 10 percent higher price. These two changes, however, were realized as straight profit.

At the same time that the patty shrank and the price increased, government regulators also reduced the allowable fat content in hamburger meat from 30 to 25 percent. The Swift frozen meat patties that White Castle had been using were 28 percent fat, but Swift soon adjusted its blend to conform with the new regulations, along with charging more for each pound of beef. Although few customers noticed either the holes or the two-cent increase separately, some noticed the combined "one-two punch" effect, without taking into consideration the higher material costs caused by the reduction of fat.

Some customers even became very critical. The *Star Reporter*, a union newspaper published by the Congress of Industrial Organizations (CIO), blasted White Castle's combined size reduction and price increase. Under the headline "World's Tiniest Hamburger Raised to 12 Cents after President Asks No Price Boosts," the article complained,

> White Castle is now one of the most expensive places in the city to buy prepared food . . . actually the White Castle sandwich is not cheap at all. Many restaurants serve sandwiches with four times as much meat as against the 48 cents that White Castle collects for the same amount. . . . This company has seen fit to sock the public with a 25 percent raise on prices, but White Castle fails to show any increase in wages.[11]

This attack was not really aimed at the hamburger itself but, rather, at what this union perceived to be White Castle's unfair labor practices. Since this union newswriter was not privy to the company's planning meetings, he could not have known that in addition to paying the higher meat costs, company managers fought for the price increase as a means to raise their operators' wages. Most of the other criticism was confined to some customers grumbling as they paid their bills. On the whole, however, White Castle's customers happily paid for a filling and satisfying meal, rarely noticing the slight increase.

In the wake of this controversy over holes and prices, White Castle also experienced a brief but potentially disastrous horsemeat scare. Old fears about the quality of ground meat were rekindled when an Indiana newspaper reported the arrest of several meat suppliers who were adding large quantities of horsemeat to their hamburger. Sales throughout the regional fast-food industry plummeted, forcing the closure of some of the smaller restaurants. Peter Pan Snack Shops gave away fifty thousand free sandwiches as a goodwill gesture to reassure its customers.[12] White Castle immediately ran large newspaper ads, reminding its customers that its patties were 100 percent beef, produced by the large and reputable Swift Company under strict government supervision. The company also placed highly visible signs proclaiming "100% Beef" on the back bars of every Castle.[13] Nevertheless, much of the public stayed far away from all types of ground meat. One manager commented, "The fact that it is definite that a lot of people in Indiana have been eating horseburger has turned a lot of people against hamburger, and I have heard many people remark that they don't want any hamburger, even if they know it's good meat." Because of its damage-control advertising, White Castle's sales suffered only marginally, but its operators were besieged by endless horseburger jokes. One truck driver came into a Castle and asked for "two without the saddle." Another customer ordered, "Saddle me two to go." White Castle endured the joking because its customers kept buying.[14]

White Castle's troubles were not over yet. Just as the horsemeat scare was subsiding in the Indiana and Chicago area, rumors briefly surfaced in Minneapolis claiming that White Castle itself used horsemeat in its hamburgers. Sparked by an anonymous tip to the Minnesota State Health Department, these rumors were quickly quieted when state inspectors found no supporting evidence. Indiana and Chicago also experienced an "aftershock" scare five months later when the trial of the horsemeat culprits renewed publicity of the issue. Although the offenders themselves received only nominal punishment, their actions caused irreparable damage to many of the region's fast-food hamburger outlets. Fortunately, White Castle's solid reputation for quality enabled it to survive the scare relatively unscathed.

The Government Intrudes on the Hamburger Business

In addition to high employee turnover, fluctuating prices, and food shortages, White Castle had other problems. The drastic increase in government regulations and restrictions severely hampered the company's operations and often drove up the cost of doing business. The phenomenal growth of government on all levels, and its greatly increased role in all facets of American life, was an unintended consequence of the combined Depression-World War II era. Before 1930, local governments issued—but only sporadically enforced—health and labor codes, and the federal government largely limited its intervention to establishing standards for food purity. White Castle, for example, invited the government to inspect all the beef it used.

Since White Castle maintained the highest food standards possible, most regulatory agencies of the federal government, such as the Food and Drug Administration and the Department of Agriculture, rarely interfered in the company's operations. The federal Wage and Hour Department once penalized White Castle for incomplete record keeping and for not displaying a poster outlining current wage and hour laws. The Internal Revenue Service was the only other federal agency ever to cite White Castle for any infractions, but even these were nothing more serious than correcting accounting errors and paying small penalties. Billy Ingram firmly believed in playing by the rules, and this belief kept federal regulators at bay.

More troublesome were the state and local government agencies. Managers in the home office and throughout the many White Castle areas were constantly confronted with new local rules, laws, and ordinances affecting their business. For example, as late as the 1950s, New York State law still forbade women from working at night in any capacity, a restriction that meant that White Castle either had to employ enough men for the night shift or shut down the Castles at night. In times of low unemployment, the New York Castles were frequently closed, with White Castle losing a significant amount of revenue. The Minnesota Department of Agriculture condemned all of White Castle's Orange Crush faucets in the Minneapolis-St. Paul area, contending that the drinks dispensed to customers were of inconsistent quality. A White Castle manager asked the state official why, after dozens of inspections, these dispensers were now deemed to be faulty. He replied that his agency "had not had the personnel to enforce more than half of the codes, but recently, due to an increased budget allocation, they had been able to increase the number of inspectors." To accommodate this new enforcement, White Castle bought new drink faucets and resumed its Orange Crush business. In New York City, however, White Castle had to serve Orange Crush that was not even orange, since city ordinances prohibited artificial colorings in soft drinks. City officials in Clifton, New Jersey, suddenly decided that a new Castle being built should have an additional dressing room, so the architectural plans had to be redrawn. The state labor board in Indiana sanctioned White Castle for not allowing operators formal "lunch hours."

The most common annoyance was from the city health departments. Some health measures were reasonable and necessary, such as requirements in most cities for all food service workers to have periodic chest X rays to screen for tuberculosis. Other regulations were not so necessary. In Cincinnati, for example, the health department cited a Castle for low water pressure in its dishwasher. Hammond, Indiana, health inspectors erroneously gave a Castle a low "C" rating, instead of its usual "A+," because of a mix-up in the increasingly voluminous paperwork. After much bureaucratic wrangling, the Castle's flawless health rating was restored. Indianapolis health authorities repeatedly cited White Castle for the large volume of litter created by curb customers discarding cups, sacks, and hamburger cartons along the roadside, forcing the company to clean the trash for two miles in every direction. White Castle graciously responded by cleaning up the trash and printing "Don't Be a Litterbug" on all its paper packaging, leading all other restaurants in this litter-prevention effort.

Managers in every White Castle area had to contend with a complicated array of codes and orders constantly appearing or changing. Many of these rules applied to only one area, and many directly contradicted those of other areas. To minimize the confusion, General Counsel Russ Saxby announced in 1957 that he had compiled "a library of city ordinances" pertaining to sanitation, health, parking lots, and related regulations. The fact that White Castle served only top-quality food in a pristinely clean environment never seemed to be enough. Although burdensome, White Castle sought to comply with all health department mandates and, as a result, usually earned the highest possible ratings.[15]

Zoning commissions and city planning departments also presented problems for White Castle. The town of Oak Lawn, Illinois, for example, passed an ordinance prohibiting all hamburger and hot-dog stands within the town limits. White Castle successfully appealed this rule and was eventually granted an exception, but many other chains were excluded for years. Other cities, such as Louisville and Chicago, built new expressways and turnpikes to alleviate the traffic on main thoroughfares but by so doing often ruined the business of the Castles on those particular avenues. Developments that many planning commissions termed *urban progress* often meant financial disaster for many downtown Castles.

Although city and state ordinances were often irksome and costly, what Billy Ingram and his management staff usually hated most were policies and laws handed down from Washington. New federal laws in the early 1950s stipulating minimum wages and hour limits greatly affected White Castle's business. With its chronic labor shortage and a forty-hour work-week, combined with new minimum wages and mandatory time-and-a-half overtime pay, meant a huge payroll increase for White Castle. Long a critic of big and intrusive government and an opponent of the taxes to pay for it, Ingram bristled at what he perceived to be additional and unfair burdens. On many occasions he publicly railed against the growing presence of government in the marketplace. "I constantly chafe at the rising taxes, the government regulations, limitations, shortages, rising prices, and restrictions that do not allow us to do the things we would like to do." A believer in free enterprise, he added, "Our employees also earned $658,444.21 which they didn't get because that was the sum that we were required to deduct from their checks as withholding taxes." In 1952, Ingram's longtime friend and St. Louis area manager, Bruce LaPlante, summed up the company's sentiment even more bluntly: "The present screwballs in Washington who are running things should be made to stew in their own juices. Merely losing the election next time is too good for them." LaPlante's wish only partially came true; the Democrats did in fact lose the White House that very year, but regulation, control, and supervision over business continued at every level of government.

On a lesser scale, White Castle also was troubled by a rash of crime, violence, and accidents during the early 1950s. Since the founding of the company, most Castles stayed open twenty-four hours a day, long making them prime targets for nighttime crime and disorderly behavior. Beginning in the final years of World War II, however, White Castle experienced a rapid upsurge in crime, including assaults, robberies, and other types of thefts. By the end of the 1940s, armed robbery became a somewhat regular event at Castles across the country.

In March 1949, for example, a lone gunman robbed a Louisville Castle but escaped with only $14.50. That same month, another robber entered a St. Louis Castle, holding a hammer in his pocket as if it were a gun and demanding money. When the operator noticed that "the gun" was actually a hammer, he and a group of customers began beating the robber with ketchup and mustard bottles. The robber pleaded for mercy and then fled without a cent. One customer, remembering the ketchup and mustard shortages during the war, remarked, "It's a shame to waste ketchup and mustard on a robber." In Indianapolis, a masked man entered a Castle, fired one shot, and escaped with $111.85. In Chicago, an area supervisor carrying the day's receipts form numerous Castles was carjacked by a gun-wielding assailant whom police later deemed unbalanced. The supervisor escaped unharmed, with all the money intact. Not all incidents turned out so well. In St. Louis in 1952, supervisor Junior May was beaten up in the area office by two robbers and then forced to open the office safe. They escaped with $7,878.16 but were soon apprehended, tried, and sentenced to nine years in state prison. Junior May survived, was hospitalized for two weeks, and eventually returned to work.

Other violence also became increasingly common at White Castles. Being open during the late night hours made Castles and Castle operators vulnerable to vandalism and assaults. Manager Howard Lewis used to refer to the period after 1:00 A.M. as the "degenerate run," in reference to the many drunk patrons and homeless men coming in at night. In one instance, four drunk youths broke windows and threw Orange Crush on the female operators. Immediately after this incident, Ingram ordered that phones be installed in all Castles and parking lots for the safety of the operators and customers. In Chicago and other cities, roving street gangs terrorized curb customers and employees in the Castle lots, causing the company to hire Pinkerton security guards for protection. In Columbus, two nighttime customers exchanged gunshots after arguing over a parking space. In several cities, White Castle area offices lost valuable business machines and petty cash to after-hours burglaries.

Less violent but much more costly to White Castle was the growing practice of customers' either eating and then leaving without paying or simply grabbing a sack full of carryout burgers and running out the door. This practice of "dining and dashing" became a weekly occurrence at many Castles, and the company enlisted the help of local police to track down offenders and recover damages. Once curb service became a norm, some motorists began driving off without paying; a practice that became popularly known as *drive-outs*. In an effort to curtail these losses, many Castles switched to having customers pay when they ordered, instead of the old practice of paying after they had eaten their meals. This did not eliminate all drive-outs or fleeing carryout customers, but it greatly limited the company's losses.[16]

Less malicious but perhaps much more destructive and costly to the company were the automobile and truck crashes into many Castles. Crashes were not unexpected, considering that most of the older urban

Castles were built within feet of the curb and often occupied busy street corners. And as the number of American-owned automobiles almost doubled in the decade following World War II, traffic accidents became much more common overall. Unfortunately, many of these new auto and truck accidents involved the front windows and counter rooms of White Castles. Many also occurred during late night hours, with cars driven by intoxicated drivers. The worst incident was when an eighteen-wheel tractor-trailer lost control and plowed into the front of St. Louis's Castle No. 27. Despite extensive damage to the Castle, no one was seriously injured in this crash, or in any of the many others. With the exception of a few bumps and bruises, most of the damage was limited to the Castles themselves, ranging from broken glass to complete destruction. In fact, Ingram once joked that these crashes sometimes gave the company good reason to renovate and update the older Castles.

The Rise of Modern Fast-Food Competition

The combined problems of labor turnover, food shortages, crime, and increasing regulation all paled in comparison to the threat of the new competition coming from the growing regional and national fast-food chains. Competition in itself was nothing new to White Castle, and it was always willing to accept a challenge. Billy Ingram had been a dedicated fighter ever since the business wars of the 1920s with competitors such as White Tower and White Clock and throughout the ensuing years of protracted lawsuits. In those earlier days, White Castle beat down all challengers and reigned for years as the undisputed industry leader. Although Ingram did not win the hamburger fight in the 1950s, he did not lose either. He simply chose to fight using his own rules and values.

Most of the booming fast-food restaurant chains grew as a result of widespread franchising, using investor capital to expand their name. Since he started the company in 1921, Ingram expanded only when he had the necessary capital on hand, never wanting to build his empire on credit or with investment money. But now the business world was changing, and Ingram would not allow White Castle to change with it.

Beginning in the early 1950s, a new type of franchised restaurant chain appeared on the horizon and crept closer throughout the decade. These new franchised chains built larger, more modern restaurants, capable of serving a multitude of customers. They introduced new methods of food preparation and customer service. There is no dispute that White Castle originated the hamburger industry and probably shaped the first generation of fast food, lasting from 1921 to roughly 1950, but it eventually relinquished its lead. In many ways, these new chains began the second generation of the fast-food hamburger industry that White Castle started. Contrary to popular belief, however, the hamburger trade in the 1950s was not really dominated by the giant fast-food chains that proliferated in the latter part of the decade. The era of McDonald's and Burger King was still a few years away. Rather, the 1950s was a time when the fast-food industry adapted to the changing needs of the buying public, and in turn, the public adapted to fast food. When McDonald's and Burger King finally arrived on the scene, American consumers were ready for their long-term reign. Their arrival and ascendance signaled the beginning of the third generation of fast food in America and around the world.

Big Boy Sets the Pace for Suburban Eating

Most of White Castle's competition during the 1950s came from smaller regional chains or from companies using more traditional restaurant approaches. As early as 1949, Castle managers began reporting on the competition to the home office, observing such things as "a new stand opened recently, using girls wearing cowboy uniforms who look real cute," or "a new stand opened with most of the building glass." In Louisville, one stand opened featuring a five-cent hamburger, and another, advertising "the World's Best Hamburger." White Castle manager Willard Offner scoffed at this claim, noting that the new stand "only has five stools, so perhaps he doesn't believe his own advertising." Twin Cities manager Roscoe Guymon reported that "there seems to be a deluge of hamburger stands being built in St. Paul and Minneapolis," adding that many were perilously close to existing Castles. Chicago managers spruced up several of their Castles in response to a "very attractive new hamburger shop being constructed with curb service and air conditioning," which was said to cost more than $70,000 to erect. In New York City, L. M. Shackelford reported that "gas stations have closed, and soon afterward eating places appeared with 'opening soon' signs . . . so far the effect of the competition is in doubt. We hope our customers will not forget us."

After the Korean War ended, White Castle began encountering even better organized and prosperous chains in many of its major market cities. The first competitor that presented a serious threat to its business was a predominantly midwestern chain of drive-ins called Steak N Shake, which was started by A. H. Belt in Normal, Illinois, in 1934. In addition to featuring hamburgers, Steak N Shake's operation reflected a White Castle influence in its slogan "Takhomasak."[17] Bruce LaPlante in St. Louis was the first to sound the alarm about this new competition, reporting to other managers in 1951 that "Steak N Shake has opened two more drive-ins, making a total of seven. Park-Moor is building another on Highway 66 near [Castle] No. 24, which makes five. They all seem to be doing lots of business even though their service is slow and their prices are higher than ours." Chicago manager Howard Lewis commented about Steak N Shake that "it looks as though we are going to have some competition in various locations." By 1953, this chain was proliferating in almost every White Castle city. After Steak N Shake opened two additional restaurants, LaPlante complained in the monthly General Letter that the new chain "has thrown an iron curtain of drive-ins around the city, tapping every main artery and community. We are not lamenting, alibiing, or tossing in the towel, but we are merely stating the facts and hoping that the same doesn't happen to you."[18]

Unfortunately, more of the same was happening everywhere, with Steak N Shakes and similar businesses springing up at a rapid rate. Soon Steak N Shakes appeared in Indianapolis and quickly captured a share of that market. Area managers everywhere began to assess the growing competition on a weekly basis and tried to take measures to control the spread of this chain. Despite their best efforts, however, more hamburger outlets appeared in its cities at an increasingly rapid rate.

Another growing restaurant chain that managers saw as a potential threat was Howard Johnson's, which began on Cape Cod, Massachusetts, in 1935. Since Howard Johnson's offered a diverse menu including fried clams and featuring ice cream, White Castle officials first thought that it would not be a direct competitor.[19] Indeed, when one appeared in Louisville directly across from a prosperous Castle, area manager Willard Offner joked, "The only thing that we can determine for sure is that they have twenty-eight more flavors of ice cream than we do. Later, as Howard Johnson's continued to build new drive-in-style restaurants and began selling many more hamburgers, White Castle managers started to take its presence more seriously, studying its progress and analyzing its products and prices.

Curiously, Billy Ingram's initial approach was nonconfrontative, as he believed—correctly—that the public's ever growing hunger for fast-food hamburgers could support several chains. Spokesman Benny Benfer told area managers not to worry about any potential competition because "we are still serving better hamburgers and our Castles are cleaner and more attractive." Not until more and bigger chains appeared did he begin to be concerned. One such chain was a franchised drive-in from California known as Big Boy. Started as a ten-stool diner in 1936 by twenty-one-year-old Robert Wian, this hamburger chain grew throughout the West under the name "Bob's Big Boy," soon finding success as a combination coffee shop and drive-in restaurant. The Big Boy name came from the trademark double-hamburger sandwich that Wian created in 1937.[20]

While his own Bob's Big Boy restaurants spread from coast to coast, Wian also sold franchises to other entrepreneurs around the country. One large-scale franchisee was the Cincinnati-based Frisch Company, which opened scores of Frisch's Big Boys restaurants throughout the Midwest. White Castle first noticed the growth of Frisch's in 1954 in its hometown of Cincinnati. In his first mention of Frisch's, area manager Russ Moore joyfully reported to the home office about a vicious dispute between owner Dave Frisch and his employees. But Moore's tone soon changed in his next report, focusing instead on Frisch's growing popularity and sales in Cincinnati. After Frisch's opened a new drive-in directly across from Castle number 14 on Montgomery Road, Moore wrote that "at the present rate they are building they will have us pretty well hemmed in before long." He added optimistically, "There is some talk that maybe they are moving too fast."

One place that Frisch's was moving to was Columbus. In August 1954, Columbus manager Benny Collins reported the opening of a new Frisch's, and he seemed most worried about the popularity of its double-decker hamburger. In addition to the arrival of Frisch's itself, Collins was alarmed at the proliferation and popularity of "Big Boy" imitators. "We did not think at the time that Columbus would be deluged with the number of places featuring a similar sandwich. During the past year, we have had ten new drive-ins serving this type of sandwich, and the competition gets keener all the time." By the fall of that year, Frisch's was heavily advertising its Big Boys on radio, television, and billboards throughout both these cities.

In downtown Cincinnati, long a White Castle stronghold, Frisch's built a modern restaurant that potential customers had either to walk or drive past to reach the closest Castle. Moore termed this positioning *threatening*. After Frisch's opened several new restaurants close to the Castles in the Columbus area, Collins commented that "this is quite an operation and we will probably be hurt at these Castles." His fears became reality: by the end of 1954 Frisch's had become the dominant force in the Cincinnati and Columbus restaurant markets. Assessing his area's performance, Moore conceded that Frisch's growing popularity accounted "for a slight decrease in business." Unfortunately for White Castle, Frisch's started to expand beyond the Ohio state line. While the Cincinnati and Columbus areas were still reeling from the new competition, Frisch's moved into Indianapolis and Louisville where it avoided directly competing with existing White Castles, instead focusing on the growing suburban markets and building drive-ins near new shopping plazas and supermarkets.

In addition to Frisch's, other chains capitalizing on this new trend toward suburbanization resulted in a major setback for White Castle. Since its beginning, White Castle had viewed itself as a predominantly urban operation, for years concentrating on serving a walking or streetcar clientele. The newer chains, without established traditions or customers, thus were better able to serve this changing society, building their restaurants out in the suburbs to accommodate the eating needs of the growing middle class.[21] Burdened with its many existing restaurants, White Castle tried to adapt its older buildings to both the greater volume of customers and the fast-growing automobile culture. White Castle's competitors such as Frisch's and Steak N Shake, however, had the advantage of being able to erect its new restaurants wherever they chose. This advantage did not go unnoticed at White Castle. Offner in Louisville complained about all the new hamburger outlets opening in the suburbs, pointing out that such competition "will draw all the customers away from our Castles which are either downtown or on the fringe."

At the same time, the rapid decline of some urban neighborhoods hurt White Castle's traditional business. In Cincinnati, a White Castle manager observed that the "tearing down of large inner city apartment houses causes a considerable drop in business." For a brief time, White Castle seemed frozen in the past while its competitors reached toward the future. In suburban St. Louis, competitor Park-Moor built a new drive-in featuring an enormous steel and fiberglass carport for motorists to eat under. Howard Johnson's, Frisch's, Steak N Shake, and others all installed customer intercoms at every parking space as a means of expediting service and trimming labor costs. Offner sadly admitted that "our customers are giving these places a 'looking over' and tryout," often switching their hamburger loyalty in the process.

Fortunately for the city-bound White Castle, this explosion in suburban fast-food hamburger chains was almost self-destructive for the newcomers.

By 1957, Willard Offner happily reported a hamburger war among Frisch's, Ranch House, and other chains: "The various hamburger chains of Louisville . . . have about squared off for a competitive battle . . . there has been a good bit of advertising with major price reductions." He proudly added, "We do not expect to indulge in any such competition."[22] White Castle, in fact, occasionally benefited from these wars among the new chains. When Ranch House offered a two-for-one special, the large customer turnout resulted in a two-hour wait for burgers. Scores of discouraged but still hungry customers showed up at the area's White Castles, where they were fed promptly, giving White Castle a huge increase in hamburger sales. Offner remarked, "When restaurants featuring almost the same menus and the same prices start building next door to each other, it is almost sure to hurt someone, and in many cases, very badly."

In addition to building restaurants in the optimal suburban locations, several of the new chains offered a wide array of new products, often trying to create a more upscale image. For example, Ranch House, a growing competitor in Louisville and St. Louis, began featuring a two-patty hamburger similar to the Big Boy, with cheese and a spoonful of tartar sauce for the hefty price of forty-five cents. Most of the new chains also featured one or more flavors of milk shakes or "frosted malted milks," which was not surprising, since some of them had evolved from either ice-cream stands or drugstore soda fountains.[23] All newcomers also served huge amounts of french fries, a product that most White Castles had abandoned a few years earlier.

Most of the chains offered a basic, streamlined menu, with hamburgers the common denominator of the industry. Each chain also either had its own distinctive food over which it claimed ownership or some gimmick in terms of service for which it was known. For the next forty years, the fast-food industry was a breeding ground for product innovation and imitation, always advertising each new variation and nuance. Although White Castle also frequently experimented with products during that time, flirting briefly with trendy foods, it defied the norm of the times by sticking to its basic, time-tested products: hamburgers, coffee, and Coca-Cola.

The Rise of Competition from National Chains

Just as White Castle was finally learning how to compete successfully with the regional drive-in chains, even more contestants entered the hamburger business, further changing the rules and level of competition. By the end of the decade, a new wave of "self-service" restaurants began overtaking drive-ins, White Castle-style hamburger counters, and diners throughout the country. These new restaurant chains featured straightforward menus, very quick service, uniformity, standardized food, and reasonable prices.

One of these new chains was Insta-Burger-King, which started in 1954 in Miami. Founded by partners James McLamore and David Edgerton, Insta-Burger-King—whose name was later shortened to Burger King—was based on McLamore's simple philosophy: "There are only two things that customers have, time and money—and they don't like spending either one of them, so we better sell them their hamburgers quickly." McLamore was right; hamburger customers wanted their food fast, and Burger King became popular by delivering it that way. Having achieved success in Miami, McLamore and Edgerton then franchised their business throughout Florida and eventually throughout the nation.[24] By 1956, Willard Offner in Louisville noticed "a new Florida concern" in the suburbs, which he referred to as the "Hamburger King." Two years later, he reported that there was still only one "Burger King" in the Louisville area and that the regional chains such as Steak N Shake still were more of a threat.

Following the success of Burger King, another early, nationally franchised chain, known as Burger Chef, appeared on the scene. Burger Chef eventually opened more than one thousand outlets, spanning much of the eastern half of the United States. Decked out in turquoise, orange, and white, these stands featured a limited, no-frills menu of milk shakes, french fries, and, of course, hamburgers. Burger Chef's slogan was "We sell millions nationwide." True to its claim, Burger Chef saturated some regional markets, selling millions of hamburgers, but it never represented a significant challenge to White Castle's business. Carrols was yet another hamburger chain achieving widespread prominence, opening hundreds of restaurants nationally. Similar to Burger King and Burger Chef, however, Carrol's never became a major competitor of White Castle. A new chain that did offer some competition to White Castle was Henry's. This was a self-service-style hamburger restaurant started by the Bressler family in Chicago that also owned a thirty-one-flavor ice-cream chain. The Bresslers carefully planned and built their operation in a way guaranteed to be successful. And successful it was, with Henry's causing great concern among White Castle managers as it spread into new areas.[25]

Among the new national chains appearing in the late 1950s, only McDonald's presented a life-and-death threat to White Castle. Although it had been in existence since the early 1940s, McDonald's was a creature of the West Coast, long thriving in the suburbs of Los Angeles and slow to spread eastward. Founded in 1937 by brothers Maurice and Richard McDonald as an orange juice and hot-dog stand near the Santa Anita racetrack in Arcadia, their food-stand business steadily grew during the 1940s, switching its main offering from hot dogs to hamburgers in response to local preferences. From 1940 to 1948, the new McDonald's restaurant in San Bernardino was primarily a drive-in, with the hamburgers delivered to customers by female carhops. In 1948 the brothers decided to eliminate the carhops, pare down their menu to only hamburgers, "and just made the whole thing a cheap, efficient operation where people wouldn't have to wait." Calling it "McDonald's New Self-Service System," the McDonalds reduced their burgers from two ounces to 1.6 ounces and offered a standard sandwich premade with ketchup, onion, and pickles. At the same time, they lowered their price from thirty-five to fifteen cents.

The McDonalds' "new" system actually was just a speedier and more streamlined version of White Castle's, emphasizing quick service and inexpensive hamburgers. Nevertheless, the McDonalds did it in a way that hungry customers clamored for. After a brief transition from drive-in to self-service, the McDonalds' business grew rapidly, attracting lines of more than two hundred customers. As the crowds grew even larger, the brothers devised a way to premake even more burgers and to keep them warm under infrared heat lamps. Theirs was the first hamburger company to use such a system. As their business prospered, the McDonalds replaced their original octagonal building with one that had a more distinctive architecture and was more conducive to their new style of walk-up, self-service business. The brothers' trademark red-and-white-tiled building had a sloped roof and giant twin neon arches spanning the entire length.[26]

Soon after designing and erecting their new hamburger stand, the McDonald brothers further expanded their business through franchising. Starting in 1953 they advertised their franchising offer in several national restaurant trade magazines and soon sold twenty-one franchises. Chicago salesman and entrepreneur Ray Kroc noticed the advertisements and decided to visit the McDonalds' San Bernardino operation to take a closer look. When he saw the throngs of customers lined up for fifteen-cent hamburgers, Kroc became an immediate believer in "the McDonald's System." Soon after his visit to California, Kroc became McDonald's national franchising agent, in 1955 selling himself his first McDonald's franchise, which he located in Des Plaines, Illinois. Within a year, Kroc had sold twelve additional franchises in Illinois and Indiana, and one hundred more by the end of the decade. Years later, after buying complete rights to the company and name from the McDonald brothers for $2.7 million, Kroc tried to downplay the company's California roots, focusing on the Des Plaines store as the company's birthplace. Regardless of origin, however, by the mid-1950s the powerful McDonald's chain was on the offensive, quickly spreading its name and its new standard for service across the nation.[27]

White Castle first took formal notice of the McDonald's onslaught in 1958, when Indianapolis manager Virgel Whitt announced that "the Mac-Donald [*sic*] chain is operating two units in our area . . . and it appears competition is going to get keener in our city." From that point on, virtually all discussion of competition focused on McDonald's. The next month, the Cincinnati White Castle managers reported that McDonald's and Henry's arrived amid "quite a bit of publicity." They seemed even more dazzled by McDonald's highly publicized vow to open one thousand additional restaurants nationwide within the next three years. Castles in the Chicago area resumed selling french fries in response to their immense popularity at McDonald's. After observing his first McDonald's opening in the fall of 1958, Offner in Louisville confidently stated, "We do not feel that the competitive situation is going to lessen . . . but we should be able to hold our own." Four months later, however, he admitted that the "hamburger field is getting a little overcrowded in Louisville and . . . there will eventually be some consolidations or some of them will go out of business. I doubt if all of them can survive."[28] We do not know whether Offner was including his own company in that assessment.

White Castle's senior management staff at the home office in Columbus was slow to comment on the competitive threat, even in private company correspondence. It was as if formal recognition of these competitors would be an admission that White Castle's reign over the fast-food hamburger industry had finally come to an end. With the arrival and spread of McDonald's, however, the years of denying the existence of their competitor had to end. In the April 1959 General Letter, Chicago manager Arthur L. Schultz publicly announced the threat from Ray Kroc's burgeoning hamburger empire.

> We never worry too much about drive-in competition, but we must admit that either now or sometime in the future most drive-ins do take some business that we may have had or that we could get in the future. The McDonald chain, one of the fastest growing operations in the Chicago area, has opened its 25th drive-in within the area. The most recent one at 48th and Cicero makes a total of 100 units which had a total business of twelve million dol-

lars in 1958. They hope to do twenty-five million in 1959. They also hope to add 200 units throughout the country by 1960. They opened their first two units in 1954, and they bragged about several things, one being that they put the hamburger on the assembly line. This is accomplished by frying in advance and wrapping the hamburger and placing it in a steam table arrangement. They also talk about no tipping, no jukeboxes and no carhops and that they have dentists, salesmen, farmers and veterinarians running their units. Most of their operation proves this out.[29]

Schultz ended his report optimistically, predicting that "as long as we keep up our standards, we need never fear they will become a serious threat as far as competition goes." A month later, Billy Ingram's son Edgar echoed Schultz's optimism, writing,

> For months we have seen news releases and publicity in all the restaurant magazines and in newspapers about new organizations going into the quick-lunch or hamburger business. There is an imposing array of these, including Henry's, the Gold Point System, the Ranch House, Richard's, McDonald's, Frisch's, and probably some others which you can recall.

The younger Ingram went on to point out the shortcomings of any system based on franchising: "Anyone, if he has the money, regardless of whether or not he knows anything about the quick-lunch business, can get into this business very quickly." He was appalled at the chains' lack of amenities such as indoor seating, air conditioning, or curb service.

Edgar Ingram also criticized the food quality of most of these new chains, citing their widespread use of heat lamps and describing the competitors' french fries as "fairly limp" and their hamburger buns as "varying greatly." In his final assessment of the competition, Ingram weakly acknowledged the threat by ordering "that in each town where we have competition we should look at it very critically to determine if they have anything in their method of operation that is superior to ours." He concluded more confidently: "To me, that we operate all our own units, that we strive to serve the most food value for the least amount of money in the cleanest surroundings . . . will give us the foundation to outlive any competition."[30] With these words, White Castle was admitting that a new day had dawned in the hamburger business, which could be a bleak one for the company's future.

Amid the shortages and price hikes and growing competition, White Castle experienced another blow in the 1950s. Longtime White Castle hostess Ella Louise Agniel, more popularly known as Julia Joyce, died suddenly on April 23, 1952, in an automobile accident on Long Island while returning to New York from a friend's funeral. Everyone in the company was stunned by the loss. Her obituary in the company *House Organ* praised her twenty years of dedicated service, crediting her with bringing the hamburger "to thousands of women in the various cities in which White Castle operates." At the time of her death, Agniel was concentrating her marketing efforts on the women's clubs in the newly created suburbs on Long Island. Billy Ingram was especially saddened by Agniel's death, for he knew that her work marketing White Castle's hamburger sandwich to the middle class during the 1930s was instrumental to the company's continued prosperity during that difficult era. He also knew that her untimely departure left a significant void in the company at another troubled time.[31]

The combined setbacks, losses, and external threats during the 1950s placed White Castle in an increasingly precarious position. The company's sales in the early part of the decade were erratic, with only modest growth throughout the next several years. That is, White Castle's sales remained stagnant while both the economy and the competition growing rapidly. The company was quickly losing market share in this booming era of fast food, and the number of Castles remaining open was dropping as well. Being a resourceful businessman, Billy Ingram resolved to reverse this trend. For the remainder of the decade, he tried once again to strengthen his company, probably not intending to recapture the industry lead but determined to return White Castle to a sound footing.

Billy Ingram Leads White Castle Back to Prosperity

As one might expect, Billy Ingram was troubled by White Castle's continuing misfortune ever since the disastrous circumstances of World War II. The company's troubles only seemed to multiply as each year passed, despite the best efforts of Ingram and his management team. Indeed, they found themselves in a constant struggle just to survive or to keep up with their new competition. As a former industry leader, Ingram hated to be in such an unfavorable position. He remembered the 1920s, when all entrants into the hamburger business sought to duplicate White Castle's buildings, products, and methods. With these days in mind, he decided to rebuild his company in exactly the same manner he had built it the first time, emphasizing White Castle's basic strengths of cleanliness, quality food, and motivated service.

In 1950, Ingram reminded his management staff of the company's founding principles and announced a renewed emphasis on those principles. He first ordered that sanitation and cleanliness be made a priority, explaining that "our Castles are, as a whole, in better condition than any time in the past, but the demands for higher standards are apparently increasing and we must study our processes and our results if we wish to stay out in front." In this same vein, Ingram outlined a schedule for modernizing all the company's buildings.

Feeling the pressure from the growing competition, Ingram also advised enhancing White Castle's food products, noting,

> There are probably many things we can do that will improve our products. The buns, meat, and other ingredients of our sandwich should be studied for that purpose. Our method of cooking, particularly our timing, should be carefully considered in an effort to not have sandwiches overcooked, or carried too long on the griddle. Coffee, pastry, and other items should not be regarded as unimportant.

He also returned to his favorite emphasis on sales and service, warning that "in meeting the new and excessive demands of our business, we have perhaps in some cases become lax in salesmanship. . . . From . . . what I have observed, I believe there is possibility for improvement." Ingram was not attempting anything revolutionary; he was merely returning to his own proven strategies. Later that year, he reinforced his message by reminding managers that "I believe that we make the best sandwich that people can buy for the money. We have the knowledge and understanding to correct any faults we may discover." These thoughts became White Castle's long-term business strategy for recovery throughout the 1950s, emphasizing clean and modern buildings, the best food possible, and a talented and energetic sales force.

Ingram assigned the task of modernizing the White Castle buildings to the venerable Lloyd Ray whose construction department had originally constructed most of the Castles. Ray drew up a six-year plan either to renovate the buildings or tear them down and construct new ones. In conjunction with the Porcelain Steel Building division, he first compiled a list of what modifications each Castle needed for improvement and then established a manufacturing and construction schedule.

Each month in the manager's General Letter, the current renovation's progress and plans for new construction for the coming month were reported. When a Castle was either structurally flawed or too small for current needs, the building was demolished and replaced by what some managers referred to as a "Super Castle." These new Castles were labeled *super* because of their much greater size, generous seating capacity, and both exterior and interior walls made of porcelain enamel. Constructed primarily to compete with the newer chains' larger buildings, these Castles measured forty-five by fifty-five feet. In addition, most were built either on the periphery of a city or farther out toward the new suburbs.

The first Super Castle to open was in suburban Louisville in July 1956. Billy Ingram attended the grand opening. Awed by his new Castle, he commented that "the [32] front room is especially inviting and beautiful . . . and the setting of this Castle is most interesting because of the grass and trees along Eastern Parkway." He added, "All of us, I feel sure, are impressed with the possibilities for the future." The future was further away than Ingram implied. Not many more of these big suburban Castles were built during the 1950s, with the company's emphasis instead on improving or replacing profitable Castles in more traditional markets.

The goal of serving "the best food possible" was much more difficult to meet. In the early days in Wichita, Ingram and his partner, Walt Anderson, selected cuts of meat, often supervised the grinding, and personally taught all their operators how to shape a hamburger patty by hand and how to fry it correctly to the company's specifications. As the company expanded, the partners delegated these duties to managers and eventually to multiple layers of management staff and trainers. Instead of ordering meat by the pound from Billy Dye's Wichita meat shop, White Castle bought hundreds of tons of preformed and frozen patties each year from the Chicago-based Swift Company. Although Ingram insisted on uniformity in all facets of the company's operation and instituted safeguards to ensure quality, the magnitude of White Castle's business made adherence to his strict criteria difficult. The high employee turnover further compounded this problem. In some years, Castle operators would last only a few weeks or months before quitting. Recognizing these difficulties, Ingram tried to create a more stable work force and to train his operators more thoroughly in the proper way to cook a White Castle hamburger.

Another difficulty in improving food preparation and quality during the 1950s was the fact that some of White Castle's food items kept changing, either to match a competitor's newest items or to respond to customer demand. Compared with the 1920s when the menu consisted of only coffee, hamburgers, cola, and pie, White Castle's offerings in the 1950s were much more diverse.

The test kitchen at the home office was constantly experimenting with new products while at the same time trying to perfect its hamburgers. Given the popularity of the Big Boy sandwich and other, larger hamburgers offered by other chains, White Castle introduced and test-marketed its "King Size" hamburger in April 1958. This consisted of a three-ounce meat patty with added condiments, plus a new slogan, "Now the Castles have a King!" White Castle customers were not enthusiastic. The Columbus area, which was test-marketing this new burger, reported in early summer that "the King-Size hamburger is not doing well.[33] We had placed much enthusiasm in the King-Size sandwich . . . and we are still trying to get it off the ground." This attempt to compete in the bigger-sandwich market did not go well, and so was White Castle's last effort.

In addition to big hamburgers, White Castle also resumed selling milk shakes to meet customer demand. Although White Castle had served them briefly during the 1940s, it stopped because they took a long time and were cumbersome for the operators to fix. Another reason was that some managers believed that the milk shakes' 10 percent butterfat content ruined customers' appetites for additional hamburgers. By the mid-1950s, however, milk shake technology had improved along with their popularity. To make the milk shakes, the company bought new Sweden Shake machines for each Castle. Although these shakes were never a large segment of White Castle's business, company managers deemed them necessary to satisfy customer demand.

Another move to keep up with the competition's products was White Castle's return in the late 1950s to offering french fries. The company had removed fries from its menu during the Korean War because of a shortage of potatoes and because many of the managers believed that frying them in hot grease was dangerous for the operators. But by the middle of the decade, french fries had become a fixture in the fast-food industry. Commenting in 1959 on White Castle's slow return into this market, Chicago manager Schultz stated, "We have always thought that french fries and hamburgers went together like ham and eggs, but like a lot of other things, we were just a little slow in taking advantage of this.[34]

Not all White Castle's new food offerings were imitative and trendy; some were sincere attempts to better serve its customers' needs. One example was the fish sandwich. Realizing that hamburgers sales dipped considerably during Lent, White Castle searched for a popular meat substitute. Targeted at Catholics abstaining from meat, this fish sandwich was offered only on Fridays. Billy Ingram was at first opposed to the idea, remembering the poor sales performance of the fish sandwich offered during World War II.

The fish patty was made from cod, halibut, or haddock, and contrary to Ingram's expectations, it thrived in White Castle's many heavily Catholic cities, such as Chicago, St. Louis, and New York, and thus became a permanent addition to White Castle's menu. With this item, White Castle won back a significant share of the market—at least on one day each week.[35]

The food items that helped White Castle rebound during the 1950s were its famous hamburgers and coffee. Whereas other companies built their business on bigger hamburgers or ornate buildings, White Castle concentrated on improving the original articles. Billy Ingram spent hours testing and comparing different coffee beans. He became convinced that the best beans were shipped into New York City, so he signed a contact with Arnold and Alborn of New York to buy 800,000 pounds of coffee. A salesman from that company came to the 1956 White Castle managers' meeting and lectured for two days on the way to make better coffee.[36] Despite his coffee and information, the areas reported no increase in coffee sales for the following year. Next, Ingram had the idea of building his own plants to roast the beans to his exact specifications, but this plan never materialized. Instead, he switched coffee vendors again, buying from Wallingford Coffee of Cincinnati. This proved to be a satisfactory business relationship that continues today.

Throughout much of the decade, the company devoted most of its energy and resources to selling more and better hamburgers. Ingram believed that his product offered the finest quality and value on the market: "Our product fills a fundamental need and desire of the public, and we are undoubtedly achieving a constant and overall improvement in its production." Company employees on all levels continuously experimented with the seasonings, cooking times, amount of onions, and condiments. When one manager suggested adding the flavor enhancer monosodium glutamate to the hamburger mix, Ingram rejected the idea, pointing out, "The White Castle cooking process and the onions are enough."[37]

Nonetheless, Ingram continually sought to improve on his sandwich's quality and taste. Maintaining that "flavor and palatability cannot be overemphasized," in 1955 he hired Professor L. E. Conkle of Ohio State University to determine the degree of flavor and moisture that hamburger meat loses when frozen. Soon after that, he contracted with the Battelle Memorial Institute in Columbus to examine the effects of "quick freezing" on buns and hamburger patties.[38] Ingram even experimented with wrapping the onion-covered burgers in wax paper to "eliminate the onion odor when sandwiches are taken home in automobiles."

Later in the decade, when the pricing norm for hamburgers was fifteen cents or more, Ingram once again fought against his managers' request for a price increase. In 1957, he predicted that White Castle's lower hamburger prices would "allow us to survive" while "our competition will decline by 25% in major cities. His prediction was correct: White Castle's net hamburger sales grew every year during the 1950s. Although White Castle ended the decade with considerably fewer restaurants than it had in 1929, the overall hamburger sales per Castle were nearly four times higher. Ingram may have lost his dominance over the fast-food industry, but he still sold more than 100 million hamburgers in both 1958 and 1959. Despite the onslaught from the huge competitors, White Castle continued to sell hamburgers.

Although Ingram was passionate about his hamburgers, he was even more passionate about his employees. He never wavered in his belief that capable and courteous Castle operators were the company's greatest strength. He also was concerned that White Castle had been unable to attract and hire higher-caliber employees since World War II. Accordingly, in addition to updating the buildings and improving the hamburgers, Ingram decided to improve his employees' training and motivation. He began by hiring the Research Institute of America to teach his management staff better instructional techniques and how "to get along with employees."[39] White Castle also began rotating supervisors and managers every quarter to different Castles to lessen personality conflicts or preferential treatment, and the company sent many managers to Dale Carnegie courses to polish their communication and interpersonal skills.

White Castle also spent more time on the operators themselves. Its goal was to make employees feel more positive about the company. First, the company constantly reminded its employees of the benefits of working at White Castle. It printed numerous booklets outlining the extent of its insurance coverage, describing the retirement system, and urging everyone to participate in the savings plan. Employees often received letters citing examples of sick employees or their children who benefited from the generous Blue Cross and Blue Shield coverage, about money that employees earned through the annual bonus, or about Castle employees retiring to a life of leisure.

In addition, air conditioners, exhaust vents, showers, and telephones were installed for the employees' comfort. Because most employees were women, White Castle also changed the operators' uniforms to conform with changing women's fashions and provided stockings at their wholesale price. Meals were supplied free to all employees while working. Employees always received a large cake from the company on their birthday. These company efforts did seem to inspire greater employee allegiance, since the turnover decreased steadily during the decade.

Better training his managers and giving more consideration to employees was not the goal of Ingram's plan but, rather, just the means of achieving it. He agreed with Bruce LaPlante's assessment that happier workers would achieve greater productivity and profitability. Accordingly, as the employees' working conditions improved, the company expected more efficiency and reliability. The Chicago area implemented a new program called "Speed in Operation" to underscore the need for better, faster service. The company as a whole monitored food and service quality more closely by sending inspection teams of area managers to Castles throughout the country. Once White Castle reestablished strict standards for service, it demanded that they be observed. Even in this era of labor shortages, the company dismissed employees who did not perform to the company's expectations. Nonetheless, the company still rewarded a positive attitude and loyalty. When one elderly female operator could no longer cook or change money because of her cataracts, the company created a new and probably unnecessary position of "Castle custodian" just so she would still have a job.

Broadcasting the White Castle Message to the People

The world of advertising changed while Ingram was restoring his White Castle System to good health. Television sets appeared in millions of American homes during the 1950s, giving birth to a new medium of advertising. The growing fast-food hamburger chains quickly realized television's potential and spent great amounts of money buying commercial slots. White Castle, however, was slow to realize its value, or even that of radio advertising. Both Billy Ingram and his advertising director Benny Benfer still believed that print advertising and hamburger coupons were the most effective ways to advertise the company.

As the competition heated up in the early 1950s, coupon-sale weeks became increasingly common in most Castle areas, consuming virtually all their advertising budgets. But area managers began to question this practice, seeing that radio and television exposure gave their competitors a distinct advantage, and some experimented with radio and television commercials. The White Castle leadership was still not very receptive. In 1956 when Chicago manager Howard Lewis asked Benfer for money for radio ads in Chicago, Benfer replied,

> We have used radio and TV advertising during the past two and a half years and there is no evidence that either of these mediums have ever brought enough people to the Castles to warrant its continuance or to justify the money expended on it . . . advertising is designed to do one thing and that is to get people to come to the Castles and sample our product. This has been accomplished by the medium or coupon advertising in the newspaper.

This issue was debated at the 1956 managers' meeting in Columbus. Billy Ingram quickly backed his advertising chief, saying that White Castle already has "a three-part advertising: a fine product; efficient and courteous service; and clean, wholesome, attractive, and sanitary buildings." He doubted that "any other form of advertising would be successful as these three, and without them no advertising would be effective too long." This response sent the area managers into an uproar. They wanted new advertising that was not tied to coupons for free hamburgers, since they viewed that approach as ultimately more expensive. Ingram defensively retorted, "You're saying that we don't know what is good or bad in advertising? I don't want to substitute advertising for quality operations, as these should always remain our goals." Benfer added that he distrusted radio- and television-advertising salesmen "who are not interested in what the advertising will do to help the sales of a product, but [who] are interested primarily in their own business, which is selling advertising." Again defending his preference for print ads, he concluded, "You must go down to where the ducks are to get ducks."

From there the discussion broke down for the morning. When the meeting resumed for its afternoon session, Ingram opened with a conciliatory comment, saying that through debate and argument "we can reach both understanding and deeper comradeship." Although nothing was resolved that week, the managers soon started allocating limited funds earmarked for radio and television advertising, often allowing area managers the discretion to spend it.

Almost without exception, these managers used their advertising money to reach the children of the 1950s, who accounted for 36 percent of the total population of the United States in 1955, with fifty-four million youngsters eating 40 percent of the nation's food. Marketing studies of the era indicated that 81 percent of American mothers consented to buying at least one item each week asked for by their child. With these statistics in mind, White Castle managers resolutely went after the children's market. Castle advertising was almost exclusively focused on kids. Louisville's Offner led the pack by sponsoring a children's television show called *The Cactus and Randy Show*, a live daily afternoon show in which the main characters wore cowboy attire and hosted games and guests. White Castle employees were present in the studio during the broadcast, feeding hamburgers to the characters and awarding coupons for three free sandwiches to the children and parents in the studio audience. Billy Ingram even appeared on the show once, passing out hamburgers to the crowd. Periodically throughout each show, "Cactus" would munch a hamburger and proclaim it to be "cowboy good." *Cactus and Randy* became quite popular with the children in Louisville. Offner observed, "We have a good many customers between the ages of four and twelve. A good many times we see as many as five or six of these children in a Castle at a time. We are inclined to believe that a good many of these children are coming in due to our television program . . . we also are inclined to believe that some of the parents are becoming customers due to the influence of some of the children." The old print ads were designed to offer good price and value to adults by giving away free hamburgers, but this new approach was to reach these same adults through their children. This company emphasis on children and family business pervaded all areas.

Most of the media advertising was directed to young customers. Some areas offered hamburger boxes that could be folded into the shape of a castle. Other cartons had trading cards printed on them, with prizes such as footballs and flash cameras given to children who collected the entire set. Other areas featured displays with railroad or space travel themes; New York experimented with small kiddie rides at their Castles. All Castles offered bibs for small children. Since families usually did not sit at the counters, most Castles installed tables for better family-style seating.

By the end of the 1950s, most White Castles had changed from being almost exclusively adult to being more family focused. Even more important, radio and television advertising had become an integral part of White Castle's marketing approach. The managers predicted that this new strategy would generate the same level of sales without the large-scale hamburger giveaways, and they were right.

White Castle at the End of the 1950s

Fast-food hamburgers became formalized in the 1950s as truly "America's food." Long the favorite on urban streets for more than thirty years, hamburgers migrated to the suburbs during the 1950s where they were readily claimed. As the national giants emerged, however, confusion reigned as to the exact origin of this eating style. Ray Kroc's massive propaganda machine soon taught a new generation of young Americans that he was the "Father of Fast Food." Old-timers and those involved in the restaurant industry, however, knew the truth about the start of the fast-food hamburger. They knew that Billy Ingram was almost single-handedly responsible for selling hamburgers to America. In the March 1957 issue of *Fast Food Magazine*, the industry's trade publication, Ingram was publicly lauded as the "Grandaddy of the Hamburger." The article recounted the story of White Castle's beginnings, crediting Ingram with being the man who made White Castle and White Castle as the company that created the industry. More articles and many newspaper and radio interviews followed, widely recognizing Ingram's significant accomplishments. The *Chicago Tribune* hailed him as an innovator, saying he "created his own competition as he expanded." All proclaimed him to be the undisputed founder of fast food.

By the close of the decade, White Castle was once again strong and ready for the future. Ingram's operation was smaller than it had been twenty years earlier, but it also was more streamlined and much more profitable. The larger franchised chains had already eclipsed White Castle in terms of size and scope, but the tenacious little company held on and continued to flourish. Even more significant than White Castle's resurgence in the late 1950s was the rise of its growing mystique. As fast-food chains proliferated, White Castle and its famous hamburgers still enjoyed a loyal following built up in its more than thirty years in business. By this time, almost two generations of urban Americans had grown up along with White Castle, and many counted the small burgers as their favorite food. As the nation became more mobile after the war, some of these loyal customers moved to non-White Castle areas, could no longer get their burgers, and yearned for them. As early as 1954, a resourceful Louisville woman paid White Castle to airfreight twelve hamburgers to her brother living in Los Angeles. The company readily complied, packing the burgers in dry ice and taking them to the airport. The brother received his cherished meal the following day, complete with precise reheating instructions. This transaction started a practice of shipping burgers to distant fans that lasted for thirty years until White Castle began marketing frozen hamburgers in grocery stores nationwide. This also underscored the fact that some customers saw White Castle as more than just a mere hamburger. The 1950s was when this budding fanaticism about White Castle first began to surface. As other hamburger options presented themselves, consumers could choose McDonald's, Burger King, Steak N Shake, or an endless variety of other places for their meal. To a White Castle fan, however, none of these franchised hamburger factories would do. For the next forty years White Castle enjoyed—and continues to enjoy—a large group of loyal followers who regularly sought out and often traveled great distances to have a White Castle hamburger.

In 1958, Billy Ingram, nearly eighty years old, handed over the day-to-day control of the company to his son Edgar. Because the elder Ingram was not yet ready for retirement, he decided to spend the winters in Miami and return to either Columbus or his Canadian retreat in the summers. But Ingram soon grew bored in Miami with no business to oversee, so he built three new Castles in the area, even though that city was already saturated with fast-food hamburger chains. Disregarding the competition, Ingram was frustrated that Floridians averaged only one hamburger per visit, and he was determined to change this trend, just as he had done in the rest of America.

6

White Castle in the Age
of McDonald's

American society changed drastically in the three decades between 1960 and 1990. Much happened during this tumultuous time, alter-
ing how Americans lived their lives, viewed their country, and even how
they ate their meals. The middle class completed its exodus from the city to
suburbia, in the process repositioning society's wealth and redefining the
dominant culture. The stereotypical family of the 1950s mutated into entirely new forms. Deeply entrenched gender roles and stereotypes began to
crumble, often allowing many American women greater mobility and responsibility. Unlike previous brief wartime stints in the workplace, women
broke out of their imposed domesticity of the 1950s, pursued lifetime careers, and frequently raised their families alone. A brief yet profound wave
of political liberalism rocked America in the late 1960s and early 1970s, resulting in numerous reforms that were quickly balanced by a lengthy conservative spell. Americans experienced an unpopular and divisive war, riot-
ing in their major cities, and the assassination of one president and the res-
ignation of another. An inflationary economy sent wages and prices
skyrocketing before settling down to a more modest climb. As a result, by
1990 American workers enjoyed only a fraction of the buying power that
their parents had had in 1960. Both spouses often worked at full-time jobs
outside the home just to maintain some semblance of a 1950s middle-class
lifestyle. The tools of work and the toys of play also changed drastically.
Heralded as an almost divine blessing, technology boomed during these
years at a pace never before seen by humankind, integrating the television,
computer, and other electronic gadgetry into nearly all facets of everyday
life. This technological revolution even extended into eating. In kitchens
across America, microwaves replaced radiant heat as the primary means to
cook food quickly. Actually, the preparation and consumption of food were
even further sped up by other changes and innovations of this era. To an increasingly large degree, the tradition of the family meal itself was removed

from the home to the nearby fast-food outlet. By 1990, the daily consumption preferences of the majority of Americans confirmed fast food as an integral part of the mainstream diet. The quest for public acceptance of the hamburger that Billy Ingram had launched almost seventy years earlier was now complete and, for better or worse, overwhelmingly victorious.

The period between 1960 and 1990 was the heyday of fast food. McDonald's and Burger King secured their hold as the reigning powers in the industry, fending off competition from upstart powerhouses such as Wendy's, Arby's, and Jack-in-the-Box and spreading their names and products around the globe. During these years, fast food graduated from the simple hamburger and its variations to a seemingly infinite multitude of new product offerings. Restaurant chains packaged chicken pieces, tacos, egg rolls, and heavily modified cuisines from every corner of the world into the fast-food or "quick-service" format. By 1990, fast food had a variety of new faces and meanings, offering customers nearly every conceivable food product across the counter, with the option of "eat here or carry out."

As the fast-food industry continued to change, the White Castle System held on to the simplicity of featuring hamburgers, Coke, and coffee.[1] This continued emphasis on its original strengths was a double-edged sword lacking the flash to dominate in an increasing glitzy industry in which the label *new* was constantly applied to an endless series of products yet still retaining a legion of loyal traditionalists. Abiding by Ingram's prohibition against expanding through the use of borrowed money, White Castle's growth stagnated relative to others in the industry. Meanwhile, McDonald's and Burger King, franchising at a phenomenal rate and catering to the needs of growing suburbia, spread to almost every small town in America and then on to almost every developed or developing nation. As these giant chains proliferated to tens of thousands of units, White Castle remained comparatively small, adding a few Castles each year and moving into suburban markets only when its own capital became available.

White Castle actually was a quiet success story between 1960 and 1990. By the 1960s Billy Ingram had grown quite cautious and conservative about expansion, and after his death in 1966 his son Edgar did not greatly alter the company's direction. White Castle continued to grow slowly, remaining quite profitable and proving to the industry that big need not mean better and that urban dwellers still ate hamburgers, too. In a sense, White Castle actually celebrated its own anachronism, recognizing and capitalizing on the unique and even humorous nature of its business and products. In an even more real sense, White Castle remained committed to its locations in urban neighborhoods, and hence to the past, because that was where its Castles were. With limited capital and a conservative approach to expansion, conversion from an urban-based company to a predominantly suburban chain was just not practical. Instead, White Castle firmly retained its urban clientele, despite dramatic changes in class and ethnicity. In many ways, White Castle spent these three decades becoming comfortable with its own unique identity and niche while at the same time learning to compete in a new and increasingly savage fast-food industry. Competing in this new forum meant playing by new rules and subtly adapting to a new generation of consumers in terms of products, service, and marketing. While still retaining its allegiance to the urban areas, when the company added new Castles, they often were on busy suburban thoroughfares. Lagging behind the other chains, television and radio eventually became the preferred media for White Castle advertising. Most important, White Castle survived a generational transition in its industry, learning to walk the narrow line between attracting new customers, accustomed to the flash and hype of "modern" fast food, while still accommodating the possibly simpler tastes and the needs of its long-standing clientele. With this dual purpose in mind, the company continued to prosper and gradually grow during these years, with the pace of expansion greatly accelerating in the late 1980s under the direction of Edgar's son E. W. "Bill" Ingram III.

The Growth of the Franchised Giants

By the end of the 1950s, the nationally franchised hamburger chains set the pace of the quick-service restaurant industry. Ray Kroc's empire of McDonald's franchises approached one thousand units, with the Florida-based Insta-Burger-King chain lagging behind by several hundred. By 1970 both companies had expanded to many more new locations across the country, with McDonald's reaching more than fifteen hundred units, leading the industry in both sales volume and marketing trends. Although each company owned a small core of its own restaurants, most of their rapid growth was achieved by selling franchises to local or regional entrepreneurs. Although such franchising was not a new practice in American business, it reached a fever pitch by the late-1960s. It even became common for existing restaurant chains to begin buying franchises from the growing giants. Accordingly, by 1980, there were 6,200 McDonald's in the United States and 1,185 overseas, with those numbers doubling by 1990.[2]

With the success of McDonald's and Burger King, numerous entrepreneurs tried to imitate or improve on their operations. Just as earlier entrepreneurs sought to replicate White Castle's booming success in the 1920s by creating similar White Towers, Royal Castles, or White Huts, in the 1960s and 1970s hundreds capitalized on the McDonald's and Burger King phenomenon by either purchasing costly franchises or starting their own chains. Once again playing on familiar-sounding names, the leader Burger King was quickly joined by Burger Queen, Burger Chef, and others. Burger Chef briefly stood out as the most successful of these sound-alike imitators, growing even larger than Burger King prototype and, at one point in the late 1960s, even rivaling McDonald's in the number of franchised restaurants. Started in 1957 by the manufacturer of Burger King's Instabroiler, General Equipment Company, Burger Chef incorporated the same automatic broiling method and made a comparable hamburger.[3] Similar to the confusing White Castle-White Tower competition two generations earlier, many customers failed to discern a significant difference between the Burger King and Burger Chef chains in either name or product and often used the two names interchangeably and almost generically.

Although Ray Kroc was able to keep tighter control over the more distinctive McDonald's name, his was the operation most frequently targeted for imitation. The founder of Burger Queen, George Clark, recalled that "most everybody copied McDonald's, either through observing or maybe they copied subconsciously. . . . Our food was exactly the same as McDonald's. If I had looked at McDonald's and saw someone turning hamburgers while he was hanging from his feet I would have copied it." Clark's admission was more frank than most, but his actions were typical in the fast-food world. McDonald's symbolized success and huge profits, and newcomers into the industry sought to replicate all aspects of its operation. Above all else, independent entrepreneurs and fledgling chains all fixated on Ray Kroc's mastery of standardization in all aspects of the business, from the kitchen to the bookkeeping to the building construction.[4] Despite its undisputed lead, McDonald's still waged an extremely competitive war in the fast-food marketplace. As Ray Kroc explained, "It is ridiculous to call this an industry. This is not. This is rat eat rat, dog eat dog. I'll kill 'em, and I'm going to kill 'em before they kill me. You're talking about the American way of survival of the fittest."[5]

Using the McDonald's model, new local, regional, and national fast-food chains proliferated during the 1960s and 1970s. Familiar names such as Hardee's, Carrol's, Jack-in-the-Box, and Red Barn based their new chains on this proven formula of selling standardized hamburgers at a low price. Defying the odds in terms of both available capital and a regional unfamiliarity with fast food, Hardee's grew from a small restaurant in Greenville, North Carolina, in 1961 to a chain of more than nine hundred outlets fourteen years later. Beginning with "a red and white-striped building like McDonald's in the early 1960s" and later shifting to Burger King's brown-and-orange color scheme, Hardee's offered "a self-service system and menu featuring fifteen-cent hamburgers."[6] Once again using the McDonald's methods of self-service, standardization, and relentless franchising, Hardee's grew into one of America's leading fast-food companies, often spreading to small rural towns, as opposed to the more conventional pattern of opening outlets in the suburbs. This deviation from the McDonald's norm was significant because Hardee's built a thriving hamburger chain in areas previously deemed impossible but, even more important, because it brought the fast-food hamburger to still another segment of the population.

Wendy's was an even more improbable success story, beginning in an urban and suburban market seemingly already saturated with fast-food hamburgers. Undaunted by the size and following of the existing giants, former Kentucky Fried Chicken manager R. David Thomas began his new chain with a lone outlet on Broad Street in downtown Columbus, Ohio, in 1972. Despite the pessimists on Wall Street and a looming recession, Thomas believed that American consumers wanted bigger and better hamburgers than those currently offered by the major chains. Accordingly, his first Wendy's featured a square, quarter-pound ground beef patty that was more than twice the size of the McDonald's hamburger. Thomas also charged his customers almost three times as much for his basic hamburger, fifty-five cents compared with McDonald's eighteen. His hunch about consumer tastes proved to be correct: "By the end of 1972, Wendy's had nine outlets with annual sales of 1.8 million dollars." By the end of that decade, hundreds of Wendy's sprang up across America, joined by thousands more in the 1980s. In almost every location, the new Wendy's were directly and successfully competing with a McDonald's, a Burger King, or both.[7] Besides beginning a billion-dollar industry, Thomas proved to Wall Street, the restaurant industry, and the world that the public had an insatiable appetite for good hamburgers and would pay even higher prices to get them. Thomas also made his fast food even faster by using drive-thru windows at all his outlets, forcing McDonald's and Burger King to follow suit.[8] His success, in turn, provided inspiration and attainable goals for an even newer generation of entrepreneurs, who plunged into the industry with renewed fervor. Thomas did not, however, reinvent the wheel. He and those who came later merely modified the McDonald's concept somewhat or improved it, just as the McDonald brothers had done with the White Castle concept thirty years earlier.

Fast Food: Not Just Burgers Anymore

A further refinement or, rather, a further mutation of the White Castle-McDonald's fast-food hamburger approach took the form of Kentucky Fried Chicken, Arby's, Taco Bell, Pizza Hut, Long John Silver's, and other, similar chains. These chains largely copied the fast-food hamburger format, merely substituting other food products in the place of the hamburger sandwich. Clever entrepreneurs offered chicken pieces, roast beef sandwiches, fried fish fillets, and Americanized tacos and burritos as alternatives to the more traditional fare of hamburgers and hot dogs. Despite these new chains' different products, most were similar to McDonald's in appearance and marketing. Their buildings, both inside and out, were suspiciously reminiscent of McDonald's and Burger King; they sold their new chicken, sandwiches, tacos, or fish sticks in wrappings nearly identical to those of hamburgers; and they lined the same suburban corridors.

In fact, the only aspect of the hamburger business that these chains actually changed was the hamburger itself. Many of these chains were predicated on the assumption that consumers responded to the convenience of the carryout, quick-service foods, rather than just to hamburgers. This assumption actually was a fairly safe one, since White Castle, Burger King, McDonald's, and many of the other chains had offered different sandwich options for many years, proving that there was a viable market for them. For example, White Castle had offered fish sandwiches off and on since World War II, with great success, and McDonald's introduced its cheese-topped Filet-O-Fish in 1962.[9] The sales records of both companies proved that customers bought fish and other offerings right along with their hamburgers and that there was money to be made. Soon burger alternatives collectively comprised a significant share of the fast-food market, although never seriously rivaling the dominance of the hamburger.

Fried chicken emerged as the most popular offering among these alternative foods. As early as the 1950s, newly franchised chains began appearing along the highways, specializing in selling battered and deep-fried pieces of chicken. Using pressurized oil fryers to cook his chicken quickly, A. L. Tunick founded his Chicken Delight chain in 1952 and sold more than four hundred new franchises within a decade. But Tunick's success was soon eclipsed by retired Kentucky restaurateur Colonel Harlan Sanders, who got into the fast-food business almost by accident. Since the 1930s, Sanders had owned a popular service station, motel, and restaurant on U.S. Route 25, catering to motorists traveling between the Midwest and Atlanta and Miami. Featuring pan-fried chicken, Sanders' restaurant—first called "Sanders' Servistation" and later "Sanders' Court"—became an almost legendary oasis for travelers in the days before four-lane interstates, even winning notice in Duncan Hines's 1939 guide, *Adventures in Good Eating*.[10]

Sander's popular and thriving business folded in 1955, however, when Interstate 75 was built seven miles to the west, becoming the preferred thoroughfare for travelers and diverting his once-loyal customers beyond easy reach. With no customers to eat his chicken, Sanders had to sell his property at public auction and retire to live on his Social Security income. This unwanted retirement did not last long, however. Years earlier he had shared his chicken recipe and cooking methods with other restaurant owners, at a royalty cost of four cents for each chicken cooked. At the urging of his friend, hamburger stand owner Pete Harman, the sixty-six-year-old Sanders began an aggressive campaign in 1956 to market franchises for his chicken, driving from state to state demonstrating his product to restaurateurs. His terms were simple; franchisees gained the rights to the company name and "secret recipe" in exchange for a five-cent royalty on every chicken that the franchise operators sold.

Based in Salt Lake City, Harman became Sanders's first franchisee, creating the name "Kentucky Fried Chicken" and quickly changing the focus of his business from hamburgers to chicken. As the popularity of his chicken grew, Sanders soon sold hundreds of franchises and eventually became the high-profile pitchman for the booming fast-food chicken industry in America.[11] His image became synonymous with the company and, to some degree, with the industry itself. Other prosperous chicken chains, such as Church's Fried Chicken which was founded in San Antonio, Texas, in 1952, grew up alongside Sanders' Kentucky Fried Chicken, yet they never achieved the same popularity. Even after he sold his company rights in 1964, Sanders remained in the public spotlight, wearing his trademark white suit and goatee, assuming a larger-than-life persona that much of the public thought was a fictional character like the Magic Burger King or Ronald McDonald.

While most of the hamburger alternatives came in hamburger-size portions in familiar boxes or wrappings, one franchised food product was distinctly different from the norm. Before the 1950s, pizza was often confined to the Italian enclaves of large eastern cities and was considered by many Americans to be exotic or "foreign." By the end of the decade, however, it began to be found across the country, showing up more and more in midwestern and western cities. The franchising of pizza restaurants began in 1954 with the creation of the Shakey's Pizza chain, which spread to more than one hundred locations by 1960. Although widely franchised and primarily located in suburbia, Shakey's did not truly qualify as "fast food" because most of its business was eat in, as opposed to carry out, attempting to replicate urban pizzerias, albeit with player pianos and pinball machines for the customers' entertainment.

As pizza became more popular, it soon spread beyond the traditional pizzeria-style restaurant. In 1958, two Wichita college students, brothers Frank and Dan Carney, started serving pizzas from a small, six-hundred-square-foot restaurant that they called Pizza Hut. Unsure of exactly how to make pizzas when they first opened and using a recipe borrowed from a friend, the Carney brothers introduced this new food to the people of Wichita, who responded to it with the same enthusiasm that they had for Walt Anderson's hamburgers nearly forty years earlier. Selling small pizzas for ninety-five cents and large ones for a dollar and a half, primarily on a carryout basis, the Carneys' business was so successful that they started a second store within six months and four more the following year.

When one of Pizza Hut's first managers wanted to open his own shop in Topeka, the Carneys lent him the money to buy the original Pizza Hut franchise. This franchise was just the first of many, with the Pizza Hut chain growing to six company-owned stores and 250 franchised outlets by 1967. After Pizza Hut stock went public in 1969, the infusion of new capital allowed the company to grow to more than two thousand stores by 1976. As the company expanded, the new Pizza Huts were constructed with simple yet spacious dining rooms and offered greatly expanded menus to its eat-in clientele.[12]

Although Pizza Hut distanced itself somewhat from a strict definition of fast food, it began a trend that swept the country and dramatically changed Americans' eating habits. Entrepreneurs everywhere entered the business, first starting as individual carryouts and many expanding into chains of varying sizes. By the mid-1970s, Pizza Hut had become more a American Italian restaurant, and so fast-food pizza companies such as Domino's and

Little Caesar's filled the niche of "pizza only" shops, selling millions of piz-zas every year on either a carryout or a car-delivery basis. By the end of the 1970s, pizza was deeply embedded in the American palate and often a weekly fixture at family meals. With the inclusion of such items as fried chicken and pizza, fast food was no longer limited to being sold "by the sack" but now was offered in a wide variety of buckets, barrels, and broad, flat, white boxes.

Other new hamburger alternatives varied to a still greater degree, mak-ing safe forays across ethnic lines. Some of these variations even grew di-rectly out of the hamburger tradition. Telephone repairman Glen Bell was a frequent customer at the McDonald's early San Bernardino carryout, and he was impressed enough by its operation to build a similar business.[13] Similar to hundreds of other entrepreneurs, Bell openly copied McDon-ald's entire operation, with one noteworthy exception: he supplemented the hamburger menu with bland, Americanized tacos that quickly became his featured, and most popular, item. Responding to the demand for his tacos, he named his new stand "Taco Bell" and soon dropped hamburgers from his offerings.[14] Once again, however, Bell and his numerous imitators did not stray too far from the traditional American palate. Harvey Leven-stein attributes the success of Taco Bell's fare to being "no more spicy or un-American tasting than hamburgers" and just being a slightly different vari-ation of the already popular pizza concept, noting that "the step from pizza to tacos was hardly more daring than the one that led Americans of the 1950's from pasta to pizza."[15]

Regardless of how readily Americans accepted these modified tacos and burritos, Taco Bell and the other fast-food taco chains had to overcome im-mense distrust and prejudice among consumers against Mexican restau-rants, believing them to be dirty. In response to this sentiment, Taco Bell and other taco-centered chains omitted all overtly Mexican symbols or ar-chitecture from their outlets, emphasizing that these were American restau-rants that happened to serve somewhat Mexican ethnic food. Taco Bell, for example, traded its symbol of "a sleeping Mexican in a sombrero" for an in-nocuous pastel-color bell. Despite these changes, many American con-sumers still believed that eating at Taco Bell to be adventurous experimen-tation with exotic "foreign food," although according to Levenstein, "It is questionable whether anyone but Mexicans should have considered it for-eign food."[16]

Other, less celebrated chains featuring more traditional hamburger al-ternatives flourished at a similar rate. In 1964, brothers Forrest and Leroy

Raffel founded a "McDonald's style" restaurant in Boardman, Ohio, featuring roast beef sandwiches, soft drinks, and milk shakes. Because their first choice of names, "Big Tex," was already taken, the Raffel brothers used their initials to devise the name Arby's. Avoiding the gleaming metal and shiny plastics common to most other fast-food chains, the Raffels constructed their new restaurants out of natural woods and stone walls, contriving an Old West decor. The Raffels also charged considerably higher prices for their roast beef than their competitors charged for their hamburgers. Certainly on one level, they intended this earthy decor, skewered beef roasts prominently cooking in view of the customers, and higher prices "to attract a more discriminating customer." Architectural historian Philip Langdon goes beyond these more obvious marketing aspects, contending that their choice of building style and materials was a dramatic rejection of McDonald's "futuristic structural modernism" that typified fast-food outlets in the 1950s and early 1960s.[17]

Aside from these architectural developments, Arby's proved that by using various price structures, decor, and marketing approaches, different fast-food chains could win over different socioeconomic classes. In short, as the fast-food industry became even more segmented in terms of products and locations, some chains began to target factors such as income level, ethnicity, or age. All the major chains became conscious of their clientele and how their patronage could be protected and enhanced.

The aggregate effect of all these new foods and decors was that eating fast food became a more varied and interesting experience, luring customers into chain outlets on a more frequent basis. Few diners hungered for hamburgers at both lunch and dinner, day in and day out, soon growing tired of the monotonous fare. By the 1960s, however, those frequently dining out at fast-food restaurants could select from an increasingly diverse selection of meat, poultry, and fish, in addition to pizza and tacos. Eventually, outlets featuring such items as "fast-food" Chinese egg rolls, Greek gyros, and submarine sandwiches sprang up in the few open spaces remaining on "Hamburger Alley" or "the Strip," providing still more alternatives to fast-food customers seeking their daily meals. No longer just a fried beef patty or a piece of chicken, by 1970 fast food took on multitude of new forms, with meat possibilities ranging from seasoned lamb to stir-fried shrimp. Without question, frequent fast-food diners never needed to eat the same meal twice in one week, often enjoying as much diversity of choices as they could get from more formal restaurants or even grocery store shelves.[18] Despite this new diversity in these fast foods, the hamburger retained its undisputed supremacy in the ever-changing marketplace. Americans still loved their hamburgers and enthusiastically chose them over all other options. Even though an endless array of chains featuring hamburger alternatives such as pizza, chicken, Mexican, seafood, and "budget steaks" had taken root by 1977, hamburgers still accounted for more than half of all fast-food sales in the United States.[19] Originally starting with Anderson and Ingram's simple White Castle sandwich, the hamburger went on to become a diverse product in itself, double-stacking with Bob's two-patty Big Boy in the 1930s, later growing to a quarter pound or more at other chains, and finally wearing an endless variety of vegetables, sauces, and even other meats such as bacon. Most fast-food customers developed distinct preferences for the burgers offered by particular chains, carefully differentiating between standardized fried patties delivered in a "no option" format from their "flame-broiled" rivals, supposedly cooked and topped to individual taste. While some customers swore allegiance to a particular hamburger and chain, many others decided their burger choices by whim or mood. Sesame and poppy seeds adorned round buns, and "secret sauces" provided mystery to many new burgers. Variations such as taco burgers and pizza burgers abounded, encouraging frequent customer defection from one chain to the next. Some chains featured their uniform factory-frozen patties with pride while others advertised the bonus of their hand-formed patties made from fresh ground beef. White Castle's original diminutive onion-laden sandwich became just one of many ways to enjoy a hamburger. Although still universally a beef patty between two buns, the hamburgers' specific incarnations proved endless. Just as tacos, fish fillets, and eggrolls offered a break from fast-food monotony, this new generation of diverse hamburgers also gave customers significant choices for their meals. One thing was certain: despite differences in onion, tomato, or special sauces, Americans still regularly clamored for the hamburger as their primary food. The rise of the giant fast-food chains, and even the challenges from competing products, only further confirmed the hamburger as America's food.

Fast Food Enters Corporate America

Already corporate powers in their own right, the growing profitability of the fast-food chains made them attractive acquisition targets to the even larger corporate behemoths that systematically purchased them in the late 1960s and early 1970s. Some chains, such as Burger Chef, were originally divisions of larger companies eager to cash in on the hamburger craze. Later sold off to the even larger General Foods in 1968, Burger Chef proved to be one of the less lucrative fast-food investment properties. Other chains, such as the rapidly expanding Burger King, which was purchased by baking-goods giant Pillsbury, were better earners for their parent companies. In most cases, the purchasing corporations were already involved in some other area of the food industry and were merely diversifying their holdings. In some cases, these companies may have realized that the growth of fast food in America during the 1960s meant more consumers eating away from home and thus a decrease in their traditional market base of raw food products prepared for family meals. Food conglomerate Ralston-Purina bought the booming Jack-in-the-Box drive-thru chain in 1970 from founder Robert O. Peterson; international liquor and specialty-food pow-erhouse Heublein bought Kentucky Fried Chicken from Louisville pro-moter John Y. Brown Jr. for $280 million worth of company stock; United Brands purchased the A&W drive-in chain; Consolidated Foods bought the regional midwest L&K chain in 1968; Imasco acquired Hardee's in 1974; Pepsico bought Pizza Hut in 1977 and Taco Bell a year later; and Royal Crown bought Arby's.[20] Anticipating huge profits, these corporations rushed headlong into the fast-food business, acquiring either regional or national chains and making the chains' founders enormously wealthy men. By the end of the 1970s, most of the major chains belonged to larger cor-porate families, and as a result, many often expanded at even faster rates with infusions of capital from their parent companies. As with any mergers or acquisitions, these corporate alliances ranged from harmonious to dis-astrous. The inclusion of these chains into the umbrella of corporate Amer-ica, however, had even a greater significance than just the mingling of money and the issuance of shares: the fast-food industry, once considered only a temporary trend, was finally accepted and recognized by Wall Street and economists as a legitimate sector of the national economy.

The Criticism of Fast Food Grows

The public first viewed the new generation of fast-food chains with won-der. Family visits to the new McDonald's were treats for most children and a welcome time saver for weary parents. To a public already enamored with anything "modern," the golden arches and perfectly identical burgers seemed like the culinary equivalent of television and space travel technology. Fast food and especially McDonald's become living symbols of American prosperity and innovation, and therefore of American superiority over the rest of the world. To a lesser degree, this public awe spread to many of the other new chains. A barrage of television commercials sparked widespread curiosity about these new restaurants and their products. But as McDonald's became entrenched from coast to coast as a leading source of America's food, critics of both the company and the cuisine proliferated. Beginning in the 1960s and accelerating through the 1980s, criticism of fast food appeared in medical journals, the popular press, and books. Journalists, consumer advocate groups, physicians, and political groups all decried the power of the leading chains, complaining about issues ranging from monopolistic business tactics to nutritional irresponsibility. They cited academic studies proving the high fat content of fast food, testimonies from small local restaurant owners driven from business by the major chains, government investigations into the exploitation of teenage laborers, and warnings about the dangers of excessive homogeneity.

In 1989, the *New England Journal of Medicine* published a study showing that fat comprised between 40 and 55 percent of the calories in typical fast-food items such as french fries and hamburgers.[21] In 1988, *Consumer Reports* stated that "a steady diet of typical fast-food items would overload you with protein, fat, and calories while shortchanging you on vitamins, minerals, and fiber."[22] Other nutritional advocates warned consumers of fast food's high cholesterol content and encouraged a return to the presumed healthier eating habits of the past.[23]

Frightened by these reports and exposés, the leading chains rushed to accommodate more health-conscious consumers by offering alternatives to their traditional fare. Salad bars or ready-made salads became new standards on the overhead menu displays, in addition to new sandwiches claiming a lower fat content or fewer calories. McDonald's publicly atoned for past sins by making a highly publicized switch from animal to vegetable oil for its french fries and offering other products with greatly reduced fat. Interestingly, despite the dire warnings from consumer groups and the medical community, the buying public did not respond enthusiastically to these new offerings. After a brief flirtation with lower-calorie and lower-fat products, many fast-food diners soon returned to their quarter-pound patties and deep-fried chicken pieces.

Critics also attacked the fast-food chains for their working conditions, their use of teenage workers, and the comparatively low wages paid throughout the industry. Most chains mechanized each function in their restaurants. Food was often produced on an assembly line, with automatically timed cookers, frozen patties, and premeasured soft drink servings, thereby requiring workers to have only a cursory understanding of the food preparation process and to know only how to interact with machines and customers.

Cooking hamburgers in these outlets provided little latitude for creativity. By design, the chains usually hired young, unskilled workers and quickly taught them how to perform virtually every function in the restaurant, though not expertise in any particular area. The purpose of this approach was to minimize the effect of high employee turnover, to make each employee expendable. The result was low wages and little employee bargaining power. Many of the chains in this newest generation of fast food, such as McDonald's and Burger King, raised their net profitability by hiring from the abundant pool of baby-boomer teenagers.

Fast-food chains routinely paid these teenagers only federal minimum wages and constantly lobbied for the creation of even lower "youth minimums." Critics charged that some of these companies rose to power and wealth reliant on the exploited labor of teenagers. This reliance on teenage labor by the major franchised chains and minimum wage pay structure further lowered the status and desirability of working in a fast-food restaurant. For years, the scene in most chain-franchised outlets was one of a dozen teenaged workers wearing paper hats following the directions of a tie-clad male manager in his twenties. Neither oblivious to negative publicity nor willing to greatly increase their labor costs, McDonald's and other chains began their own media blitz to publicize how working in a fast-food operation was an ideal first job for young people, the starting point for many successful careers. Instead of directly addressing the issues of wages or exploitation, these chains pointed to their civic involvement, charity work, and more positive hiring practices, such as the employment of handicapped workers.

By the end of the 1980s and the end of the baby boom, the franchised chains no longer had at their disposal an endless supply of young workers to make and serve their tacos, pizzas, hamburgers, and chicken. With fewer teenagers to employ, some chains actively recruited retired persons and unskilled adult women returning to the workforce after raising families.[24] Despite the greater age, experience, and maturity of these new employees, the working conditions remained the same, and wages remained consistently low throughout the industry, since paying low wages was a key ingredient in many chains' profitability.

Still other critics warned that the growing fast-food culture was forcing an excessively homogeneous diet on the American people. Indeed, Americans consumed 50 percent more chicken and beef in 1976 than they had in 1960, mainly because the fast-food chains usually served only those two meats. The chains' generally limited menus further limited people's exposure to food. Soft drinks, iceberg lettuce, and ketchup were fast-food mainstays and soon ranked among the most often consumed foods in the nation. Vegetables offered on fast-food salad bars often set the parameters for overall vegetable consumption, thus affecting production choices for growers. Richard Pillsbury points out that traditional American favorites, such as turkey, sweet potatoes, and green beans, faded into the background because these are not the food offered on "Hamburger Alley." Pillsbury observes that the industry "shifted roles from being the product of our foodways to being the cause of them."[25] Although he is certainly correct, this trend began much earlier. Just as Billy Ingram had sold both the sandwich and the idea of the hamburger to an earlier America, Ray Kroc, Ronald McDonald and others now taught modern consumers to enjoy specific fast food such as Big Macs, Whoppers, and Egg McMuffins. The only real difference was the size and scope of the endeavor. These lessons now even began at younger ages, teaching small children about fast food through brightly decorated Happy Meals and honey-dipped Chicken McNuggets.

The Demise of the Weaker Giants

Many of the fast-food chains disappeared from sight just as quickly as they appeared. In 1968, the United States had 136 franchised chains specializing in hamburgers, hot dogs, or chicken, and the future seemed bright.[26] But by the end of the 1980s, some of the largest chains had either sold their last outlets to competitors or just closed their doors. The last of this crowd was Burger Chef, which finally sold off its remaining assets to the Hardees System. Enjoying a solid position in the late 1960s as the "number two" chain in the industry, Burger Chef began to unravel in the early 1970s and was soon on the auction block or, more accurately, was sold at a salvage sale. Although Burger Chef was the largest chain to vanish, it was certainly not the only one. The central Atlantic Gino's peaked at 303 company-owned units by the late 1970s but quickly descended into financial ruin after attempting to expand into California. Gino's eventually sold its properties to Hardee's and Marriott and faded away.[27]

Carrol's, a Syracuse, New York-based hamburger chain shrank from 160 outlets in the late 1960s to approaching bankruptcy a decade later. Unable to compete with McDonald's, Carrol's closed all its outlets in 1981 and immediately resurrected seventy-six of them as the more competitive Burger Kings. As a result of this switch, the profits for each unit shot up within the first year. Recognizing the power of affiliating with a giant chain, Carrol's president David J. Connor later commented, "These are the same restaurants at the same locations with the same people. All we did was change the name."[28] Nonetheless, a large and formerly profitable company succumbed to the growing dominance of the national chains.

The L&K chain of Marion, Ohio, in the early 1950s America's largest hamburger chain, decided to sell its hundreds of restaurants to other firms and redirect its energy and resources into the motel business. Even perennial White Tower ceased to exist as a chain in the 1980s, although disassociated White Tower restaurants still can be found in many cities.

Different variables accounted for each of these fast-food failures, but many common threads can be detected. Some analysts point to larger corporate ownership as a key factor in the closure of these chains. Burger Chef began as an appendage of a larger manufacturing concern, only to be sold to General Foods as an investment during its boom period in 1968. Burger Chef's largest franchisee later attributed the chain's collapse to General Equipment's overemphasis on developing better equipment and ignoring the management structure. Others believe that in addition to other problems, General Foods managers made poor real estate-planning decisions.[29] The conventional wisdom among many in the industry is that many conglomerate executives just did not understand the need for flexibility and quick response in the ever-changing fast-food industry.

Other theories blame the failure of many fast-food chains on the erratic economy rather than corporations or individuals. Industry analyst Robert Emerson points to the recession of 1973/74, resulting from the disastrous oil embargo, as the primary cause of the major failures. Although overall fast-food sales remained strong during the recession, profitability was not evenly distributed across the industry. Thus chains such as McDonald's and Burger King prospered and rapidly expanded, but Gino's, Borden's Burgers, Wetson's, Burger Chef, and others began a precipitous decline. Still other chains struggled just to hold on to their market share and remain in the black.[30] Emerson contends that those chains that fared well during the recession reinforced their dominant positions in the industry and often swallowed up their weaker competitors. But those chains that endured hardship and forced retrenchment during the crisis never fully recovered and eventually slipped out of existence.

White Castle's Role in the New Generation of Fast Food

Even as the giant franchised chains solidified their hold on the American appetite between 1960 and 1990, White Castle maintained its control over a narrower, yet quite profitable slice of the fast-food market. White Castle actually spent the first part of this era learning to compete with a new book of rules. The widespread franchising, numerous hamburger alternatives, and new advertising vehicles greatly altered the industry to which White Castle had given birth years earlier. Beginning the 1960s with only ninety Castles, White Castle barely qualified as even a medium-sized hamburger chain. Some observers at the time predicted that White Castle would soon disappear in the wake of the these larger chains, taking with it the era of small, urban, porcelain eateries. Such pessimism about the future of the company was not unwarranted, considering looming factors such as urban decline, oversaturation in the hamburger business, and changing population patterns. Despite the overwhelming odds and adjustment to rapid changes, however, White Castle survived the "burger wars" and found a viable role in the industry.

The 1960s was not the first time that changing lifestyles and economic realities forced Billy Ingram and White Castle to reevaluate their position and their customer base. A hamburger market did not exist when Ingram started the White Caste System in 1921, so he went out and created one. Within a decade, a hamburger-hungry following extended from Wichita to New York City, including every major city in between. Just as Ingram's hamburger craze took root, the Great Depression appeared, threatening the life of this fledgling fast-food industry. Although many of his imitators and competitors failed during the 1930s, Ingram used this adversity to his own advantage, by broadening his customer base to include the middle class and even increasing the number of his Castles. Ingram even kept his company profitable during World War II, albeit in a reduced form, as the nation faced shortages and other extreme hardships. Although daunting, facing the onslaught of McDonald's and the rapidly changing market of the 1960s seemed mild compared with the task of creating an industry and then shepherding it through two of the worst calamities in American history. With his son Edgar overseeing the day-to-day operations, Ingram began the

1960s with his usual optimism. Later, in his eighties, he often reflected on past glories and achievements. At least in public statements, Billy Ingram tended to speak more about the past than the present. At the 1965 annual managers' meeting, he closed the session with these remarks:

> Our business has been wonderful. The reports that come in weekly amaze me. I can't help but to think constantly of the activities of the people in the Castles and the pressure that is put on them from time to time. I don't know where we are going. We don't know where we are going. We don't know whether we should add equipment to our units or whether we should put our units nearer together. I think that time will, in some measure, solve a lot of these things. I think that we are in a wonderful era of success.[31]

In keeping with his lifelong perspective, these last words from Billy Ingram to his managers were optimistic and intended as inspirational. His benign view of the hamburger business was certainly different from Ray Kroc's image of rats eating other rats. To the end, Billy Ingram's approach to his employees, customers, and even his competitors was kind and honorable. He did not live to attend another managers' meeting but died in May 1966.

White Castle continued after Billy's death, but being competitive and profitable in this new era of fast food in the 1960s required more than just success in the past and optimistic words for the future. Indeed, Ray Kroc did have a realistic image of the modern fast-food industry. Edgar Ingram quickly realized that competing head-to-head with the franchised giants would not work, so instead he decided to capitalize on White Castle's unique image and strengths. Under his leadership, White Castle held on to its existing market share and even extended it.

Ingram did this by identifying White Castle's existing customer base, targeting its marketing efforts toward this base, and changing every aspect of its business to accommodate these customers' needs or desires. He directed the development of new food products, a wide variety of advertising strategies, and a new wave of Castle construction. But in addition to doing battle in the increasingly fierce fast-food marketplace, his reign over White Castle was plagued by racial controversy in the cities, militant consumer activism, and growing unionism in the restaurant business. Having been his father's understudy for more than thirty years, Edgar competently dealt with each obstacle. He also maintained his father's approach to the hamburger business, emphasizing quality, cleanliness, and service in every facet of the operation. Nonetheless, his leadership style could be best described as cautious. Not the promoter and motivator of people that his father was,

Edgar Ingram was known instead as a careful and detail-oriented manager, always planning and looking ahead.

The greatest difference between his and his father's management styles was that Edgar seemed more inclined to delegate authority and responsibility, seeking out qualified subordinates to perform specific tasks. For example, Ingram had the new advertising director, Gail Turley, begin a comprehensive media effort to bring in customers. Sharply contrasting with the former ad chief, Benny Benfer, who believed only in the value of newspaper coupons, Turley was convinced that effective television and radio advertising was necessary.

Little thought or strategy had gone into previous advertising campaigns, and almost nothing had been done to measure their effectiveness, other than to count how many coupons were returned during each hamburger sale. Now, with far fewer advertising dollars to spend than its larger rivals had, White Castle had to maximize the effect of every bit of advertising. Rather than just printing coupons in newspapers and calculating their return rate, Turley systematized the entire process of marketing and advertising. After establishing White Castle's customer base, Turley then designed the advertising to reach them most effectively. He also developed a "customer profile," identifying the primary juvenile customer as a child between six and twelve years old, with teenagers the second largest cohort. His surveys also showed that males aged nineteen to twenty-five were the largest adult cohort eating at the Castles, with females in that same age bracket making up the second largest group.

Turley also discovered from these surveys why customers patronized White Castle: first, for the taste of the White Castle hamburger; second, for the inexpensive price; third, for quality; and finally, for cleanliness and convenience. With this knowledge of who his customers were and why they came to White Castle, Turley designed and directed a comprehensive advertising campaign to reinforce their patronage and to attract others to the Castles. In addition to radio advertising, White Castle spent more and more money on buying television time. Turley saw television as an effective way of reaching children, citing the positive experience of other fast-food companies.

By 1970, television was a regular means of Castle advertising in every market, broadcasting the slogan "The White Castle Hamburger. Without It, All Hamburgers Would Taste the Same." Impressed by the favorable public reaction in Columbus to the White Castle commercial before the *Lassie* show each Sunday evening, Ingram praised the use of television ads, noting that "even though [they are] expensive, [they] can be very effective."[32] Turley thus advocated even greater usage of television and the production of several different commercials, pointing out that it would "be impossible to make a commercial that would suit everyone, as tastes and beliefs vary" and warning against the one-station, one time-slot syndrome, such as White Castle's local sponsorships of *Lassie*. He also suggested the novel approach of spoofing White Castle's image in radio and television ads, explaining,

> This is an effort to place emphasis on those things which are distinctive about the White Castle hamburger; its size and the fact that it is square and also to recognize the fact that sometimes laugh at our products and convert this into a selling point, i.e. "They also laughed . . . then they tasted."

Turley's idea to use the more comical aspects of White Castle's products was not well received by the managers. What they did like was the fact that both radio and television advertising brought more customers to the Castles.

Even though White Castle recognized the necessity of modern advertising, Edgar Ingram constantly reminded his managers that there had to be substance behind the commercials. In 1971, he stressed to his management staff at their annual meeting that quality products and good service were more crucial than advertising to attracting and retaining customers.

One of Ingram's first official directives was that each shipment of ground beef be sampled in "test sandwiches" and that he receive regular reports on them. He wanted even more detailed reports if any meat was found to be inadequate and returned to Swift.[33] Like his father, Edgar took great pride in the fact that White Castle made hamburgers "using good steady grade of lean meat, and no imported beef in our product."[34] White Castle bought beef from both Armour and Swift, and Ingram constantly compared the quality of each. A few years later, he reinforced this attention to meat quality by issuing quality control test kits to area managers, enabling them to spot-check the meat on a regular basis.

In 1969 Ingram commissioned the Ohio State University College of Agriculture and Animal Sciences to replicate the 1930 University of Minnesota study of the nutritional value of White Castle hamburgers. The 1930 study had proclaimed White Castle's burgers to be a nutritionally ideal food, but Ingram was cautious about making such sweeping claims again. As America became increasingly health conscious in the late 1960s and early 1970s, few consumers would believe that hamburgers ranked among the healthiest food options. Aware of this, Edgar's expectations for this new study were quite modest. When he commissioned it, he stated frankly,

In many instances the results of this type of study are advertised in a misleading way. . . . We would want to use the test results in a completely truthful manner, and that even if they are not used in an advertising campaign, we would want to be in a position to assure our own people that we are serving a first-class product.[35]

After Ohio State completed the analysis, White Castle's director of research and sales promotion, Bill Long, announced that "the tests to date are encouraging, but we definitely will not want to state that one can only eat White Castle hamburgers and maintain a stable diet, as there is not enough of the four basic food groups." Edgar concluded this discussion of the research by saying, "Although we would not want to advertise that a person could live on White Castle products alone, we will have the satisfaction of knowing we are doing a good job."

This emphasis on quality control resulted partly from White Castle's pride in its products but also from the rise in consumer activism and government regulation. Consumer research groups began publishing exposés of poor food quality at other chains, and Edgar Ingram wanted to make sure that White Castle did not become a target of these reports. The company used the defense of having nothing to hide, monitoring its own food quality so carefully that no one else could find fault.

Racial unrest and conflict more directly affected White Castle than other fast-food chains in the 1960s because most of the outlets of the leading franchised chains were located in predominantly white suburbia, whereas most of White Castle's restaurants were in urban neighborhoods that had become heavily African American since World War II. Although White Castle never segregated its restaurants and was long known among African Americans as a place where they would be readily served, a frequent complaint arose in the early 1960s that White Castle employed very few black workers. In fact, in many cities the company had no black employees, which was particularly troubling as blacks comprised an increasingly large percentage of White Castle's customer base.

White Castle's managers quickly realized that they were at fault in this situation, and they immediately took corrective steps. Confronted by growing criticism and a brief boycott in New York City in July 1963, White Castle actively started recruiting more black workers and soon achieved an acceptable racial balance in its workforce. In addition, the company printed and distributed booklets entitled "All Rights," outlining its policies against employment discrimination. The controversy over race, however, did not end there, continuing throughout the remainder of the decade. The home office directed area and Castle managers to maintain detailed "records of nondiscrimination" in the event that White Castle's hiring or employment practices were questioned. Although the issue did arise on numerous occasions, White Castle was never cited for any further incidents of racial discrimination.

Crime and violence remained the most pressing problems for White Castle in the 1960s. As a primarily urban institution open around the clock, these troubles were not new to the company, having begun during World War II. At that time, White Castle took steps to protect its female operators from assault and harassment. In addition, because they were open in the early morning hours, the Castles were frequently robbed. To some degree, White Castle accepted these risks early on as the inevitable result of staying open all night in cities. In the early 1960s, however, violence and crime had escalated well past the point of tolerance, and White Castle was forced to invest heavily in security measures. In light of the growing violence and the money it entailed, Ingram instructed his management staff to close at night all those Castles that they deemed necessary for the employees' safety.

Because White Castle was an all-night—or at least a late-night—urban restaurant, it often became a haven for the homeless and the "people of the night." Since the brightly lit Castles were sometimes the only oases on dark city streets, people spanning a broad range of economic class and occupation came in for hamburgers and hot coffee. White Castles served at night mostly shift workers going to and from factories, nighttime workers such as police officers and cab drivers, and people leaving bars, but they also attracted many nocturnal street people seeking warmth, shelter, or toilet facilities in the early morning hours. In the absence of suitable shelter facilities, many used White Castle's rest rooms to bathe as best they could. White Castle accepted these customers from the street—or anyone else for that matter—with great toleration, excluding them only if they caused a significant disturbance. Their volume accelerated in the 1970s and 1980s as the overall number of homeless persons rose following the movement to deinstitutionalize the mentally ill. White Castle still welcomed all customers as long as they purchased coffee or food items and did not cause a disturbance. The liability to White Castle for this open acceptance policy was that other, more mainstream patrons sometimes felt uncomfortable among the homeless, and their discomfort led many to seek out other places for a late-night meal or snack, resulting in lower sales for many of the downtown Castles. In some areas, working-class and middle-class customers became wary of visiting White Castle and similar restaurants in the late evening and early morning, and many Castles soon became stigmatized as unsavory places.

Despite the combined problems of crime, violence, and vagrancy, White Castle maintained its operations in urban neighborhoods. For the construction of newer Castles, however, most of the managers agreed that either the suburbs or the solidly working-class sections of the cities were preferable to the inner city.

The Rise of Suburban Castles

By the late 1960s, White Castle was still expanding very slowly. The company began the decade with ninety outlets and had only 112 ten years later. This lack of new building frustrated Ingram, who knew that the company could make even greater profits by edging out toward the suburbs, but he did not have enough capital to start a large-scale expansion. The area managers grew concerned that the slow rate of expansion was hindering the employees' upward mobility, thus offering them little incentive for careers with the company. Although sales and profits continued to remain strong throughout the 1960s, the company was relatively "cash poor" due to a large sum owed to the Internal Revenue Service.

When Billy Ingram died in 1966, he left the company to his family, who were then responsible for a huge inheritance tax. This liability was especially burdensome, since most of the inheritance was in the form of the company itself, rather than cash or other forms of wealth that could be liquidated to pay the taxes. The Ingrams agreed that the company should stay intact, and to do that, all available cash reserves had to be used to pay the government. To forestall rumors, Edgar quickly reassured his managers that no part of the company would be sold, nor were any mergers or changes planned. Maintaining this status quo also meant a moratorium on expansion. With so much money committed to the tax debt, there was little left to build new Castles. The company's general counsel announced that the company was in sound fiscal shape but warned managers to "brace for expenditures in the near future."[36] The next year, he elaborated: "The company is in good financial position with good prospects for future profits. . . . However, the requests for capital expenditures must be, and are being controlled to provide for 'planned growth' with proper provision for present and future commitments." The White Castle managers thus understood that few new Castles would be built in the near future. Both to economize and to generate needed revenue, White Castle shut down its Miami operation and sold Billy's properties in Florida.

Other ideas were also considered as a means to obtain the capital necessary for expansion. When one manager proposed borrowing to fund new buildings, Edgar rejected the idea, explaining that "we do not want to borrow from outside sources, as this ends up with representatives sitting on our board, and once this occurs, they begin running our business, which is certainly something we would prefer to avoid."[37] But he made it clear that significant building would commence as soon as White Castle paid off its tax obligations.

In 1968, Ingram announced the criteria for the placement of new construction: traffic and general activity in the area, accessibility and visibility, competition (type and amount), income of the area's residents, secondary area (residential, commercial, or industrial), and growth in the area. The managers agreed that these factors pointed to building most of the new Castles in the suburbs. At the same time, however, some still wanted to keep a foothold in White Castle's traditional urban neighborhoods, citing its vast existing customer base. Moving in the opposite direction of its franchised competitors, White Castle maintained its urban strength while venturing out into McDonald's and Burger King's suburban territory.

By the mid-1970s, however, many of the larger franchised chains were going in the other direction; having already saturated the suburbs, they had begun turning their marketing sights on urban consumers.[38] McDonald's and Burger King soon appeared in busy downtown areas to accommodate daytime customers, but most of their outlets closed either at the end of the business day or near sunset. The chains also opened outlets in selected urban residential areas, usually with hours and services similar to those at their suburban locations. Before long, the major chains became fixtures in most American cities, offering stiff competition to existing restaurants and driving many established eateries from business. Despite the major chains' successful encroachment into the cities, White Castle held on to most of its customers and market share. Although it never posed a serious threat to McDonald's and Burger King's dominance of the suburban market, White Castle gained a permanent, if relatively small, foothold in the new shopping malls and housing tracts.

White Castle's presence in suburbia accelerated in the late 1970s when Edgar Ingram retired and his son, Edgar Waldo "Bill" Ingram III, took over the company. Following his graduation from college in 1972, Bill began working at White Castle as an administrative assistant in the accounting department, assuming positions of greater responsibility over the next few years. In 1979 he became president and chief executive officer, with his father becoming chairman of the board.

White Castle began expanding rapidly under Bill's direction, adding nine new Castles in his first year and then almost doubling the total number of Castles within a decade. Some of the new buildings replaced outdated Castles, but most were constructed along suburban highways on the outskirts of traditional White Castle cities. Still others were built in metropolitan areas where White Castle had never been before. With the exception of White Castle's brief foray into Miami, from 1959 to 1967, the company had avoided expanding into new territories since the 1920s. The company's territory actually shrank over the decades, with Castles operating in fourteen cities in 1930 but in only ten by 1979. In the 1980s, however, Bill Ingram directed White Castle's expansion into Dayton and Cleveland, Ohio; Lexington, Kentucky; Nashville; Philadelphia; and back into Kansas City, Missouri, at a pace paralleling the company's 1920s growth. Some of these new cities, such as Dayton, filled in geographic areas between thriving Castle cities, whereas others such as Philadelphia and Nashville extended White Castle's territory in entirely new directions. Still predominantly in the northeast quadrant of the United States and still tiny in comparison to the national chains, White Castle expanded to almost three hundred restaurants and finally regained its position as a leading fast-food hamburger chain. Castles soon dotted many suburban thoroughfares, competing head-to-head with smaller specialty chains such as Rally's or Hot-n-Now and, to a lesser degree, with giants McDonald's and Burger King. White Castle was bigger and stronger than ever before and became established as a permanent player in modern fast food. This new success was just another chapter in the company's long history. Over time, White Castle went from being an undisputed industry leader to limping along as a survivor and a distant competitor to finally emerging as a distinctive and unique force in the new fast-food industry.

How Did White Castle Survive and Thrive?

Ray Kroc was right. Few competitions in the history of American business could compare with the "burger wars" of the 1960s and 1970s in either ferocity or number of casualties. Entrepreneurs built immense chains, but in a few years some of these immense chains vanished from the landscape.

Fortunes were made and then quickly lost. Industry analyst Robert Emerson describes the "endless shakeout" in the fast-food industry, pointing to the rash of chain failures and mergers in the 1970s and the constant peril to all but the strongest chains.[39] While many of the larger chains perished, White Castle not only survived throughout this modern "shakeout" but actually grew into a much stronger company. White Castle proved itself as a survivor after the Great Depression and World War II, but the growth of the fast-food giants and the resulting drastic changes in the hamburger industry should have finally claimed White Castle, as it did many of the older chains. White Towers became boarded-up eyesores along deteriorating city streets. Big Boy stood alone outside an increasing number of empty restaurants. Once numbering in the hundreds, Kewpee's dwindled to fewer than a dozen individually owned outlets. For the most part, the earlier generations of fast food passed away, leaving the industry to the young and vibrant McDonald's, Wendy's, Hardee's, and Burger King.

Surprisingly, White Castle was not among the many casualties. Logically, White Castle should have died along with these others, but instead it only grew. The reasons for its remarkable survival and prosperity, however, defy both marketplace logic and business trends in recent history. In a world where bigger chains grew to dominate and set the pace of competition, tiny White Castle ran at a slower speed, advertising far less than most other chains and selling simpler products. Some people claim that White Castle's key to survival was its consistently lower hamburger prices, but most of White Castle's customers always knew that the small, five-holed square burgers were proportionately just as expensive as McDonald's or Burger King's larger sandwiches. That is, many customers compensated for the hamburger's small size by eating between four and ten "White Castles" at a time, with their average bill comparable to that at most of the other chains. Thus low price was not really the key to White Castle's survival.

Certainly the ambience of most White Castles did not draw in customers. Unlike the major chains, which frequently designed and redesigned their dining rooms, White Castle remained simple and spartan. The interiors of the more modern Castles were still crafted in the same Porcelain Steel Buildings shop that produced the Castle interiors of the 1930s. Instead of customers ordering their food across open, sweeping counters as they did at many modern chains, most Castles still have a formidable chest-high stainless steel barrier and windows separating customers from operators. White Castle customers order their burgers and coffee at three or four openings in this wall. Compared with the major chains, other parts of the

Castle interior also remain sparse, offering diners booths consisting of basic formica tables with brightly colored, molded-plastic seating. Different from the rest of the industry, White Castle never indulged in comfortable or ornate furniture, potted plants, faux café settings, children's play areas, or large statues of their mascots. (White Castle, in fact, never even devised a mascot.) Above all else, it is a safe guess that few customers ever went to White Castle for the lavish or constantly updated decor. By the early 1990s, White Castle's interiors anachronistically still resembled many fast-food outlets of the 1950s, with some definite aspects of even earlier days.

Why White Castle continued to thrive is not easy to determine. It was inexpensive, but not extraordinarily so; it was usually clean and neat, but by no means truly attractive; and its selection of offerings was slim in comparison to that of other chains. White Castle had capable managers to direct operations and expansion, but so had the defunct Burger Chef, White Tower, and Gino's chains. Yet despite the odds, White Castle continued to grow between 1960 and 1990, attracting an entirely new generation of loyal customers. True to its origins, White Castle specifically targeted the working class in much of its advertising, as opposed to other chains, which appealed to a broader constituency or even just to the middle class. This directed marketing succeeded in attracting a large cohort of working-class customers. These customers provided substantial revenue, but they were still not the secret to White Castle's success. The primary reason for White Castle's growth and prosperity is not so readily quantifiable by industry analysts nor easily understood by anyone not enamored with White Castle or its hamburgers. The truth about its success is actually quite simple: White Castle has a legion of loyal fans who yearn for only White Castles, while McDonald's, Burger King, and all the other chains only share a multitude of hungry and often fickle customers.

Discerning this difference between "customer base" and "devoted followers" is crucial to understanding why White Castle still thrives. White Castle has a large loyal following most easily equated with the thousands of admirers of the rock band The Grateful Dead who traveled around the country and the world attending each concert or with the millions of people worldwide compulsively collecting information, memorabilia, and artifacts from the television show *Star Trek*. Just as the famed "Deadheads" or "Trekkies" formed virtual cults around the repetitive music or the rerunning episodes, White Castles' fans built a culture around the company and its food. Also comparable to the Deadheads and Trekkies, much of the rest of the population wondered in amazement as to why otherwise rational people would fixate on such offbeat phenomena. Even more than these other cultish followings, White Castle fanatics span virtually all ethnicities, social classes, and age groups. These fanatics abound everywhere, paying homage to White Castle in a variety of ways. Many people scour antique shows and shops searching for coveted White Castle stoneware artifacts from yesteryear. This year the Princeton University Band sponsored its ninth annual White Castle hamburger-eating contest, with the winner consuming more than thirty burgers. A poetry society centered on White Castle annually holds a nocturnal meeting at a Castle in Columbus, Ohio, reading their newest odes to the burgers and the culture. The Internet is now peppered with numerous "unofficial" home pages celebrating different aspects of White Castle, each showing a tally of tens of thousands of "visitors" to their site. For decades, burgers packed in dry ice have been shipped to White Castle fanatics across the country and around the world. Some devotees even stuff their Thanksgiving turkeys with mashed and minced White Castles. Such quirky affection for White Castle is a great social equalizer. Castle dining areas often form a socioeconomic "common ground" where truck drivers eat alongside physicians who eat next to the homeless. True to the results of the 1960s marketing survey, many customers came to White Castle for the unique taste of the hamburgers, but for many others the White Castle experience was more than just simply eating fast-food hamburgers. Deadheads often imbued the Grateful Dead's music with meaning, and Trekkies often view the words of Mr. Spock and Captain Kirk as profound prophecy. On a more realistic and earthly level, White Castle is similar. Although rarely articulated as such, eating at White Castle for many diehard fans is a symbolic act performed on a regular basis, ranging at intervals from daily to annually.

The notion of ritualistic eating is not limited to White Castle but, rather, is an ancient practice commonly discussed by anthropologists and historians. Feasts and feast days abound throughout the human past. To devoted White Castle fans, the act of eating at White Castle just follows in that legacy. Food has always had greater cultural meaning than just being mere sustenance, and the act of coming to White Castle represents different meanings to many different people. To some it means going home. It is not uncommon for suburbanites to nostalgically return to their old neighborhoods to dine at the White Castles they knew in their youth. To the most avid fans, the simplicity of White Castle brings them back to what they perceive to be a simpler world in a simpler time. In this sense, coming to White Castle for many modern people possibly has the same effect that busloads of suburban tourists derive from gazing at the Amish in rural areas. Simple hamburgers sold in very spartan surroundings are reminiscent of earlier days. In addition to this return to simplicity, on a more conscious level many White Castle customers revel in the fact that they are participating in something that they deem historical. Most have a vague idea about the company's history and know that they are in some sense eating America's original fast-food hamburger. On any day in any Castle, it is actually quite common to hear customers discussing the company's history while waiting in line for their sacks of burgers. These avid fans are among the very few Americans who still remember that fast-food hamburgers existed before Ray Kroc and his McDonald's propaganda machine and appreciate the tradition of White Castle. To the "uninitiated," the allure of White Castle seems most odd and unappealing. Why anyone would crave these quirky little burgers is a mystery to many. Some people just do not like White Castle, especially those who disdain onions, the close mingling of social classes, or the stark surroundings. Visitors smell onions as they walk in the door and often leave with the scent clinging to their clothes. Many others dismiss White Castle out of hand, without ever venturing in to taste a burger. Over the years, customers coined a multitude of derisive or sarcastic terms for the company and its hamburgers, including *porcelain palace* and *sliders*. (After successfully dodging the term *slider* since the 1930s, White Castle finally embraced it and featured it in its advertising but changed the spelling to Slyder for copyright reasons.) These commonly used nicknames in themselves are enough to keep many queasy diners at bay. Interestingly enough, White Castle aficionados use these slang terms with great affection, not deterred by the criticisms of the weak stomached. For these fans a trip to White Castle is like nothing else. Rather than eating uniform and picture-perfect Big Mac's or Whoppers, they prefer their hamburgers tiny, cooked in and laden with pungent onions, buns steamed to an almost custardlike consistency, sharply contrasting with the crispness of the pickle slices. Their devotion to these small burgers and to the company itself has been the unlikely secret to White Castle's continued prosperity.

Epilogue
White Castle's Role in History

Like an septuagenarian still running marathons, White Castle continues to compete with other, stronger and faster chains and still enjoys remarkable health. Remaining a vibrant and growing company after more than seventy-five years in the hamburger business, White Castle currently owns approximately three hundred restaurants distributed across fourteen cities in the United States. In addition, the company also still operates its subsidiary, Porcelain Steel Buildings, and recently began a thriving frozen-food plant that makes and distributes White Castle hamburgers to grocery stores across the country. The company's overall combined sales for 1995 exceeded $325 million. White Castle also recently announced a new partnership with the franchised chain Church's Chicken, in which the two companies will share space and personnel in some of their restaurants, but with each selling its own food products. This new expansion, combined with six new franchised stores in Mexico City, point to a bright future for White Castle.

When Billy Ingram first emblazoned the phrase "A National Institution" on all his company's letterheads, food packaging, literature, and mugs, he optimistically proclaimed his expectation that White Castle would eventually spread from coast to coast. Over the years, the turbulence of history and the realities of capital and competition dampened this dream, but in the 1950s he still alluded to the notion of growing nationally. Although White Castle possibly reigned over the industry in the 1920s and 1930s, its star was soon eclipsed by larger and more powerful fast-food chains. These companies, such as McDonald's and Burger King, eventually became the national entities that Billy Ingram long dreamed of becoming. They exist in virtually every town in America, making their hamburgers accessible to every American consumer. Their many thousands of outlets dwarf White Castle's few hundred. In the corporate sense of the phrase, these newer chains can more rightfully bear claim to being America's "national institutions."

In another sense, however, Billy Ingram far exceeded his goal of creating a "national institution," although not as he specifically intended nor strictly to White Castle's advantage. While his hamburger chain grew to only a relatively modest size, his innovations took the country by storm, creating not one but two new significant national institutions. As the first purveyor of the hamburger in a systematic or concerted manner and as the originator of the modern fast-food "carryout" concept, Ingram created the national institutions of both the fast-food industry and the first truly distinctive American cuisine. He turned the hamburger from being considered virtually inedible to becoming the daily meal for millions of Americans.

The fact that Americans consume ten of millions of hamburgers each day is important for a multitude of reasons. One reason is purely economic. Americans spend many billions of dollars every year buying these burgers, fueling the growth of the fast-food industry and making it a major component of their modern economy. Millions of American jobs, ranging from cattle herders to slaughterhouse workers to part-time fast-food counter operators, depend on the health of this thriving industry. Much of the nation's cattle production winds up in fast-food wrappings, with hamburgers comprising more than 75 percent of the total beef consumed away from home.[1] Hundreds of tertiary industries also thrive in support of both beef production and retail fast food. These combined industries are driven by enthusiastic consumer demand. In 1994, fast-food restaurants in the United States served more than five billion burgers, increasing their total sold by almost 3 percent from the previous year. Consumers like them and consumers buy them, with 86.6 percent of all Americans ordering some type of hamburger sandwich at least once in 1994. This frequency of consumption indicates that the hamburger is both undeniably America's favorite meal and a significant commodity in the American marketplace.

Perhaps even more important than becoming America's preferred daily fare, the hamburger grew to become an even larger cultural and ethnic symbol, emerging as its most identifiable ethnic food. As the twentieth century began, America lacked its own distinctive ethnic cuisine and or other ethnic identifiers. Much of the population was either foreign born or were first- or second-generation Americans, still strongly identifying with the cultures of their homelands. English was both the dominant language and the prevailing ethnic norm in the United States at the time, and becoming "more American" in many ways meant conforming to a modified British ethnicity. Immigrant groups concentrated in ethnic enclaves resisted this conformity, but many gradually lost their sons and daughters to the majority culture. The presence of these many newcomers, however, conversely started to erode the Anglo-Saxon Protestant grip on American culture. Immigrant foods and immigrant ways soon invaded the restaurants and traditions of the dominant groups. The internal migration of African Americans from the South to the North added still other influences to the mix. America became a polyglot of languages, cuisines, and religious beliefs, undermining the old standard of British American ethnicity and replacing it with a kaleidoscope of cultural norms. Waves of immigrant Irish, Poles, and Italians created majorities in many major cities, resulting in a shift of both political and cultural power. Some turn-of-the-century social critics bemoaned the threat to Anglo dominance, warning that the United States was on a collision course with cultural chaos. Fearing this rise of "foreign" influence, many Nativist guardians called for an end to unrestricted immigration and for firm laws protecting English as the only official language. When the United States entered World War I in 1917, the country seemed destined to become even more divided by ethnicity, race, and region. Wartime and the years immediately following, however, reversed this trend. Rather than further fragmenting society, World War I and the early 1920s laid the foundation for a truly separate and distinctive American ethnicity. Conscripted troops from all ethnic backgrounds were thrown together in crowded barracks, forcing their recognition of commonalities and dispelling divisive stereotypes. After the war, boundaries between diverse groups were further weakened by the inception of new radio networks, motion pictures, and national advertisements for the booming consumer culture. For the first time, Americans in Albany, New York, laughed at the same jokes and danced to the same orchestras as Americans in Albuquerque, New Mexico. Automobiles became more affordable, soon physically linking communities and people closer together. The pace of all these combined changes was truly revolutionary. Within a decade, America's culture and ethnicity became increasingly homogenized and distinctive from that of their European cousins, enjoying new technologies, generating new art forms, and establishing a new sense of national identity. And yes, by the end of the 1920s, much of America was also enjoying the same hamburger sandwich as their common ethnic meal. Americans hungered for an ethnic food, and the hamburger appeared at just the right time to satisfy their need.

Without a doubt, the long-term effects of Billy Ingram's little burgers have been nothing less than incredible. While the size of the fast-food hamburger industry and the immense popularity of the hamburger itself are both obvious and quantifiable, scholars and social commentators from all political directions frequently point to even greater, if less tangible, social and political significance. Scholars and social critics discuss "fast-food culture" with meanings that go far beyond the actual food, making the term a metaphor for everything from other quick-service industries to excessive standardization in both culture and consumption patterns. Forgetting the actual origin of the fast-food industry, some even use the term *McDonaldize* as a synonym for creating a mass culture. In many corners, "fast food" and its numerous cultural connotations are demonized as most insidious threats to individuality, higher culture, and public health. Many critics mistakenly hark back to an idealized time before fast-food hamburgers of culinary heterogeneity and healthy eating among the masses, often indicting fast food as a primary culprit for what they perceive to be the deterioration of society. Their criticism of the hamburger and even the broader "fast-food culture" as homogenizing factors in society are accurate, but possibly only negative from their perspective. The same homogenizing trend that they criticize can be just as easily interpreted as the reinforcement of a single American ethnicity, which other political camps would herald as positive. Criticisms of fast food as a nutritional evil, however, are misplaced. To a large extent the nostalgic view of these critics is wildly distorted: the majority of Americans in the past never maintained a healthful or vitamin-enriched diet, and the introduction of fast-food hamburgers neither helped or hindered that norm. The fast-food industry that White Castle spawned, in fact, perhaps significantly improved the collective diet by providing the public with food that was usually standardized and uniform in terms of content and hygienic preparation. Although certainly not the "healthy" diet now known to modern science, fast-food fare is often no less nutritious than most of the meals eaten by Americans in earlier times. Similar to popular foods of any era, fast foods, and particularly hamburgers, appeal to the common palate, regardless of numbers concerning calories, cholesterol, or fat. The fact remains that fast-food critics comprise only a small slice of society, and despite their persistent ballyhoo, the vast majority of Americans remain passionate and unapologetic fast-food lovers.

Some theorists stretch the significance of fast food even further. Acknowledging that the fast-food hamburger is indeed America's ethnic food, some contend that this sandwich developed into an effective tool of United States foreign policy, claiming that the hamburger, Levi's blue jeans, and other Western material goods had more to do with tearing down the Berlin Wall than concepts such as democracy or freedom. Their ideas do have merit. Fast-food restaurants, along with our grocery superstores, are America's modern "amber waves of grain," symbolizing its vast abundance of food and material wealth and its excessive consumption. As communication ties strengthened with the Soviet bloc countries in the late 1980s, their people became more and more aware of the disparity in wealth and material goods between the two worlds. These people could then figuratively peer over the walls and see what they did not have. McDonald's moved into Moscow, providing an even closer look for Soviets at what Americans eat. Within a few short years after that, totalitarian regimes were toppled throughout Eastern Europe, and some semblance of capitalist consumer cultures took hold. This is not meant to suggest that the introduction of the hamburger simply inspired a wave of revolutions but, rather, that the burger, in conjunction with other perceived opulence from the Western world, only sharpened oppressed appetites yearning for both liberty and creature comforts. It is conceivable that these many revolutionary movements were more about freedom for capitalism than about freedom for the individual. Conversely, exporting capitalism and selling products may have been the true intent of the Western powers which long encouraged the downfall of communism. Despite the cold war rhetoric about fighting to guarantee freedom, democracy, and human rights to the peoples living under Soviet domination, today many Western nations excuse violations of these principles by Boris Yeltsin's regime in exchange for its protection of Russian capitalism. Perhaps the hamburger was even more the goal than just merely being the tool.

On a less dramatic or strategic level, fast food also has "Americanized" much of the developing world. Many streets in the second- and third-world cities are lined with McDonald's, Burger Kings, Wendy's, and many locally owned fast-food imitators. In fact, most American chains now own or franchise outlets outside the United States and Canada. In the past decade, White Castle has even attempted franchised operations in Malaysia, Korea, Japan, and now in Mexico. The aggregate effect of this exporting of fast food and other material goods is the subtle introduction of American culture around the world, far less brazen than earlier British imperialism and colonization, but with the similar outcome of spreading a cultural umbrella over other societies. Similar to the British three centuries ago, the purpose of this cultural imperialism is blatantly commercial. As American culture spreads to these other lands, so does the growing demand for American-made or -directed consumer goods. Fast food, along with a plethora of other American products, is now a booming commodity in the new global marketplace. McDonald's has more than two thousand restaurants in Japan alone, serving more than two million hamburgers each day.[2] In some sense, what became "American food" in the United States during the 1920s may now be on the road becoming a "world food." Although the possibility is absolutely dreadful to some, perhaps the entire planet will someday be "McDonaldized."

Billy Ingram obviously never intended to create a national ethnic food, much less a weapon of international policy; he just wanted to sell as many hamburgers as he possibly could. As a small-city entrepreneur, Ingram initially aspired only to make a good profit and grew as demand carried him. There is no precise or quantifiable reason that his chain became so popular, resulting a nationwide craze for these little burgers. Customers simply liked his products, and word spread about this new food. As with almost everything that occurs in history, variables of timing and location played a crucial role in his success. Ingram founded his chain at a watershed period in modern history, a time of great demographic and technological change, and a time when America was redefining itself. Ingram started his chain offering a good product at a good price in clean surroundings; all features appealing to customers of any era More than even his sound approach to business, however, it is likely that Billy Ingram, White Castle, and the hamburger were just in the right place at the right time. A little luck, a lot of hard work, and a hungry populace opened the door for White Castle's hamburgers to become America's food.

Notes

NOTES TO CHAPTER 1

1. Richard Osborn Cummings, *The American and His Food* (New York: Arno Press, 1970), 41–42.

2. Raymond Sokolov, *Why We Eat What We Eat: How Columbus Changed the Way the World Eats* (New York: Touchstone/Simon & Schuster, 1993), 148–49; Harvey Levenstein, *Revolution at the Table: The Transformation of the American Diet* (New York: Oxford University Press, 1988), 3–9.

3. Robert Wiebe, *The Search for Order, 1877–1920* (New York: Hill & Wang, 1967), 44–45.

4. John Whiteclay Chambers, *The Tyranny of Change: America in the Progressive Era, 1890–1920* (New York: St. Martin's Press, 1992), 119–20.

5. Waverly Root and Richard de Rochemont, *Eating in America: A History* (New York: Morrow, 1976), 354.

6. John Mariani, *America Eats Out* (New York: Morrow, 1991), 80–81; Paton Yoder, *Taverns and Travelers* (Bloomington: Indiana University Press, 1969), 142.

7. Levenstein, *Revolution at the Table*, 11–12.

8. David Nasaw, *Going Out: The Rise and Fall of American Amusements* (New York: Basic Books, 1993), 65, 81–82; Roy Rosenzweig, *Eight Hours for What We Will* (Cambridge: Cambridge University Press, 1983), 53; Richard Pillsbury, *From Boarding House to Bistro* (Cambridge, Mass.: Unwin Hyman, 1990), 21–23.

9. Root and de Rochemont, *Eating in America*, 319–21.

10. Mariani, *America Eats Out*, 43.

11. James Trager, *The Chronology of Food* (New York: Henry Holt, 1995), 400.

12. Mariani, *America Eats Out*, 44.

13. Interestingly, the same company that originated to meet the needs of the burgeoning rail industry in the nineteenth century failed to accept the first contract offer for in-flight food service on air carriers early in the twentieth century, believing that air travel did not have a viable future.

14. Roy Rosenzweig, *Eight Hours for What We Will*, 53.

15. Nasaw, *Going Out*, 13–14.

16. Levenstein, *Revolution at the Table*, 60–61.

17. Philip Langdon, *Orange Roofs, Golden Arches* (New York: Knopf, 1986), 9.

18. Root and de Rochemont, *Eating in America*, 336.

19. Ibid., 337.

20. Mariani, *America Eats Out*, 70, 77–78.

21. Ibid., 74.

22. Levenstein, *Revolution at the Table*, 190–91.

23. James Trager, *The Chronology of Food*, 345.

24. James Olson, *The Ethnic Dimension in American History* (New York: St. Martin's Press, 1994), 135; Alan Kraut, *The Huddled Masses* (Arlington Heights, Ill.: Harlan Davidson, 1982), 98–99.

25. Mary Douglas, ed., *Food in the Social Order* (New York: Russell Sage Foundation, 1984), 116–17.

26. Rosenzweig, *Eight Hours for What We Will*, 60–61, 187; Mariani, *America Eats Out*, 108–9.

27. Jeffrey Tennyson, *Hamburger Heaven* (New York: Hyperion, 1993), 16.

28. Mariani, *America Eats Out*, 108–10; John Baeder, *Diners* (New York: Abrams, 1978), 141–43.

29. Trager, *The Chronology of Food*, 356.

30. Ibid., 278.

31. Nasaw, *Going Out*, 82; Mariani, *America Eats Out*, 74.

32. Trager, *The Chronology of Food*, 388.

33. Ibid.

34. Phil Patton, *Made in the U.S.A.* (New York: Penguin Books, 1992), 22–24; Mariani, *America Eats Out*, 92, 110; Root and de Rochemont, *Eating in America*, 421.

35. Trager, *The Chronology of Food*, 323, 336–38.

36. Ibid., 324.

37. Root and de Rochemont, *Eating in America*, 417–23.

38. This competition with the alcoholic beverage industry was not accidental. Many of the new drinks were seductively called root *beer* or ginger *ale* and, in the case of Canada Dry in 1907, marketed as "the champagne of ginger ales."

39. In 1902 the pharmacy industry began publishing a trade magazine entitled *Soda Fountain*, whose articles and advertisements were directed at both pharmacy and soda fountain issues, since most stores had that dual function. Its name was changed in 1932 to *Soda Fountain Magazine*; in 1941, it became *Soda Fountain and Quick Serve*; in 1945 it became simply *Soda Fountain Service* and then *Fountain Service* later that year; and finally in 1956, it was renamed *Fast Food*. Indeed, the magazine's name itself represents many of the changes throughout the century in the casual restaurant business.

40. Mariani, *America Eats Out*, 256.

41. Levenstein, *Revolution at the Table*, 164.

42. Root and de Rochemont, *Eating in America*, 317; Trager, *The Chronology of Food*, 375, 405.

43. Tennyson, *Hamburger Heaven*, 16–18.

44. Karl Witzel, *The American Drive-In* (Osceola, Wisc.: Motor Books, 1995), 49.

45. Letter from the mayor of Hamburg, New York, Richard Hansen, on official letterhead stationery, to Kim Kelly-Bartley at the White Castle System, March 10, 1992. In this letter, Hansen states emphatically that the hamburger began in his town and that all other claimants are impostors.

46. Witzel, *The American Drive-In*, 49–50.

NOTES TO CHAPTER 2

1. "Romantic Story of the Hamburger Kings," *Everyweek Magazine*, April 26, 1931, 28–29.

2. "Walt Anderson—Hamburger King," *Wichita Eagle*, December 4, 1921, 8, 1–4.

3. *Teamsters*, November 1974, 14.

4. Dick Long, "Wichita Has Made Appetizing Hamburger Popular," *Wichita Eagle* (Sunday magazine supplement), December 6, 1925, in the "White Castle" file, Office of the Wichita City Historian, Wichita Public Library, Wichita, Kans.

5. Interestingly enough, this same William Dye is credited in midwestern folklore with devising and popularizing an Americanized version of chili, in essence, creating another culinary staple of American culture. Years later, the Pizza Hut chain also began in Wichita, once again offering an Americanized version of a foreign food.

6. Jeffrey Tennyson, *Hamburger Heaven* (New York: Hyperion, 1993), 21.

7. "All White Castles Gas Heated," *Cooking in Volume* (Chicago: People's Gas, Light, and Coke Company, 1930), vol. 7 (June): 1.

8. "Walt Anderson," *Wichita Eagle*, December 4, 1921, 8, 1–4.

9. Ibid.

10. Harvey Levenstein, *Paradox of Plenty: A Social History of Eating in Modern America* (New York: Oxford University Press, 1993), 228.

11. The idea of using white paint to promote cleanliness was already a norm for the interior of lunch-counter businesses, but White Castle was the first to take "this technique a step further by proclaiming a white, sanitary atmosphere on the outside." See Philip Langdon, *Orange Roof, Golden Arches* (New York: Knopf, 1986), 9–10.

12. Long, "Wichita Has Made," *Wichita Eagle*, December 6, 1925.

13. Ibid.

14. Arthur Kallet, *100,000,000 Guinea Pigs* (New York: Vanguard, 1933), 38–39.

15. Frederick Schlink, *Eat, Drink, and Be Wary* (New York: Covici, Friede, 1935).

16. Levenstein, *Paradox of Plenty*, 46–47.

17. "White Castle Food Experiment Department Opens," *Wichita Eagle*, May 27, 1928.

18. Tennyson, *Hamburger Heaven*, 24.

19. Thomas C. Dolly, "The Bottom Line," Entrepreneurial Leadership Center, Bellevue College, Winter 1991/92, 2–4.

20. Long, "Wichita Has Made," *Wichita Eagle*, December 6, 1925.

21. Although such strict physical examinations may seem excessive today, remember that during the 1920s, the prevalence of tuberculosis, scarlet fever, and infantile paralysis caused great fear of public contact.

22. White Castle *House Organ*, June 18, 1927.

23. "How an Idea Built on Nickels Does Business in the Millions," *Restaurant Management*, August 1935, 81–85, "White Castle" file, Office of the Wichita City Historian, Wichita Public Library, Wichita, Kans.

24. White Castle *House Organ*, June 18, 1927.

25. White Castle *Hot Hamburger*, December 1925.

26. "40,863 Will Be Distributed to Firm's Employees," *Wichita Eagle*, December 13, 1928, 19.

27. "How an Idea," *Restaurant Management*, August 1935, 81–85.

28. White Castle System Company sales records (approximated), Ohio State Historical Society, managers' meeting minutes, 1925.

29. *Hot Hamburger*, February 1926.

30. More precisely, until the 1960s when three White Castles were temporarily opened in Miami and until the 1980s when the company permanently expanded into Nashville and the Philadelphia metropolitan area.

31. White Castle *House Organ*, September 27, 1927.

32. White Castle *House Organ*, November 17, 1927.

33. White Castle *House Organ*, March 5, 1927.

34. Ibid.

35. "Romantic Story," *Everyweek Magazine*, April 25, 1931, 28–29.

36. Michael Parrish, *The Anxious Decades* (New York: Norton, 1992), 74.

37. Edgar W. Ingram, "All This from a 5-Cent Hamburger," address to the Newcomen Society, 1964.

38. "5¢ Burger," *Wichita Eagle-Beacon*, November 23, 1982.

39. *Wichita Eagle-Beacon*, September 3, 1982.

40. All available information on early competitors and White Castle's actions against them is located in the "Competitor Files," White Castle System Legal Department, Home Office, Columbus, Ohio.

41. Harrison Shutt, "Kewpee's Hamburger History," *Allen County Reporter*, vol. 49, 1993, published by the Allen County (Ohio) Historical Society.

42. Tennyson, *Hamburger Heaven*, 32.

43. Langdon, *Orange Roofs, Golden Arches*, 34.

44. "The Krystal Company at a Glance," Krystal Company, Chattanooga, Tenn., April 10, 1989.

45. Langdon, *Orange Roofs, Golden Arches*, 41.

46. Although White Castle predated Krystal by almost a decade, until recently their respective histories were almost parallel. Each endured the same ups and downs over the decades, and again until recently, both remained solely family owned and controlled.

47. Levenstein, *Paradox of Plenty*, 51.

48. Such confusion still persists. Today it is quite common for people to reminisce about the "White Castle" in their city or town that never had any White Castles. When pressed, though, they often remember that it was actually a White Tower or another White Castle imitator.

49. "White Tower" file, White Castle System Legal Department, Home Office, Columbus, Ohio.

50. "White Tower System of Eating Houses v White Castle System of Eating Houses," case no. 3855, United States District Court for the Eastern District of Michigan, Southern Division (Report of the Special Master, May 25, 1933).

NOTES TO CHAPTER 3

1. White Castle *House Organ*, July–August 1935.

2. Jeffrey Tennyson, *Hamburger Heaven* (New York: Hyperion, 1993), 34–35.

3. Minutes of the 1934 annual White Castle managers' meeting, on file at Ohio State Historical Society, Columbus, Ohio.

4. Harrison Shutt, "Kewpee Hamburger's History," *Allen County Reporter* 49 (1993): 16.

5. John F. Love, *McDonald's: Behind the Golden Arches* (New York: Bantam, 1986), 12.

6. Company sales figures, reported in the *House Organ*, December 1930.

7. Minutes of the 1933 annual managers' meeting, Columbus, Ohio.

8. White Castle *House Organ*, December 1930.

9. White Castle *House Organ*, July–August 1935.

10. White Castle *House Organ*, May–June 1932.

11. Telephone interview with Bruce LaPlante, September 5, 1996, St. Louis, Mo. LaPlante worked for White Castle for more than forty-five years, first as a manager in Chicago and then, for the remainder of his employment, as an area manager in St. Louis.

12. In a small way, Walt Anderson may have actually combined the hamburger business and aviation in May 1929 when he supplied a group of his fellow Wichita Rotarians with lined and insulated hamburger bags for their airplane trip to a convention in Dallas. After a bumpy ride, which was typical for early air travel, one Rotarian cabled Anderson from Dallas joking, "My first one leaked. Have this batch tested." It is hard to determine whether Anderson was responsible for any inventions beyond the hamburger.

13. Purchase agreement between Walter Anderson and Edgar Waldo Ingram, March 19, 1933, on file in the White Castle System Legal Department, Home Office, Columbus, Ohio.

14. White Castle *House Organ*, May 1933.

15. White Castle *House Organ*, July–August 1935.

16. "Buys Factory Site in City," *Columbus Dispatch*, July 10, 1934, 1.

17. Interview with Jimmy King, Wichita, Kans., June 1994.

18. Ibid.; and an interview including King's son, Wayne King.

19. White Castle *House Organ*, September–October 1934.

20. Minutes of the 1935 annual managers' meeting, Columbus, Ohio.

21. Wichita, in fact, proved to be Billy Ingram's true "hometown." After living in Columbus for more than thirty years, he directed that he be interred in a Wichita mausoleum after his death.

22. Interview with Jimmy and Wayne King, August 1994, Wichita, Kans.

23. White Castle *House Organ*, July–August 1935.

24. White Castle *House Organ*, May 1929.

25. Minutes of the 1931 annual managers' meeting, Columbus, Ohio.

26. White Castle *House Organ*, July–August 1935.

27. John Jakle and Keith Schulle, *The Gas Station in America* (Baltimore: Johns Hopkins University Press, 1994), 21.

28. Minutes of 1930 annual managers' meeting, Columbus, Ohio.

29. Edgar W. Ingram, "All This from a 5-Cent Hamburger: The Story of White Castle," address to the Newcomen Society, 1964.

30. White Castle *House Organ*, September–October 1933.

31. Ibid.

32. White Castle General Letter to Managers, April 1934 and May 1934, at the Ohio State Historical Society, Columbus, Ohio.

33. At that time, it was widely believed in the restaurant industry—except for the Harvey chain—that women were a liability as servers, based on the assumption that male customers lingered after their meals to talk to them and that women were otherwise undependable.

34. White Castle *House Organ*, February 1933.

35. Harvey Levenstein, *Paradox of Plenty: A Social History of Eating in Modern America* (New York: Oxford University Press, 1993), 11.

36. White Castle *House Organ*, July–August 1934.

37. White Castle *House Organ*, May–June 1935.

38. Minutes of the 1936 annual managers' meeting, Columbus, Ohio.

39. White Castle *House Organ*, May–June 1936.

40. White Castle *House Organ*, September–October 1937.

NOTES TO CHAPTER 4

1. Minutes of the 1942 annual managers' meeting, Columbus, Ohio.

2. White Castle *House Organ*, December 1937.

3. Gerald Nash, *The Crucial Era: The Great Depression and World War II, 1929–1945* (New York: St. Martin's Press, 1992), 120.

4. White Castle *House Organ*, January 1941.

5. In November 1942, the title of this column was changed from "White Castle in the Army" to "White Castle in the Armed Forces."

6. White Castle *House Organ*, September–October 1941.

7. Manager's General Letter, July 1942.

8. Manager's General Letter, July 1943.

9. White Castle *House Organ*, September–October 1942.

10. White Castle *House Organ*, November–December 1942.

11. Manager's General Letter, April 1942.

12. Nicholas Lemann, *The Promised Land: The Great Black Migration and How It Changed America* (New York: Vintage Books, 1992), 8.

13. Nash, *The Crucial Era*, 173.

14. Ronald Schaffer, *America in the Great War: The Rise of the Welfare State* (New York: Oxford University Press, 1995), 94–95.

15. Loren Baritz, *The Good Life: The Meaning of Success for the American Middle Class* (New York: Harper & Row, 1982), 178–82.

16. Manager's General Letter, April 1942.

17. White Castle *House Organ*, November–December 1942.

18. Alan M. Kraut, *The Huddled Masses: The Immigrant in American Society, 1880–1921* (Arlington Heights, Ill.: Harlan Davidson, 1982), 84–85.

19. White Castle *House Organ*, July–August 1942.

20. White Castle *House Organ*, November–December 1942.

21. Ibid.

22. Manager's General Letter, September 1944.

23. Minutes of the 1943 annual managers' meeting, Columbus, Ohio.

24. Michael E. Parrish, *The Anxious Decades* (New York: Norton, 1992), 470–71.

25. Harvey Levenstein, *Paradox of Plenty: A Social History of Eating in Modern America* (New York: Oxford University Press, 1993), 82–83.

26. Letter from U. Grant Sain, Columbus, Ohio, to R. L. Butler, Chicago, August 3, 1942, on applying for additional sugar allocations and citing specific difficulties in the application process; in the "Rationing 1941–1945" file, White Castle Collection, Ohio Historical Society.

27. Memo from Maurice F. Benfer to all managers, February 17, 1942, "Subject: Rationing Sugar to Customers." Benfer describes the criteria for sugar usage.

28. Letter from Les Sampson, Detroit, to U. Grant Sain, Columbus, June 9, 1942, concerning problems with sugar thefts and angry customers.

29. Letter from U. Grant Sain, Columbus, to Les Sampson, Detroit, June 19, 1942, ordering Sampson not to violate rationing codes by accepting advance shipments of sugar from wholesalers.

30. Levenstein, *Paradox of Plenty*, 93.

31. Ibid., 83.

32. The nickname "Coke" became so popular among the troops overseas that the

company finally copyrighted it after the war and began featuring it on the bottles alongside the more formal name.

33. Memo from Maurice F. Benfer to all managers, February 17, 1942; Manager's General Letter, August 1942.

34. Memo from Maurice F. Benfer to all managers, May 8, 1942, discussing the reduction in mug size as a conservation measure.

35. Memo from Maurice L. Benfer to all managers, February 24, 1943, discussing coffee shortages throughout the system and the different measures being taken.

36. Letter from R. F. Burgdorf, Indianapolis, to M. F. Benfer, Columbus, January 7, 1943, discussing the use of chicory as a coffee extender; Benfer's reply to Burgdorf, January 8, 1943.

37. Report on coffee substitutes; Manager's General Letter, April 1943.

38. Manager's General Letter, December 1942.

39. Manager's General Letter, February 1943.

40. Minutes from the 1943 annual managers' meeting, Columbus, Ohio.

41. Marc Scott Miller, *The Irony of Victory: World War II and Lowell, Massachusetts* (Urbana: University of Illinois Press, 1988), 141–42.

42. Manager's General Letter, September 1943.

43. Letter from William J. Bauerle, Columbus, to L. M. Shackelford, New York City, May 9, 1943, concerning meat purchases from possible black market source; Shackelford's reply to Bauerle, May 15, 1943.

44. Manager's General Letter, September 1942.

45. White Castle report on meat substitutes and extenders, distributed to managers by M. L. Benfer; reports and proposals by Central Soya Company.

46. Levenstein, *Paradox of Plenty*, 89.

NOTES TO CHAPTER 5

1. Norman L. Rosenberg and Emily S. Rosenberg, *In Our Times: America Since World War II* (Englewood Cliffs, N.J.: Prentice-Hall, 1995), 71–73.

2. Loren Baritz, *The Good Life: The Meaning of Success for the American Middle Class* (New York: Harper & Row, 1982), 182–85.

3. Stephanie Coontz, *The Way We Never Were* (New York: Basic Books, 1992), 28–30; Brett Harvey, *The Fifties: A Woman's Oral History* (New York: Harper Perennial, 1993), 44–46.

4. Manager's General Letter, March 1948.

5. Manager's General Letter, July 1948.

6. Manager's General Letter, March 1953.

7. Minutes of the 1953 annual managers' meeting, Columbus, Ohio.

8. Manager's General Letter, February 1951.

9. Copy of the original "suggestion sheet" and company analysis of this new product on file in the "White Castle Collection," Ohio State Historical Society.

10. Minutes of the 1951 annual managers' meeting, Columbus, Ohio.

11. Manager's General Letter, March 1951.

12. Jim Horan, "Speaking Out," *Fountain & Fast Food Service*, March 1952, 29. The only known collections of this publication are at the New York Public Library and the Library of Congress.

13. White Castle *House Organ*, April 1952.

14. Manager's General Letter, February 1952.

15. Minutes of the 1957 annual managers' meeting, Columbus, Ohio.

16. Manager's General Letter, April 1951.

17. Michael Karl Witzel, *The American Drive-In* (Osceola, Wisc.: Motor Books, 1994), 150–51.

18. Manager's General Letter, August 1953.

19. Philip Langdon, *Orange Roofs, Golden Arches* (New York: Knopf, 1986), 26–27.

20. Jeffrey Tennyson, *Hamburger Heaven* (New York: Hyperion, 1993), 46–50.

21. Marie Berube, "Fast Food on Best Behavior Clicks with the Suburban Set," *Fountain & Fast Food*, May 1955, 50–51.

22. Manager's General Letter, January 1957; Bob McCleary, "The Customer Crisis," *Fast Food*, September 1956, 35.

23. Marie Berube, "100% Women Handle This Operation," *Fountain & Fast Food Service*, March 1952, 42–43.

24. "The Insta-Burger-King Success Story," *Fast Food*, September 1959, 100.

25. Langdon, *Orange Roofs, Golden Arches*, 90–91; Bob McCleary, "Streamlining Spurs Growth of Compact Units," *Fast Food*, November 1960, 24–25.

26. John F. Love, *McDonald's: Behind the Golden Arches* (New York: Bantam, 1986), 13–20.

27. Ibid., 28–32, 45–47.

28. Manager's General Letter, November 1958.

29. Manager's General Letter, April 1959.

30. Manager's General Letter, May 1959.

31. White Castle *House Organ*, May 1952.

32. Manager's General Letter, July 1956; Betty Coffman, "Quarter Pound Hamburgers Jump Volume 60 per Cent," *Fountain & Fast Food*, February 1953, 36–37, 79.

33. Manager's General Letter, April 1958.

34. Manager's General Letter, March 1959.

35. Minutes of the 1959 annual managers' meeting, Columbus, Ohio.

36. Minutes of the 1956 annual managers' meeting, Columbus, Ohio.

37. Minutes of the 1955 annual managers' meeting, Columbus, Ohio.

38. Ibid.

39. Minutes of the 1953 annual managers' meeting, Columbus, Ohio.

NOTES TO CHAPTER 6

1. In response to customers' growing expectations, this menu actually expanded to include cheeseburgers, onion rings, children's meals, chicken nuggets, and a few

other offerings. Despite the wider selection, White Castle's mainstays still are its hamburgers, coffee, and Coke.

2. Carrie Shook and Robert Shook, *Franchising: The Business Strategy That Changed the World* (Englewood Cliffs, N.J.: Prentice-Hall, 1993), 139; Stan Luxenberg, *Roadside Empires: How the Chains Franchised America* (New York: Viking, 1985), 7–8, 210–11.

3. Richard Pillsbury, *From Boarding House to Bistro: The American Restaurant Now and Then* (Boston: Unwin Hyman, 1990), 139–40.

4. Luxenberg, *Roadside Empires*, 76–77.

5. Max Boas and Steve Chain, *Big Mac: The Unauthorized Story of McDonald's* (New York: Mentor Books, 1976), 15–16.

6. Philip Langdon, *Orange Roofs, Golden Arches* (New York: Knopf, 1986), 169–70.

7. Luxenberg, *Roadside Empires*, 2–4.

8. Robert L. Emerson, *The New Economics of Fast Food* (New York: Van Nostrand Reinhold, 1990), 9.

9. John F. Love, *McDonalds: Behind the Golden Arches* (New York: Bantam, 1986), 231–32.

10. Luxenberg, *Roadside Empire*, 32–33; Love, *McDonald's*, 231–232.

11. Ibid.

12. Shook and Shook, *Franchising*, 167–81.

13. Pillsbury, *From Boarding House to Bistro*, 94.

14. Love, *McDonald's*, 26–27.

15. Harvey Levenstein, *Paradox of Plenty: A Social History of Eating in Modern America* (New York: Oxford University Press, 1993), 234.

16. Ibid.

17. Langdon, *Orange Roofs, Golden Arches*, 99–100.

18. Richard Horwitz, *The Strip: An American Place* (Lincoln: University of Nebraska Press, 1985), 5.

19. Robert L. Emerson, *Fast Food: The Endless Shakeout* (New York: Lebhar-Friedman Books, 1979), 56.

20. Levenstein, *Paradox of Plenty*, 231; Langdon, *Orange Roofs, Golden Arches*, 104; Emerson, *The New Economics of Fast Food*, 3; interview with Ed Hutchman, Marion, Ohio, December 6, 1996; Luxenberg, *Roadside Empire*, 240.

21. Connie Roberts, "Fast Food Fair: Consumer Guidelines," *New England Journal of Medicine*, September 14, 1989, 752–56.

22. Emerson, *The New Economics of Fast Food*, 50.

23. *Nutrition Monitoring in the United States: A Progress Report from the Joint Nutrition Monitoring Evaluation Committee* (Hyattsville, Md.: U.S. Department of Health and Human Services, 1986), 8.

24. Ester Reiter, *Making Fast Food: From the Frying Pan into the Fryer* (Montreal: McGill–Queens University Press, 1991), 8.

25. Pillsbury, *From Boarding House to Bistro*, 107–8.

26. Charles L. Vaughn, *The Vaughn Report of Franchising Fast Food Restaurants: Six Categories of Franchises* (Lynbrook, N.Y.: Farnsworth, 1970), 3.

27. Emerson, *The New Economics of Fast Food*, 11; Emerson, *Fast Food*, 167, 252–53.

28. Luxenberg, *Roadside Empire*, 120.

29. Pillsbury, *From Boarding House to Bistro*, 140.

30. Emerson, *The New Economics of Fast Food*, 9.

31. Minutes of the 1965 annual managers' meeting, Columbus, Ohio.

32. Minutes of the 1970 annual managers' meeting, Columbus, Ohio.

33. Minutes of the 1960 annual managers' meeting, Columbus, Ohio.

34. Minutes of the 1964 annual managers' meeting, Columbus, Ohio.

35. Minutes of the 1969 annual managers' meeting, Columbus, Ohio.

36. Minutes of the 1966 annual managers' meeting, Columbus, Ohio.

37. Minutes of the 1967 annual managers' meeting, Columbus, Ohio.

38. Bryce Webster, *The Insider's Guide to Franchising* (New York: Amacom, 1986), 71–73.

39. Emerson, *Fast Food*, 57.

NOTES TO EPILOGUE

1. NPD/Crest, Beef Industry Council, chart 12.

2. *U.S. News & World Report*, January 20, 1997, 57.

Bibliography

SPECIAL COLLECTIONS

The Ohio Historical Society, Columbus, Ohio
The White Castle Company Papers, 1921–1980. These papers include a complete set of the company house organs, minutes of the annual managers' meetings, monthly reports from the home office to area managers, accounting ledgers, internal correspondence, and other miscellaneous company documents.
City Historian's Office, Wichita Public Library, Wichita, Kansas
White Castle files (limited holdings)
White Castle System Home Office, Columbus, Ohio
Files from the company's legal department (materials not released to Ohio Historical Society Archives)

GOVERNMENT DOCUMENTS

Hamburg, New York. Letter from Mayor Richard Hansen to Kim Kelly-Bartley, March 10, 1992. On file at the White Castle home office.
U.S. Department of Health and Human Services. *Nutrition Monitoring in the United States: A Progress Report from the Joint Nutrition Monitoring Evaluation Committee.* Hyattsville, Md., 1986.
U.S. District Court for the Eastern District of Michigan, Southern Division. "White Tower System of Eating Houses v. White Castle System of Eating Houses." Report to the Special Master, May 25, 1933.

INTERVIEWS

Interview with Jimmy King and Wayne King, Wichita, Kansas, June 14, 1994.
Telephone interview with Bruce LaPlante, St. Louis, Missouri, September 5, 1996.
Telephone interview with Gale Turley, Columbus, Ohio, December 12, 1996.

ARTICLES

Berube, Marie. "Fast Food on Best Behavior Clicks with the Suburban Set." *Fountain & Fast Food*, May 1955.

Coffman, Betty. "Quarter Pound Hamburgers Jump Volume 60 per Cent." *Fountain & Fast Food*, February 1953.

Ingram, Edgar W. "All This from a Five-Cent Hamburger." Address to the Newcomen Society, 1964.

"The Insta-Burger King Success Story." *Fast Food*, September 1959.

"The Krystal Company at a Glance." Krystal Company, Chattanooga, Tenn., 1989.

McCleary, Bob. "The Customer Crisis." *Fast Food*, September 1956.

McCleary, Bob. "Streamlining Spurs Growth of Compact Units." *Fast Food*, November 1960.

NPD/Crest Report. Chart 12. Chicago: Beef Industry Council, 1995.

"Romantic Story of the Hamburger Kings." *Everyweek Magazine*. April 25, 1931.

NEWSPAPERS AND PERIODICALS

Columbus Citizen
Columbus Dispatch
Consumer Reports
Cooking in Volume
Everyweek Magazine
Fast Food
Fountain & Fast Food Service
Fountain Service
New England Journal of Medicine
Newsweek
Restaurant Magazine
Restaurant Management
Soda Fountain
Soda Fountain Magazine
Soda Fountain and Quick Service
Soda Fountain Service
Teamsters Magazine
Time
U.S. News and World Report
White Castle *Hot Hamburger*
White Castle *House Organ*
Wichita Eagle
Wichita Eagle-Beacon

BOOKS

Bader, John. *Diners*. New York: Abrams, 1978.

Baritz, Loren. *The Good Life: The Meaning of Success for the American Middle Class.* New York: Harper & Row, 1982.

Boas, Max, and Steve Chain. *Big Mac: The Unauthorized Story of McDonald's.* New York: Mentor Books, 1976.

Chambers, John Whiteclay. *The Tyranny of Change: America in the Progressive Era, 1890–1920.* New York: St. Martin's Press, 1992.

Coontz, Stephanie. *The Way We Never Were.* New York: Basic Books, 1992.

Cumming, Richard Osborn. *The American and His Food.* New York: Arno Press, 1970.

Dolly, Thomas C. "The Bottom Line." Entrepreneurial Leadership Center, Bellevue College, Winter 1991/92.

Douglas, Mary, ed. *Food in the Social Order.* New York: Russell Sage Foundation, 1984.

Emerson, Robert L. *Fast Food: The Endless Shakeout.* New York: Lebhar-Friedman Books, 1979.

Emerson, Robert L. *The New Economics of Fast Food.* New York: Van Nostrand Reinhold, 1990.

Harvey, Brett. *The Fifties: A Women's Oral History.* New York: Harper Perennial, 1993.

Horwitz, Richard. *The Strip: An American Place.* Lincoln: University of Nebraska Press, 1985.

Jakle, John, and Keith Schulle. *The Gas Station in America.* Baltimore: Johns Hopkins University Press, 1994.

Kallet, Arthur. *100,000,000 Guinea Pigs.* New York: Vanguard Press, 1933.

Kraut, Alan. *The Huddled Masses.* Arlington Heights, Ill.: Harlan Davidson, 1982.

Langdon, Philip. *Orange Roofs, Golden Arches.* New York: Knopf, 1986.

Lemann, Nicholas. *The Promised Land: The Great Black Migration and How It Changed America.* New York: Vintage Books, 1992.

Leuchtenberg, William E. "The Achievement of the New Deal." In Harvard Sitkoff, ed., *Fifty Years Later: The New Deal Reevaluated.* New York: Knopf, 1985.

Levenstein, Harvey. *The Revolution at the Table: The Transformation of the American Diet.* New York: Oxford University Press. 1988.

Levenstein, Harvey. *Paradox of Plenty: A Social History of Eating in Modern America.* New York: Oxford University Press, 1993.

Love, John F. *McDonald's: Behind the Golden Arches.* New York: Bantam Books, 1986.

Luxenberg, Stan. *Roadside Empires: How the Chains Franchised America.* New York: Viking Press, 1985.

Mariani, John. *America Eats Out.* New York: Morrow, 1991.

May, Elaine Tyler. *Homeward Bound.* New York: Oxford University Press, 1990.

McElvaine, Robert. *The Great Depression: America, 1929–1941.* New York: Times Books, 1984.

Miller, Marc Scott. *The Irony of Victory: World War II and Lowell, Massachusetts*. Urbana: University of Illinois Press, 1988.

Nasaw, David. *Going Out: The Rise and Fall of American Amusements*. New York: Basic Books, 1993.

Nash, Gerald. *The Crucial Era: The Great Depression and World War II, 1929–1945*. New York: St. Martin's Press, 1992.

Olson, James. *The Ethnic Dimension in American History*. New York: St. Martin's Press, 1994.

Parrish, Michael. *The Anxious Decades*. New York: Norton, 1992.

Patton, Phil. *Made in the U.S.A.* New York: Penguin Books, 1992.

Pillsbury, Richard. *From Boarding House to Bistro: The American Restaurant Now and Then*. Cambridge, Mass.: Unwin Hyman, 1990.

Reiter, Esther. *Making Fast Food: From the Frying Pan into the Fryer*. Montreal: McGill–Queens University Press, 1991.

Root, Waverly, and Richard Rochemont. *Eating in America: A History*. New York: Morrow, 1976.

Rosenberg, Norman L., and Emily S. Rosenberg. *Our Times: America Since World War II*. Englewood Cliffs, N.J.: Prentice-Hall, 1995.

Rosenzweig, Roy. *Eight Hours for What We Will*. Cambridge: Cambridge University Press, 1983.

Schaffer, Ronald. *American in the Great War: The Rise of the Welfare State*. New York: Oxford University Press, 1995.

Schlink, Frederick. *Eat, Drink, and Be Wary*. New York: Covici, Friede, 1935.

Shook, Carrie, and Robert Shook. *Franchising: The Business Strategy That Changed the World*. Englewood Cliffs, N.J.: Prentice-Hall, 1993.

Shutt, Harrison. "Kewpee's Hamburger History." *Allen County* (Ohio) *Reporter* 49 (1993).

Sinclair, Upton. *The Jungle*. New York: Heritage Press, 1965.

Sitkoff, Harvard, ed. *Fifty Years Later: The New Deal Reevaluated*. New York: Knopf, 1985.

Sokolow, Raymond. *Why We Eat What We Eat: How Columbus Changed the Way the World Eats*. New York: Touchstone/Simon & Schuster, 1993.

Tennyson, Jeffrey. *Hamburger Heaven*. New York: Hyperion, 1993.

Trager, James. *The Chronology of Food*. New York: Henry Holt, 1995.

Vaughn, Charles L. *The Vaughn Report on Franchising Fast Food Restaurants: Six Categories of Franchises*. Lynbrook, N.Y.: Farnsworth, 1970.

Webster, Bryce. *The Insider's Guide to Franchising*. New York: Amacom, 1986.

Wiebe, Robert. *The Search for Order, 1877–1920*. New York: Hill & Wang, 1967.

Witzel, Michael Karl. *The American Drive-In*. Osceola, Wisc.: Motor Books, 1995.

Yoder, Paton. *Taverns and Travelers*. Bloomington: Indiana University Press, 1969.

Index